GREAT FOOD!

Special Thanks

This book is dedicated to all of our loyal customers who have contributed to the growth and direction of Great News! over the years, and helped create the success we have attained to date. Thank you for your business, your loyalty, and your input. You have helped shape our focus, dreams, policies, classes, purchasing, and even our instructors.

A big "Thank You" to all of our wonderful associates at Great News! who work hard every day — it is their knowledge, enthusiasm, and dedication to our pursuit of excellence that keep us a leader in the industry. We are happy that they love working here, and we appreciate all of their efforts.

We are grateful for our vendor partners, who work with us to bring you new items at the best prices. Our vendors work with us in many ways behind the scenes, and over the years, these special relationships have become friendships. Together we share in the success of this exciting business.

Thank you to all of our partners, not only for their gracious support of the first Great News! Cookbook but for their wonderful products, which we are proud to carry: All-Clad, Amco, Breville, Browne, Chef'n, Chicago Metallic, Component Design Northwest, Cuisipro, Emile Henry, Epicurean Cutting Surfaces, Harold Import Company, Kaiser Bakeware, Kyocera, Le Creuset, Mauviel, Microplane, Rösle, Scanpan, Taylor, Trudeau, Vic Firth, William Bounds, WMF, Wüsthof.

We thank Tiffany Wale for her hard work and perseverance in bringing these great products in. A special thank you to Katherine Emmenegger, our executive chef and TV personality, whose great recipes and can-do attitude inspire us all.

We thank our instructors for being part of the Great News! family and bringing their good food, recipes, humor, wisdom, and energy to the table.

Thank you to Amy Stirnkorb and Bruce Glassman, our publishers, who have stayed with us during the excruciatingly long time it took us to put this book together. We are extremely happy with the final result — a chance to share a bit of Great News! with everyone.

We thank Kristin Nichols, who worked many long, hard hours organizing many fine details and being the liaison between everyone — chefs, publishers, and staff members. Hooray! Job well done.

We again thank everyone for all of their help in making our wildest dreams come true! — Devora and Ron

On the cover

A special thank you to these vendors whose products Great News! proudly features in its store:
Top row, from left: Le Creuset, Wüsthof, Emile Henry, All-Clad. Bottom row, from left: Mauviel, Cuisipro, Rösle, Scanpan.

Chefs Press, Inc.

Editorial: Bruce Glassman and Amy Stirnkorb, Chefs Press, Inc.
Design and Production: Amy Stirnkorb, Chefs Press, Inc.
Copy Editing and Proofreading: Margaret King

ISBN: 978-0-9816222-4-8

First Edition
Printed in China

GREAT FOOD!

Four Seasons of the Best Classes,
Recipes, Equipment, Techniques, and Tips

From Great News! Cooking School

Chefs Press, Inc.

Contents

NOTE: Recipes highlighted with an asterisk (*) are vegetarian or can easily be adapted to be vegetarian.

spring

summer

autumn

winter

The beautiful and
state-of-the-art classroom
at Great News! Cooking School.

Cuisinart
Cuisinart
Cuisinart
Cuisinart
Cuisinart
Cuisinart
STONEWALL KITCHE
Est 1991

The Great News! Story

Great News! Cookware and Cooking School is located in Pacific Beach, a sunny seaside community in San Diego, California. We are a destination for local cooks, foodies, chefs, and gadget hounds, but out-of-town visitors come check us out as well. (We even have the occasional celebrity sighting.) We are fortunate that word about us has spread far and wide — our reputation for great products and outstanding service is legendary in our industry. In fact, in 2011, Great News! won a prestigious award: Best Kitchenware Retailer in the USA. We were voted "Best" not only by our customers, but also by our vendors and industry partners! (Great News! was also nominated for International Retailer of the Year in 2011.)

The road to success has been long and hard, but also rewarding. Like most true success stories, ours is filled with elements of luck, misfortune, coincidence, and perseverance.

Here is our story.

Tired of the harsh winter weather in Ohio, Ron and Carol Eisenberg left Cleveland in 1976 with their three kids and two dogs to relocate to sunny San Diego. Ron, trained as a pharmacist, had worked in and owned independent drug stores.

Carol loved working and enjoyed doing the buying for the greeting card departments. Ron found that his true love was the excitement of retail rather than pharmacy work. The concept for the new business they would create in San Diego was a functional housewares store with an alternative greeting card section. The store was named "Great News!" to convey the excitement of "great new items all the time."

The transition from functional housewares, gifts, and accessories to selling exclusively cookware started slowly. For a while, Ron kept his finger on the pulse of shifting sales and the interests of his customers. In the early 1990s, he changed his buying strategy to focus strictly on cookware and kitchen items. Around this time, Carol was diagnosed with stage-4 terminal breast cancer. Together, Ron and Carol fought a 7-year battle with the devastating disease. Ron began his study of cooking by learning about Macrobiotic diets as a way to help his wife fight the cancer. Carol passed in May of 1996, and Ron threw himself into the building of his first cooking school, in the space that once held greeting cards. Thus was born the Great News! that we know today.

Ron and Devora Eisenberg, Great News! owners

During the construction of the cooking school, Ron met (in traffic school, no less!) Devora Safran, who would later become his wife. Devora, who married Ron in 2002, is an artist, designer, and great home cook who loves to entertain. Although she does not work daily at the store, Devora has worked on several cookbooks (including this one), developed the teambuilding programs taught at Great News!, and worked on the "Adventures in Food and Travel" Italian travel programs and the "Looking for the Next Instructor" contest. Her blown-glass artwork is also on display in the cooking school.

Although the cooking school brought instant credibility to the cookware store, Ron had a long way to go to build the business he dreamed of. Because he wanted Great News! to be an alternative to chain stores, Ron had to educate himself, his staff, and his customers on the technical aspects of cutlery, cookware, and kitchen appliances. The cooking school made Great News! a venue to teach not only about food preparation, but also about how to use the items sold in the store. The Great News! approach was (and still is) somewhat novel: The store wants to help customers select not only the items they think they want, but what they actually need, based on the type of cooking they do at home. We want our customers to leave knowing both how to cook and what kitchen tool is right for the job.

Today, the cooking school features a state-of-the-art kitchen that is a perfect blend of home kitchen and professional kitchen. The design is U-shaped, with a large center island finished in granite. It is an approachable, sophisticated cooking school that boasts classes on everything from baking bread to making sausage. The curriculum covers everything imaginable, from basic techniques ("How to Boil Water") to gourmet meals taught by local celebrity chef/restaurateurs. The school is home to 5 or 6 regular instructors (with their cadre of followers), and 15 to 20 guest chefs per quarter. Many cookbook authors round out the mix. On average, the school teaches 9 or 10 classes a week.

This book is partly a sample of the many exciting classes we have taught over the years — and the ones our students have enjoyed most. But remember, as our name, Great News!, reminds us, we are always on the hunt for what is new and great and up to the minute. If it's farmers' market classes, sous-vide, or fine dining, we will bring it to our fans — and let them be the judge!

Kristin Nichols, Great News! Cooking School Director

When students pass through the large double glass doors that lead from the cooking school to the retail store, they pass into a completely different, but related, world.

The 5,200 square feet of Great News! retail space is packed with quality cookware, bakeware, gadgets, cutlery, electrics, scales, linens, and gourmet food items (to mention just a few things!). This is where students can find all the items demonstrated in our classes and whatever is newest in the marketplace. Whatever it is, we have it! Moreover, we not only sell the items, we also provide instructions on the care and maintenance of the equipment.

We're proud to boast that our knowledgeable staff is legendary in the industry, partly because we are constantly working with our vendors to get the newest products and the most detailed information to pass along to our clients. We listen to the needs and interests of our customers, and respond to both our critics and our fans. This commitment to excellence is our key to success — it's what earned Great News! the honor of the Kitchenware Retailer of the Year Award.

We hope this book will give you a brief overview of who we are (as a "Mom and Pop" business) and some insight into what we do. We want you to take home a piece of Great News! that will stay with you for as long as that new piece of heirloom cookware you just bought! We're convinced that the recipes we have taught and shared over the years are a roadmap of where we have been as a business and as an industry. We have enjoyed being a part of this dynamic industry, and we are excited to share our bit of history with you on these pages.

The Food Network, Bravo, and other cable channels have transported cooking into our homes and into our lives in a new and entertaining way. They have sparked a tidal wave of

Great News! stocks hundreds of cookware items, including shelves of Le Creuset, for the home and professional cook.

interest in food and cooking, as evidenced by the wide variety of people who take our classes and shop in our store. Our customers range from singles of all ages, to newly married couples wanting to cook together, to men who really want to make and eat great food, to kids aiming to become the next Food Network star. There truly is something for everybody. We all have to eat, so why not eat well and enjoy the process?

We hope you will enjoy this book, with its great variety of recipes, menus, equipment notes, and tips. We also hope to continue to share our success at Great News! with you as we grow and evolve in the future.

As Ron always says, "Cooking is love," and we love what we do.

Happy Cooking!
DEVORA AND RON EISENBERG

Our Contributors

CAROL BLOMSTROM
As a longtime restaurateur, Carol shares some of her favorite Italian dishes with us every year.

CHRIS BRILL
As a graduate of the Culinary Institute of America and chef/instructor at the San Diego Culinary Institute, Chris brings his formal training and 25 years of experience to his position as chef at Iowa Meat Farms and Siesel's Old Fashioned Meats.

PHILLIS CAREY
Phillis has worked in the culinary arts field since 1975, authoring several cookbooks and numerous articles in magazines and newspapers, and becoming a well-regarded cooking instructor. Her recipes focus on easy-yet-elegant ideas for everyday as well as gourmet meals — all prepared with a minimum of fuss.

KATHERINE EMMENEGGER
Chef Katherine's cooking experience began in her mother's kitchen, where, as a young girl, she learned many family recipes. She is executive chef of Great News! Cooking School, teaching numerous classes, and she is a regular on local television.

STAN GLENN

Stan is an excellent instructor with years of experience and expertise as supervisor and master meat-cutter at Iowa Meat Farms and Siesel's Old Fashioned Meats.

ALLISON SHERWOOD MILLNER

Allison gave up teaching cooking to move back to her hometown to open a deli of her own. She and her husband both sleep, breathe, and live food as they create fast, fresh and homemade delicacies at Sierra Subs and Salads. With a love for all things gourmet, she is continuously exploring and inventing new specials for her eager customers.

MINEKO TAKANE MORENO

Mineko is a master of Japanese cooking and co-author of *Sushi for Dummies*. From sushi etiquette to Japanese home cooking, her classes are always a hit with students, who love her discerning taste and passion for blending traditional recipes with modern techniques.

DIANE PHILLIPS

A James Beard Award nominee, cookbook author, and chef, Diane travels the world as a student and teacher of all things cooking. She is known as the "Diva of Do-Ahead" for her planning-ahead cooking tips. It is no wonder that she lives by the motto "Cooking shouldn't feel like a root canal." She maintains a passion for the culinary arts even after the past 25-plus years in the field.

DEBORAH SCHNEIDER

Chef Deborah has a long history in the San Diego culinary scene. Her love of Mexican food and culture has inspired five cookbooks. Besides teaching, she is chef/owner of two SOL Mexican Cocina restaurants, located in Newport Beach, California, and Scottsdale, Arizona.

AISSA SHELBURN

Born and raised in the Philippines, Aissa has been baking since she was 10 years old. In 2001, she moved to San Diego to study Culinary Arts at The Art Institute of California. Since then she has worked at Great News! Cooking School, where she enjoys teaching.

MARY ANN VITALE

Chef Mary Ann is a first-generation Italian-American with a passion for sharing her traditional Italian family recipes. She owns two successful businesses in La Jolla, California — La Taverna, an intimate Italian restaurant, and Sorella della Taverna (*sorella* means sister in Italian), a to-go gourmet deli. When she's not in the classroom at Great News!, you can find her in one of her kitchens enjoying cooking and baking for others.

A Well-Stocked Pantry

Maintaining a well-stocked pantry is fundamental to being a well-prepared cook. With interesting ingredients on hand, you're free to be creative and to react to your dishes by adding that little something extra when it's needed. Here are descriptions and details about some of the basic items you should never be without.

SALT

At the cooking school, we generally use kosher salt (never iodized salt). Sea salts are in vogue; they come in many colors, shapes, and sizes with unique flavor components. Generally, they are used to finish a dish. Here's a short list of salt varieties; each delivers its own distinctive quality to a dish.

- Kosher salt is the best known; it's inexpensive and has a pure salt flavor. The coarse texture gives it more volume and makes it easy to control when salting food.
- Sea salts, available in coarse or fine texture, are a bit more expensive than kosher salt. They tend to have a marine taste and a milder saltiness.
- Fleur de sel is harvested in Brittany, France, by hand from the surface of salt beds. Its sweet marine taste and crunchy texture make it a fantastic finishing salt — one that is preferred by many top chefs around the world.
- Hawaiian sea salts are either pink, gray, or black and are very rich in trace minerals.
- Moderately priced, large-flaked Maldon sea salt from England is another great choice for both cooking and finishing.
- These days, smoked salt is all the rage. There's alderwood, hickory, apple, juniper, elm — the list goes on. Basically, any smoked salt is considered a finishing salt that can add a degree of complexity and smokiness to a dish.

PEPPERCORNS

Peppercorns, like salt, come in a wide range of flavors and colors. They are indispensable as "foundation" seasoning for almost any dish. There are numerous common varieties; each one adds a different dimension to a recipe's flavors. Tellicherry peppercorns are some of the most widely available "gourmet" varieties. There are black, white, red, pink, and green, as well as wood-smoked peppercorns, and peppercorns mixed with other flavorings, such as cayenne or lemon peel.

CHILES

Canned or dried chiles are always handy, especially if you're into Mexican cooking.

- Chipotles (smoked jalapeños) in adobo are widely available canned, but you may also find dried chipotles at farmers' markets or specialty stores.
- Chile de Arbol, Ancho/Pasilla or Guajillo chiles are all excellent to have on hand as well.

VINEGARS

Vinegars, like other basics, come in a wide variety of styles and flavors. There are fruit-flavored vinegars and Asian rice vinegars, as well as red-wine or sherry vinegars. Aged balsamic vinegars from Modena, Italy, are generally sweet and dark colored. They are usually sold in small, shapely bottles. Fine aged balsamics are used more as condiments for finishing than as a "salad dressing vinegar." The really high-quality ones are great for drizzling over strawberries, ice cream, or dried or cured meats.

OILS

Good-quality oils are a necessity in any kitchen. In addition to the staple olive oil, you'll probably want to keep corn, canola, sunflower, and soy or vegetable oil around. We like to use grapeseed oil for frying because of its high smoke point. You'll mostly want to cook with unflavored oils unless you want to impart a little extra flavor to a dish. For accents, you can use "finishing" oils, such as avocado, walnut, extra-virgin olive, hazelnut, or homemade roasted garlic oils. Sesame oil is also good to keep on hand for stir-frying or wokking vegetables.

OTHER MUST-HAVES

- High-quality dried mushrooms are good for emergencies or for nonseasonal cooking.
- Great-quality smoked paprika is a cousin to Hungarian paprika and is indispensable in any number of shrimp or pork dishes, tapas, and Spanish chorizo.
- Garlic pastes such as Sambal (Indonesian chile-garlic paste) or Sriracha (Thai chile-garlic paste) are great to have on hand to give a spicy kick to any sauce or dish. Be careful — a little goes a long way.
- Fish sauce is useful if you're into Asian cooking, especially Thai or Vietnamese.
- Low-sodium soy sauce (or Tamari, which is gluten free) is great for salting or marinating.

Basic Cooking Methods

Almost all cooking, in its simplest form, is the process of preparing food by applying heat. The following are the most common methods for cooking with heat. A general understanding of these techniques, as well as a mastery of them, will greatly enhance your culinary skills and help to ensure the success of the dishes you prepare.

BAKING is a method of fully cooking food by dry heat in an oven. During baking, steam rises from the water in the ingredients; this steam combines with the dry heat of the oven to cook the food.

BLANCHING is a method of quickly cooking raw vegetables in salted, rapidly boiling water and then "shocking," or stopping the cooking process by submerging the vegetables in an ice bath. This process intensifies and preserves the color of most vegetables.

BRAISING is a slow-cooking method, usually reserved for tough pieces of meat. A braise is always started first by searing and browning the meat on the stovetop, caramelizing any vegetables, and then adding aromatics along with stock, wine, or other liquid. Searing should be done in the same pot as braising to retain as much flavor and browned bits as possible. All of the ingredients are placed together in a rondeau, or a large, wide-bottomed braising pot, and then slowly cooked until the meat is tender.

FRYING is a method in which oil or other fat is heated to a high temperature and then used to transfer heat to the food. Sautéing, stir-frying, pan frying, wokking, shallow frying, and deep frying are standard frying techniques that differ in the type of oil, the amount of oil, and the type of pan or vessel used.

GRILLING is a fast method of cooking using radiant heat. It is basically the same as broiling. Grilling is done with high, intense heat that caramelizes the food's surface and adds additional flavor complexity.

MICROWAVING can be very useful in the kitchen — though most chefs don't recommend it as a basic cooking technique. Microwaves cook foods from the inside out, which can be handy for certain things (precooking potatoes or vegetables before adding them to a dish) but not ideal for others.

POACHING is done in liquid that is just below boiling (when the liquid's surface begins to show some quivering movement). Meats and poultry are usually simmered in stock. Fish is often poached in water, wine, or stock that is flavored with aromatics such as onion, peppercorn, bay leaf, celery, and thyme (this is also known as court bouillon). Eggs are commonly poached in lightly salted water, often with a little vinegar added. Fruit can be poached in a light syrup made with water, a little wine, sugar, cinnamon, fruit slices, peppercorns, lemongrass, ginger, or other aromatic flavoring agents. Poaching produces a delicate flavor in food while imparting some of the liquid's flavor to the finished product.

ROASTING is an oven-cooking method where food is placed in an uncovered pan. Roasting usually produces a well-browned exterior while preserving a moist interior. It's also a great way to caramelize vegetables.

SAUTÉING is a type of frying that cooks food quickly in a pan with fat or oil over direct heat. This method is most commonly used for foods that have a significant moisture content, such as fresh fruits or vegetables.

SEARING is the process of cooking the surface of food — usually meat — over intense high heat to brown the exterior.

SMOKING is a great way to add an additional layer of flavor complexity to foods — and you can smoke just about anything. Most smokers work by exposing food to smoke inside a closed cooker on low heat for a long period.

STEAMING utilizes the hot gases created by boiling a liquid to gently cook food. This method preserves delicate flavors and is perfect for cooking fragile items — such as handmade dumplings — that would fall apart during frying or other cooking methods.

WOKKING is a method of sautéing and stir-frying on very high heat in a versatile round-bottomed cooking vessel that originated in China. It is used especially in East and Southeast Asia. Woks can also be used in many other ways, such as in steaming, deep frying, braising, stewing, smoking, or making soup.

Other Useful Terms & Tips

CARAMELIZATION is a chemical reaction that occurs when carbohydrates, such as sugar, are heated to temperatures of 300°F or higher, causing them to turn brown.

CHIFFONADE. *Chiffon* is French for "rag," which refers to the fabriclike strips that result from this technique. Chiffonade is a technique in which herbs or leafy green vegetables (such as spinach and basil) are cut into long, thin strips. This is generally done by stacking leaves, rolling them tightly, and then cutting across the rolled leaves with a sharp knife, producing fine ribbons.

DEGLAZING is a method that uses liquid to remove solids from a pan or pot during cooking. While the surface remains on the heat, a liquid (water, wine, broth, stock, etc.) is added and used to loosen and dissolve the "sucs," or solid brown pieces stuck to the pan.

EMULSIFYING means to combine two liquids that normally do not combine easily, such as oil and vinegar. This is done by slowly adding one ingredient to another while whisking rapidly. This disperses and suspends one liquid throughout the other.

JULIENNE is to cut vegetables or other food products into fine matchsticks.

Measurement Equivalents

It's always helpful to have a handy reference of measurements close by.

1 tablespoon = 3 teaspoons
1/16 cup = 1 tablespoon
1/8 cup = 2 tablespoons
1/6 cup = 2 tablespoons + 2 teaspoons
1/4 cup = 4 tablespoons
1/3 cup = 5 tablespoons + 1 teaspoon
3/8 cup = 6 tablespoons
1/2 cup = 8 tablespoons
2/3 cup = 10 tablespoons + 2 teaspoons
3/4 cup = 12 tablespoons
1 cup = 48 teaspoons
1 cup = 16 tablespoons
8 fluid ounces = 1 cup
1 pint = 2 cups
1 quart = 2 pints
1 quart = 4 cups
1 gallon = 4 quarts
16 dry ounces = 1 pound

Some Notes about the Recipes in this Book

In addition to the vegetarian menus, we have identified other recipes with asterisks (*) that are vegetarian or can easily be adapted by substituting vegetable broth for meat or poultry stock/broth, or omitting a non-essential ingredient.

OLIVE OIL: At the cooking school, we keep extra-virgin olive oil on hand, but it has a low smoke point and burns quickly, so it not the best choice for frying. It is best for finishing purposes for dressings and sauces. (We also sell many varieties.)

SALT: We generally use kosher salt — never iodized salt — while cooking. We also have on hand many types of sea salts and finishing salts, as each cooking instructor has favorites. (We also sell many varieties.)

ONIONS: In general we use yellow onions unless a recipe specifies another type, like a red onion or a sweet Vidalia.

BUTTER: We regularly use unsalted butter unless a recipe calls for salted butter. You can always add salt to enhance the flavor when using unsalted butter.

FLOUR: Unless otherwise stated, recipes in this book call for all-purpose flour.

SUGAR: Unless recipes specifically ask for confectioners, powdered, super-fine, raw or brown sugar, we use granulated white sugar.

BROWN SUGAR: Unless recipes specifically ask for dark brown sugar, we use light brown sugar. Dark brown sugar adds a slightly deeper caramel flavor and darker color to a recipe than light brown sugar.

spring

spring menus

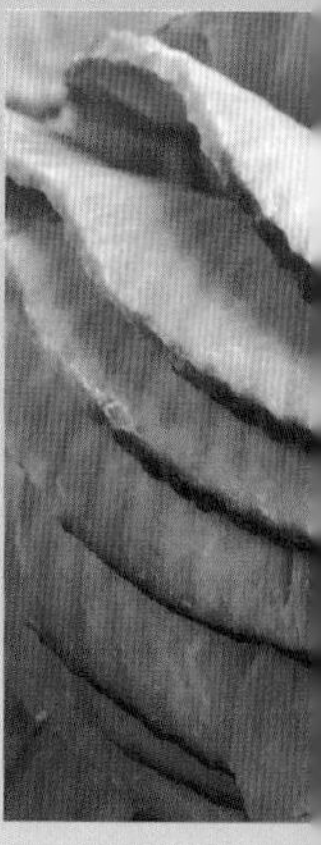

NOTE: Recipes highlighted with an asterisk (*) are vegetarian or can easily be adapted to be vegetarian.

Margaritaville Mexican Fiesta

PHILLIS CAREY

Homemade Margarita Mix • Blended Margarita • Frozen Mango Margarita
Hand-Shaken Citrus Gold Margarita • Smoky Black Bean Dip with Bacon
Shrimp Soft Tacos with Chipotle Cilantro Crema • Rio Grande Chicken Breasts with Creamy Rajas
Southwestern Spiced Rice with Black Beans and Corn
Mexican Chocolate Torte with Brown Sugar Glaze and Cinnamon Ice Cream

---

Margaritas and Mexican food are synonymous with good times in San Diego, particularly around Cinco de Mayo. In this fiesta menu, Chef Phillis shares her recipes for three styles of margaritas: blended, frozen, and hand-shaken, along with her homemade margarita mix. You will definitely want to keep some of this on hand. These delicious cocktails are paired with smoky black bean dip, soft shrimp tacos, chicken with creamy rajas (peppers and onions), and southwestern rice and black beans. The party finishes with a Mexican chocolate torte with cinnamon ice cream. Salud!

Homemade Margarita Mix

Makes 8 cups

3 cups water
3 cups sugar
2 cups fresh lemon juice
2 cups fresh lime juice

1. Combine water and sugar in a large saucepan. Stir over medium heat until sugar dissolves. Bring to a boil. Cool syrup to room temperature.
2. Mix syrup, lemon juice, and lime juice. Cover and chill until cold. Keeps 1 week refrigerated.

Blended Margarita

Makes 4 to 6

Coarse salt and lime wedges
1 1/2 cups homemade margarita mix
1 cup gold tequila
1/4 cup Triple Sec
8 ice cubes
4 to 6 lime slices

1. Rub rims of 6 glasses with lime wedges and dip rims in coarse salt. Set aside.
2. Combine margarita mix, tequila, Triple Sec, and ice cubes in blender. (Depending on the size of your blender, you may have to blend half at a time.) Process until well blended. Pour into glasses. Garnish each glass with a lime slice.

Frozen Mango Margarita

Makes 4 to 6

Granulated sugar and lime wedges
$1^1/_2$ cups diced mango, fresh or frozen and thawed
1 cup white tequila
$^3/_4$ cup Homemade Margarita Mix (see page 26)
6 tablespoons Triple Sec or Cointreau liqueur
6 tablespoons fresh orange juice
6 tablespoons fresh lime juice
3 cups ice cubes

1. Rub rims of 12 glasses with lime wedges and dip rims in sugar. Set aside.
2. Blend mango, tequila, margarita mix, Cointreau or Triple Sec, orange juice, and lime juice in a blender until smooth. Add the ice cubes and pureé until slushy. Pour into glasses and serve immediately.

Hand-Shaken Citrus Gold Margarita

Makes 6 to 8

Coarse salt and lime wedges
Crushed ice
1 cup gold tequila
$^1/_2$ cup Cointreau liqueur
$^1/_3$ cup fresh lime juice
$^3/_4$ cup fresh orange juice
$2^1/_2$ cups Homemade Margarita Mix (see page 26)
6 to 8 lime slices

1. Rub rims of 8 glasses with lime wedges and dip rims in coarse salt. Fill glasses halfway with crushed ice, if desired. Set aside.
2. Combine the tequila, Cointreau, lime juice, orange juice, and margarita mix in a pitcher. Fill a cocktail shaker two-thirds full with crushed ice. Pour in enough of the margarita to just cover the ice. Shake vigorously and pour into glasses. Garnish with lime slices and serve. Repeat as necessary.

Smoky Black Bean Dip with Bacon

Serves 8

4 slices bacon
1 medium onion, chopped
1 small red bell pepper, diced
1/2 teaspoon ground cumin
1/2 teaspoon dried oregano
2 (15-ounce) cans black beans, one drained and one undrained
1 teaspoon canned chipotle chiles in adobo, chopped
Salt and pepper
1/2 cup sour cream
2 tablespoons fresh cilantro, chopped
Tortilla chips, for dipping

1. Dice bacon and cook in a large skillet until crisp, about 6 minutes. Drain on paper towels. Pour off all but 1 tablespoon of the drippings from skillet. Add onion and bell pepper, and sauté until onion is soft, about 5 minutes. Add cumin and oregano, and cook 1 minute more. Add beans with their liquid and chipotles. Simmer over medium-low heat until slightly thickened, stirring occasionally, about 5 minutes.
2. Transfer 1 cup bean mixture to a food processor. Blend until smooth. Stir blended mixture into remaining bean mixture. Season with salt and pepper. Transfer to a bowl. Serve warm, or cover and refrigerate for 2 hours or up to 48 hours.
3. Garnish and serve. Stir half the bacon into the dip. Top with sour cream and sprinkle with cilantro and remaining bacon. Serve dip warm or at room temperature with chips.

Shrimp Soft Tacos with Chipotle Cilantro Crema

Serves 8

2/3 cup Mexican (sour) crema
1/2 cup red onion, chopped
1/3 cup cilantro, chopped
2 teaspoons canned chipotle chiles in adobo, minced
1 pound raw shrimp, cleaned and cut in half lengthwise down the back
2 tablespoons taco seasoning mix
2 tablespoons vegetable oil
8 to 16 corn tortillas, steamed to warm and soften
1 1/2 cups cabbage, finely shredded
Lime wedges

1. In a small bowl, stir together the crema, red onion, cilantro, and chipotle chiles. Set aside or refrigerate for later use. Toss shrimp with taco seasoning and refrigerate until ready to cook.
2. Heat oil in a large skillet over medium high heat. Add shrimp and sauté until barely cooked through, about 3 minutes. Reduce heat to medium low and stir in the crema mixture. Cook until just heated through, stirring frequently, about 2 minutes.
3. Assemble, garnish, and serve. Lay hot tortillas (one per taco if using traditional thick tortillas or two stacked if using the thinner store-bought variety) on serving plates or platter. Divide shrimp mixture evenly among tortillas. Top each with 1/4 cup shredded cabbage. Fold over to enclose filling and anchor shut with lime wedge. Squeeze lime over taco and serve.

Rio Grande Chicken Breasts with Creamy Rajas

Serves 8 • Marinate for 3 hours

CHICKEN

8 boneless, skinless chicken breast halves
Salt and pepper
3 cloves garlic, minced
1 teaspoon ground cumin
1/4 cup olive oil
6 tablespoons fresh lime juice

CREAMY RAJAS

3 tablespoons olive oil
3 large onions, thinly sliced lengthwise
4 poblano or 8 Anaheim chile peppers, roasted, peeled, and cut into thin strips
4 red bell peppers, roasted, peeled, and cut into thin strips
1 cup whipping cream
1 cup chicken broth
1 teaspoon dried oregano
3 cups grated Jack cheese
Salt and pepper, to taste

1. Make the chicken. Trim chicken and pound to an even 1/2-inch thickness. Season with salt and pepper. Place chicken in a wide dish. Combine garlic, cumin, olive oil, and lime juice, and pour over chicken, turning to coat. Cover and refrigerate 3 hours.
2. Make the creamy rajas. Heat olive oil in a large skillet over medium-high heat. Add onion and cook until beginning to brown, stirring frequently, about 5 minutes. Add chile peppers and bell peppers, and stir until heated through. Add cream, chicken broth, and oregano; bring to a boil. Simmer several minutes to reduce sauce slightly. Just before serving, stir in the cheese until melted. Season with salt and pepper.
3. Cook and serve. Preheat grill or grill pan and cook chicken 3 to 4 minutes per side, or until cooked through and browned. Serve chicken topped with creamy rajas.

RON'S TIP

Scanpan Non-Stick Double Grill Pans

You want to grill but don't want the hassle of schlepping all your food and pans outside or having to wait forever for the grill to heat up. Not to worry — the Scanpan grill pan is the convenient and easy way to bring the barbecue indoors. You will love the even heating of these pans, and the patented Green Tek coating is not your typical nonstick surface. The ceramic and titanium finish, 100 percent free from PFOA & PTFE chemicals, is 10 times harder than steel. This tough surface allows you to use metal utensils, and best of all, your food will brown with ease and get those beautiful grill marks. Your food will look as good as it tastes, and it will be healthier because you don't need to use fat — food won't stick. Grill meats, chicken, fish, vegetables, even fruits, and smaller items won't fall through grates. Available in both double- and single-burner sizes, these pans can handle dinners of any size.

Southwestern Spiced Rice with Black Beans and Corn*

Serves 8

6 tablespoons unsalted butter, divided use
2 cloves garlic, minced
1 cup onion, chopped
1 teaspoon ground cumin
2 cups long-grain white rice
4 cups chicken or vegetable broth
1 1/2 cups yellow corn, fresh or frozen and thawed
1 (15-ounce) can black beans, drained and rinsed
2 tablespoons fresh lime juice
1/4 cup fresh cilantro, chopped

1. Melt 4 tablespoons butter in a 4-quart saucepan. Stir in the garlic and onion, and sauté until tender, about 5 minutes. Stir in the cumin and rice, and toss until rice glistens and begins to turn white. Add the broth and bring to a boil. Stir, lower heat, and cook, covered, until the rice has absorbed the broth and is tender.
2. Immediately stir in the corn, black beans, remaining 2 tablespoons butter, and lime juice. Cover and let stand 5 to 10 minutes. Garnish with cilantro.

Mexican Chocolate Torte with Brown Sugar Glaze and Cinnamon Ice Cream

Serves 8

BATTER

4 ounces unsweetened chocolate, chopped
1/2 cup unsalted butter
1 1/4 cups golden brown sugar
1 tablespoon ground cinnamon
1/4 teaspoon salt
3 large eggs
1 teaspoon pure vanilla extract
3/4 cup flour
1 cup (6 ounces) milk chocolate chips

ICE CREAM

1 quart vanilla ice cream
2 teaspoons ground cinnamon

TOPPING

1 cup golden brown sugar
1/4 cup whipping cream
1 tablespoon unsalted butter
2 teaspoons pure vanilla extract
1/2 cup sliced almonds, toasted

1. Make the batter. Preheat oven to 325°F. Butter an 8-inch round cake pan and line with parchment paper. Stir unsweetened chocolate and butter in a heavy large saucepan over low heat until melted and smooth. Cool 5 minutes. Whisk in sugar, cinnamon, and salt. Whisk in eggs, 1 at a time, and then vanilla. Continue to whisk until batter is smooth. Add flour and whisk until just blended. Stir in chocolate chips. Pour into prepared pan, smoothing surface. Bake until tester inserted into center comes out with a few moist crumbs attached, about 30 minutes. Cool completely in pan on rack.
2. Prepare the ice cream. Soften the ice cream enough to stir in the cinnamon. Refreeze until serving.
3. Make the topping. Whisk sugar, cream, and butter in a small heavy saucepan over low heat until mixture is smooth and comes to a boil. Remove from heat; mix in vanilla. Cool 10 minutes. Whisk until thick enough to spread. Turn torte out of pan and place right side up on a platter. Spread topping over torte and sprinkle with almonds. Let stand until topping sets, about 1 hour. Cut into wedges and serve with ice cream.

Cupcake Craze

AISSA SHELBURN

Espresso Cupcakes with Espresso Bean Chocolate Frosting
Lemon Meringue Cupcakes • Devil's Food Cupcakes with Toffee Frosting
Red Velvet Cupcakes with Vanilla Bean Cream Cheese Frosting
Black Bottom Cupcakes with Malted Chocolate Frosting • Spiced Apple Cupcakes
Mexican Chocolate Cupcakes with Dulce De Leche Frosting

The popularity of cupcakes is one of the retro trends that have turned your favorite childhood desserts into the newest cool things. You have likely seen cupcake shops that offer these little individual cakes in every flavor imaginable (including savory and mini sizes). From lemon to chocolate to apple and devil's food, Chef Aissa's menu includes a wide range of our favorites. The hardest part is deciding which ones to bake and taste first!

Espresso Cupcakes with Espresso Bean Chocolate Frosting

Makes 12 to 15 cupcakes

BATTER

1 1/2 cups cake flour
2 tablespoons unsweetened cocoa powder
1/2 teaspoon baking soda
1/2 teaspoon baking powder
1/4 teaspoon salt
1 tablespoon instant espresso powder
3/4 cup unsalted butter, room temperature
1 cup granulated sugar
2 large eggs, room temperature
3/4 cup whole milk, room temperature

ESPRESSO BEAN CHOCOLATE FROSTING

3/4 cup heavy cream
6 ounces milk chocolate, finely chopped
2 teaspoons instant espresso powder
1 teaspoon pure vanilla extract
3 tablespoons chocolate-covered espresso beans, finely ground
12 to 15 chocolate-covered espresso beans, whole (for the topping)

1. Make the batter. Preheat oven to 350°F. Line cupcake or muffin pans with cupcake liners. Sift flour, cocoa powder, baking soda, baking powder, salt, and espresso in a bowl.
2. In an electric mixer, cream butter and sugar until light and creamy. Add eggs one at a time, mixing well after each addition. Scrape down bowl between each addition.
3. Alternately add flour mixture and milk in three additions, beginning and ending with the flour. Spoon batter into liners, filling three-quarters full, and bake for 20 to 22 minutes, or until a tester inserted in the middle of a cupcake comes out clean. Cool on a rack.
4. Make the frosting. Heat cream in a pan over medium heat until bubbles begin to form around the edges. Place chocolate and espresso powder in a bowl. Pour warmed cream over the chocolate and whisk until smooth. Fold in the finely ground espresso beans. Cool mixture, then whip it until it is thick and begins to hold its shape. Do not over-whip or it will be grainy.
5. Finish the cupcakes. Frost the cupcakes and top each with one whole espresso bean.

RON'S TIP

Chicago Metallic Cupcake Plungers

Everyone loves a good cupcake, and now there are so many ways to spice up these small, delectable desserts. Make any recipe into a special filled cupcake. The Chicago Metallic cupcake plunger makes it easy to fill your favorite cupcakes with cream, chocolate, custards, or anything you can dream up. The cupcake plunger removes the core of the cupcake for easy filling. You can create professional quality cupcakes in your own home and let your creativity and imagination go wild. Start filling today!

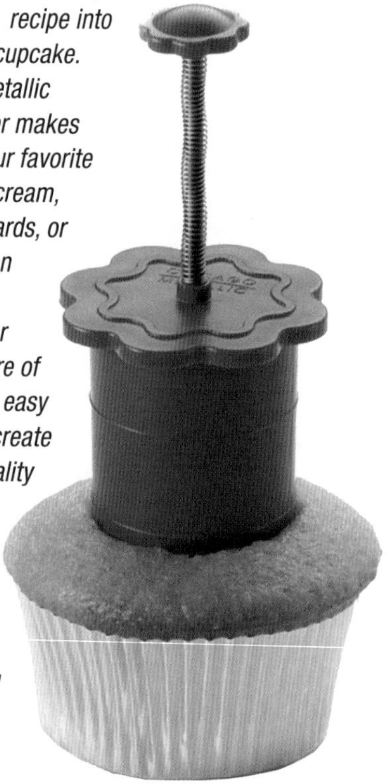

Lemon Meringue Cupcakes

Makes 12 cupcakes

LEMON FILLING

6 large egg yolks
1 cup granulated sugar
7 tablespoons fresh lemon juice
3 tablespoons unsalted butter, softened

LEMON BATTER

1 1/2 cups cake flour
2 teaspoons baking powder
1/4 teaspoon salt
1/2 cup unsalted butter, room temperature
1 cup granulated sugar
2 teaspoons lemon zest, finely grated
3 large egg whites, room temperature
1/2 cup whole milk, room temperature

MERINGUE TOPPING

3/4 cup granulated sugar
1/2 cup water
2 large egg whites, room temperature
1/4 teaspoon cream of tartar

1. Make lemon filling. Place yolks and sugar in a clean bowl on top of a double boiler over simmering water. Whisk egg mixture until ribbons form. Add lemon juice 2 tablespoons at a time. Keep cooking egg mixture until ribbons form again. Remove bowl from heat and add butter. Whisk until butter is fully incorporated. If mixture looks lumpy, strain curd into a clean bowl. Cover filling with plastic wrap pressed to the surface and cool before using, or refrigerate for up to 5 days.

2. Make the batter. Preheat oven to 350°F. Place liners in muffin or cupcake pans. Combine cake flour, baking powder, and salt in a bowl. In a separate bowl, beat butter, sugar, and lemon zest until light and creamy. Add egg whites 1 at a time, mixing well after each addition. Scrape down the bowl with a spatula to blend all ingredients.

3. Add flour mixture and milk alternately in three additions, beginning and ending with the flour. Spoon batter into cupcake liners and bake for 15 to 18 minutes. Cool cupcakes on a rack.

4. Make the meringue. Combine sugar and water in a saucepan and cook over medium-low heat until syrup registers 240°F on a candy thermometer. Occasionally swirl the pan to even out temperature. Do not stir syrup while it is cooking. Meanwhile in a clean bowl, whip egg whites with the cream of tartar until soft peaks form. If whites are ready before the syrup, keep the mixer on the lowest setting to keep egg whites aerated. If syrup is ready before the egg whites are, brush down sides of pan with clean water to decrease syrup temperature.

5. When the egg whites and syrup are ready, turn mixer back to medium-low speed and slowly pour syrup into the egg whites. Do not let the syrup touch the sides of the bowl or the whisk; otherwise, the sugar will harden in the meringue. Continue whipping the meringue until it is stiff and glossy and steam stops coming out.

6. Place lemon filling in a piping bag with a round tip. Insert tip into the center of each cupcake and pipe filling in. Pipe meringue on top of the cupcakes using a large star tip, or swirl with the back of a spoon. Lightly brown the meringue under a broiler or with a kitchen torch.

Devil's Food Cupcakes with Toffee Frosting

Makes 12 to 15 cupcakes

TOFFEE FROSTING

3/4 cup granulated sugar
3/4 cup water
1/4 cup heavy cream
1 tablespoon unsalted butter
1 teaspoon pure vanilla extract
Pinch salt
3/4 cup heavy cream, chilled
1/2 (7.5-ounce) package crème fraîche, chilled
1 cup crushed Heath Bars or other toffee candy

BATTER

9 tablespoons unsweetened cocoa powder
3/4 cup hot strong brewed coffee
1 1/2 cups all-purpose flour
1 teaspoon baking powder
1 1/2 teaspoons baking soda
1/2 teaspoon salt
1 cup granulated sugar
1/4 cup dark brown sugar, packed
6 tablespoons vegetable oil
3/4 cup buttermilk, room temperature
2 large eggs, room temperature

1. Make the frosting. To make the caramel, place sugar and water in a clean, heavy bottomed pan. Bring sugar and water to a boil over medium heat, stirring only until the sugar melts. After the sugar melts, do not stir mixture.
2. Let sugar mixture cook until sugar turns amber in color, swirling pan occasionally to cook sugar evenly.
3. When the sugar reaches the desired color and doneness, slowly pour the 1/4 cup cream into the caramel, stirring with a wooden spoon or spatula. Stir until the mixture is smooth. Add butter, vanilla and salt, and stir until butter is fully incorporated. Transfer caramel to a bowl and let cool to room temperature. Caramel sauce can be made up to 4 days ahead. Cover and keep in the refrigerator.
4. When caramel is cool, whip 3/4 cup chilled heavy cream and crème fraîche to stiff peaks. With the machine running on low, gradually add caramel sauce, and mix until caramel is fully incorporated.
5. Make the batter. Preheat oven to 350°F. Line cupcake or muffin pans with cupcake liners. Position rack in lower third of the oven.
6. Mix cocoa powder and coffee until smooth. Set aside to cool.
7. Combine flour, baking powder, baking soda, and salt in a bowl.
8. In a separate bowl, whisk sugar, brown sugar, vegetable oil, buttermilk, and eggs together until combined. Add one-third of the flour mixture to sugar mixture. Mix just until well combined. Add one-half of the coffee and cocoa powder mixture. Whisk until incorporated. Keep adding one-third of the flour alternately with coffee mixture.
9. Pour batter into cupcake liners. Bake for 15 to 18 minutes or until a tester inserted into the middle of a cupcake comes out clean. Cool on a wire rack.
10. Finish the cupcakes. Frost cupcakes with caramel cream and sprinkle with crushed toffee.

Red Velvet Cupcakes with Vanilla Bean Cream Cheese Frosting

Makes 12 cupcakes

VANILLA BEAN CREAM CHEESE FROSTING

8 ounces cream cheese, room temperature
1/2 cup unsalted butter, room temperature
2 cups powdered sugar, sifted
1/2 vanilla bean, scraped (or 1 teaspoon vanilla bean paste or pure vanilla extract)

BATTER

2 1/4 cups cake flour
1 teaspoon baking soda
1 teaspoon salt
8 teaspoons unsweetened cocoa powder
1 1/3 cups vegetable oil
1 1/2 cups granulated sugar
2 large eggs, room temperature
1 teaspoon white vinegar
1 teaspoon pure vanilla extract
4 teaspoons red food coloring
1 cup buttermilk, room temperature

1. Make the frosting. Beat cream cheese and butter in a bowl until creamy. Add powdered sugar ½ cup at a time, blending well after each addition. Add vanilla and blend until mixture is very creamy. Frosting can be made up to 3 days ahead. Refrigerate until ready to use. Whisk before using.
2. Make the batter. Preheat oven to 350°F. Line cupcake or muffin pan with cupcake liners. Combine flour, baking soda, salt and cocoa powder in a bowl. Whisk thoroughly and set aside.

3. Whisk oil and sugar in another bowl until well blended. Add eggs and blend well. Add vinegar, vanilla, and food coloring. Stir well to combine.
4. Add the flour mixture and buttermilk alternately to the oil mixture, blending well after each addition. Do not over mix.
5. Pour batter into liners and bake for 15 to 18 minutes, or until a tester inserted into the middle of a cupcake comes out clean. Cool before frosting.
6. Finish the cupcakes. Frost cupcakes with cream cheese frosting.

Black Bottom Cupcakes with Malted Chocolate Frosting

Makes 12 cupcakes

BATTER

1 ounce unsweetened chocolate, coarsely chopped
1/3 cup buttermilk
2 large eggs, room temperature
1 3/4 cups vegetable oil
1 teaspoon pure vanilla extract
3/4 cup brown sugar
1 1/3 cups cake flour
1/4 cup unsweetened cocoa powder
3/4 teaspoon baking soda
1/3 cup Dr Pepper brand soda

CREAM CHEESE FILLING

1 (8-ounce) package cream cheese, softened
1/2 cup granulated sugar
1 large egg
1/2 teaspoon pure vanilla extract

MALTED CHOCOLATE FUDGE FROSTING

3 ounces unsweetened chocolate, finely chopped
3/4 cup unsalted butter, softened
2 cups powdered sugar
1/4 cup malted milk powder
1/2 teaspoon pure vanilla extract
Milk (or half & half or heavy cream), as needed
Chocolate-covered malted milk balls (Whoppers brand is good)

1. Melt chocolate. Preheat oven to 350°F. Line muffin or cupcake pans with liners. Place chopped chocolate and buttermilk in a bowl and heat over simmering water, stirring until the chocolate melts. Do not let the mixture come to a boil or it will curdle. When chocolate is melted, remove bowl from simmering water and set aside to cool.

2. Make the cream cheese filling. While chocolate is cooling, make the cream cheese filling. Beat all filling ingredients until smooth. Set aside until needed.

3. Make the cupcakes. In a bowl, whisk the eggs, vegetable oil, vanilla, and brown sugar until well blended. Stir in cooled chocolate and buttermilk mixture. In a separate bowl, sift cake flour, cocoa powder, and baking soda.

4. Add flour alternately with the soda to the egg mixture in 3 additions, beginning and ending with the flour mixture. Spoon batter into liners about two-thirds full. Place a dollop of cream cheese filling in the center of the batter. Bake for 18 to 20 minutes, or until a tester inserted in the cake part comes out clean. The cream cheese filling will not be completely set. Let cupcakes cool on a rack.

5. Make the frosting. Melt the chocolate in the top of a double boiler. Set aside to cool.

6. Cream butter until light in color. Add powdered sugar and malt powder, and mix until smooth and creamy. Add cooled chocolate and vanilla. Mix until fully incorporated.

7. Add milk 1 tablespoon at a time until mixture reaches desired consistency. Frost cupcakes and top each with a chocolate-covered malted milk ball.

Spiced Apple Cupcakes

Makes 12 cupcakes

CARAMELIZED APPLES

1 Golden Delicious apple, peeled, cored, diced small
1/2 tablespoon unsalted butter
2 tablespoons brown sugar
1/2 teaspoon ground cinnamon
Pinch freshly grated nutmeg

BATTER

2 cups cake flour
3/4 cup brown sugar
1 teaspoon ground cinnamon
1/8 teaspoon ground cloves
1/8 teaspoon freshly grated nutmeg
3/4 teaspoon baking soda
1/4 teaspoon salt
6 tablespoons unsalted butter, softened
1/4 cup light or medium amber maple syrup
1 large egg
1/2 cup whole milk, room temperature

MAPLE CREAM CHEESE FROSTING

1 (8-ounce) package cream cheese, softened
1/2 cup unsalted butter, softened
1/3 cup light or medium amber maple syrup
1/3 cup powdered sugar
Cinnamon, for sprinkling

RON'S TIP

Chicago Metallic Muffin Trays

Have you noticed that cupcakes are all the rage lately? You may have also noticed how pricey these treats can be. So why not make your own? With the help of Chicago Metallic's muffin trays, you can save money by creating your own. Made of professional-weight aluminized steel, these pans conduct heat evenly for perfect baking and browning. The rolled lips add strength and rigidity, and prevent warping. The easy clean, nonstick surface will never chip, peel or corrode, and these pans can withstand temperatures up to 550°F. These pans can also be used for muffins, bread pudding, or single servings of Thanksgiving stuffing.

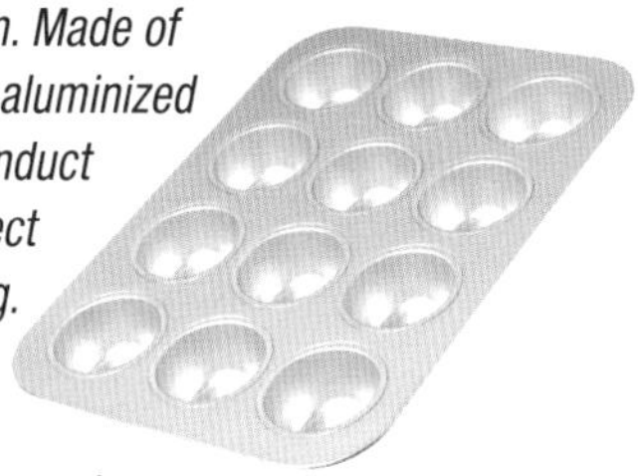

1. Caramelize the apples. Melt butter in a small sauté pan over medium-low heat. Add diced apples and cook until apples are soft. Add brown sugar and spices and toss until apples are evenly glazed. Set apples aside to cool.

2. Make the batter. Preheat oven to 350°F. Line muffin or cupcake pans with paper liners. Place cake flour, brown sugar, spices, baking soda, and salt in a bowl. Whisk to combine. Add softened butter and maple syrup and beat the mixture until smooth. Add the egg and beat to combine. Add the milk and mix well. Fold in cooled apples.

3. Spoon batter into liners, filling two-thirds full, and bake for 25 minutes. Let cupcakes cool on a rack.

4. Make the frosting. Beat cream cheese and butter in a bowl until smooth. Add syrup and blend. Taste for sweetness and add powdered sugar 2 tablespoons at a time to achieve desired sweetness.

5. Finish the cupcakes. Pipe frosting onto cooled cupcakes. Sprinkle with more caramelized apples and ground cinnamon, if desired.

Mexican Chocolate Cupcakes with Dulce de Leche Frosting

Makes 24 cupcakes • Make Dulce de Leche at least 3 hours ahead

DULCE DE LECHE BUTTERCREAM

1 (14-ounce) can sweetened condensed milk
8 teaspoons meringue powder
8 tablespoons warm water
1 1/2 cups granulated sugar
3 cups unsalted butter, room temperature

BATTER

1 3/4 cups cake flour
1/4 cup dutch processed cocoa powder
1/4 teaspoon salt
3/4 teaspoon ground cinnamon
1 1/2 ounces Mexican chocolate, finely chopped,
1/3 cup buttermilk
2 large eggs, room temperature
3/4 cup vegetable oil
3/4 cup dark brown sugar, packed
1/2 cup Dr Pepper or cola soda

1. Prepare the dulce de leche. Remove the label from the can of sweetened condensed milk. Place the can in a deep pot and cover it with water, making sure there is at least 1 inch of water above the top of the can. Bring the water to a boil and boil milk in the can for 3 hours, turning can every hour to cook milk evenly. Check the water level constantly and add more water if needed to keep can submerged in water. After 3 hours, remove the can from the water and let cool. The dulce de leche can be kept in the refrigerator for up to 10 days.

2. Make the buttercream. In a bowl, whisk the meringue powder and water until powder is dissolved. Whisk mixture until soft peaks begin to form. Gradually add sugar and beat meringue until it is stiff and glossy. Whisk in butter 1 tablespoon at a time, beating until the mixture is smooth before adding more butter. Buttercream can be made up to 4 days ahead, placed in an airtight container, and kept refrigerated. Let mixture come to room temperature and whisk until completely smooth before using.

3. Make the batter. Preheat oven to 350°F. Line cupcake pan with paper liners. Sift cake flour, cocoa powder, salt, and cinnamon in a bowl. In a separate bowl, combine chopped chocolate and buttermilk, and place over a pan of simmering water. Gently heat mixture until chocolate melts, stirring constantly. Set aside to cool.

4. In a clean bowl, whisk eggs, vegetable oil, and brown sugar until smooth. Stir in cooled chocolate mixture. Add flour mixture and soda alternately in three additions. Spoon mixture into cupcake pans and bake for 24 minutes, or until a tester inserted into the center of a cupcake comes out clean. Cool cupcakes on a rack.

5. Finish the cupcakes. When ready to serve, fold the dulce de leche into buttercream. Pipe the buttercream on cupcakes using a large star tip.

Carnivore's Delight

STAN GLENN AND CHRIS BRILL, IOWA MEAT FARMS AND SIESEL'S MEATS

Baked Ham with Maple-Mustard Glaze • Roasted Leg of Lamb with Walnut-Mint Pesto
Bacon-Wrapped Filet Mignon Stuffed with Gorgonzola and Drizzled with Balsamic Vinegar Reduction
Crown Roast of Lamb with Sun-Dried Cherry Compote and Israeli Couscous Pilaf
Hanger Steak with Merlot-Wild Mushroom Sauce
Crown Roast of Pork with Roasted Red Potatoes and Leek-Wild Mushroom Ragout

For the carnivores who come to Great News!, this cooking class is mandatory, and it is always a sellout. We recommend starting by buying the best-quality meat available. We love doing business with locals, like our friends at Iowa Meat Farms and Siesel's Meats. Not only do they provide San Diego with wonderful meat, they also know the best techniques and recipes for cooking it. Here are six amazing recipes, including lamb two ways, pork two ways, and beef two ways. The meats are paired with inviting side dishes that are designed to bring out the most flavor in each cut of meat.

Baked Ham with Maple-Mustard Glaze

Serves 12 to 15

1 (6- to 8-pound) smoked ham
1/2 cup Dijon mustard
1/2 cup whole-grain Dijon mustard
1 tablespoon dry mustard
1 cup real maple syrup

1. Preheat oven to 325°F.
2. Place ham in a baking pan and position on the center rack of the oven.
3. Combine the remaining ingredients and mix well.
4. Bake the ham uncovered for 2 to 2 1/2 hours.
5. Brush ham with the glaze, return to the oven, and bake for 10 minutes. Repeat 2 more times, baking on the glaze for 10 minutes each time.
6. Remove from the oven and let rest 15 minutes before carving.
7. Warm the extra glaze in a saucepan and serve alongside the ham.

Roasted Leg of Lamb with Walnut-Mint Pesto

Serves 8 to 10

MINT PESTO

1/2 cup fresh mint, minced
1/4 cup walnuts, toasted and chopped
1/4 cup Parmesan cheese, grated
2 tablespoons garlic, minced
3/4 cup extra-virgin olive oil
Salt and pepper, to taste

LAMB

1 (4- to 5-pound) boneless leg of lamb
6 cloves garlic, slivered
1/4 cup (or desired amount) mixed fresh herbs (rosemary, mint, oregano, parsley), minced
Salt
Freshly ground black pepper

1. Make the pesto. In a bowl, mix all pesto ingredients well. Set aside.
2. Make the lamb. Preheat oven to 350°F. Make several small slits both on the inside and outside of the lamb leg with the tip of a paring knife, and insert the slivered garlic. Season the inside and outside of the leg generously with the herbs, salt, and pepper. Tie the leg with butcher's twine. Place the lamb in a roasting pan in the oven and roast to an internal temperature of 125°F (1 to 1½ hours). Remove from oven and let rest for 10 to 15 minutes before slicing. Serve with room-temperature mint pesto.

RON'S TIP

Taylor Probe Thermometers

It is easy to overcook or undercook large pieces of meat. That's why an oven probe thermometer is always a good idea. The Taylor Probe thermometer ensures your food will be cooked to perfection because the probe pierces the meat while the attached readout remains outside the oven, keeping it clean and splatter-free. You enter your chosen temperature, and the readout allows you to carefully monitor your meats without opening the oven. This enables your oven to maintain a more constant temperature, which means cooking faster and saving on energy costs. When the set temperature is reached, the thermometer will beep to let you know your food is done.

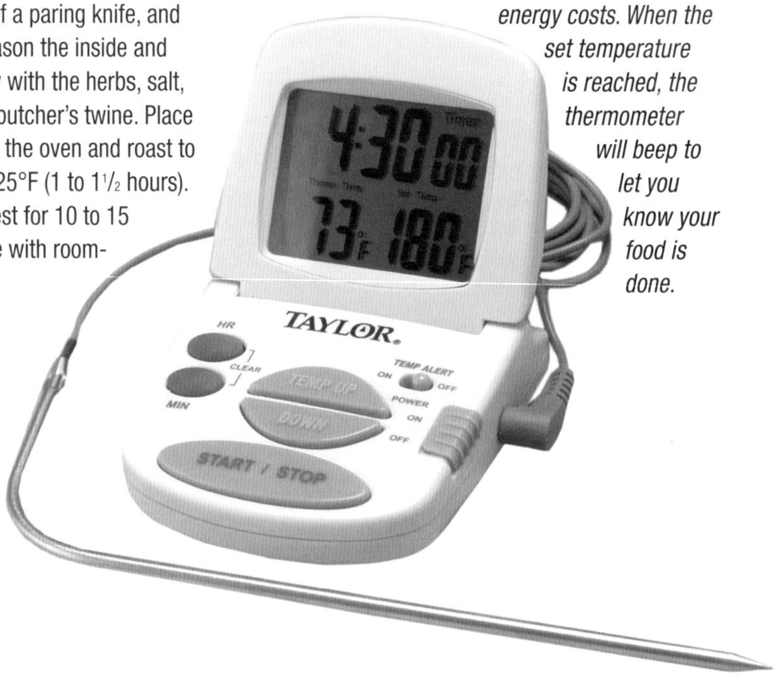

Bacon-Wrapped Filet Mignon Stuffed with Gorgonzola and Drizzled with Balsamic Vinegar Reduction

Serves 4

BALSAMIC GLAZE

2 cups good balsamic vinegar

FILET MIGNON

4 (2- to 2½-inch-thick) filet mignons
4 slices smoked bacon
3 tablespoons olive oil, divided use
1 shallot, minced
¼ cup red wine
6 ounces gorgonzola or other blue-veined cheese
2 tablespoons walnuts, toasted and chopped
¼ teaspoon fresh thyme, chopped
Salt and freshly ground pepper, to taste

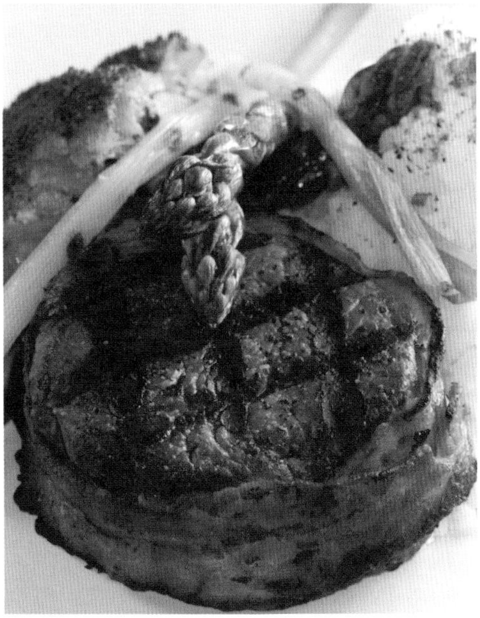

1. Make the balsamic glaze. In a small saucepan bring the vinegar to a simmer over medium heat. Reduce heat to low and gently cook until it has reduced to about ½ cup of vinegar. This process is known as reduction. What's left should be about as thick as maple syrup when cooled. This glaze, or "balsamic tar," can be drizzled over grilled poultry, pork, or even vegetables (a little goes a long way, so use it sparingly). Next time you want to dip your crusty bread in some extra-virgin olive oil, drizzle some balsamic glaze over the oil first. Keeps for weeks refrigerated.
2. Prepare the meat. Place the bacon on a parchment-lined baking sheet and cook in a 350°F oven for 5 to 7 minutes, until the edges start to curl and barely start to brown. Remove and drain on paper towels.
3. Heat a small sauté pan with 1 tablespoon olive oil. Add the shallots and sauté until translucent. Add the wine and simmer gently until it has evaporated and the pan is almost dry. Remove the shallots from the pan and let cool.
4. Combine the shallots, cheese, walnuts, and thyme, and mix well. Cut a pocket into each steak and stuff with the cheese mixture.
5. Wrap blanched bacon around filets and secure with a toothpick.
6. Cook the meat. Heat 2 tablespoons olive oil in a large sauté pan over medium-high heat until the oil starts to shimmer. Season the filets with salt and pepper. Add filets and sear for about 2 minutes per side, until nicely brown. Transfer to a rack in a roasting pan and place in a 375°F oven for about 8 to 10 minutes, or until meat reaches desired doneness. Cooking time may vary depending upon meat thickness and amount of initial searing.
7. Serve. Drizzle each filet with the balsamic glaze.

Crown Roast of Lamb with Sun-Dried Cherry Compote and Israeli Couscous Pilaf

Serves 12 to 16

COMPOTE

2 tablespoons butter
1/4 cup red onion, diced small
1 teaspoon fresh ginger, minced
1 tablespoon balsamic vinegar
1 tablespoon brown sugar
1 cup dried cherries
1 cup port wine

LAMB

1 (12- to 16-rib, about 2 1/2 to 3 pounds) crown roast of domestic lamb
Salt and pepper
Olive oil, as needed

COUSCOUS

2 tablespoons olive oil
1/2 cup onion, diced small
2 cups Israeli couscous
2 1/2 cups chicken broth or stock, boiling
1/2 cup red or yellow bell pepper, roasted and diced
1/4 cup feta cheese, crumbled
2 tablespoons fresh parsley, minced
Salt and pepper, to taste

1. Preheat oven to 400°F.
2. Make the compote. Heat a small saucepot over medium-low heat. Add the butter and onions, and cook gently without browning (sweat) until the onions are soft and translucent. Add the remaining ingredients and simmer until the cherries are soft and the liquid has thickened. Set aside until ready to serve.
3. Cook the roast. Season the roast with salt and pepper and rub with a little olive oil. Place the roast in a roasting pan in the center of the oven and cook to an internal temperature of 125°F to 130°F, about 20 to 25 minutes.
4. Make the couscous. Heat the olive oil in a small pot over medium heat. Add the onion and sauté until translucent. Add the couscous and stir until it is lightly toasted. Add the boiling stock, stir well, and bring to a simmer. Cover and simmer gently until the stock has been absorbed and the couscous is tender, about 8 to 10 minutes.
5. Remove the roast from the oven and let it rest for 10 minutes before carving.
6. Remove couscous from heat and let cool slightly. Gently fold in the roasted peppers, cheese, and parsley. Season couscous with salt and pepper.
7. Serve. Place the roast on a large serving platter. Spoon the couscous into the center of the crown. Spoon the compote (warm or at room temperature) onto the platter around the roast.

Hanger Steak with Merlot-Wild Mushroom Sauce

Serves 6

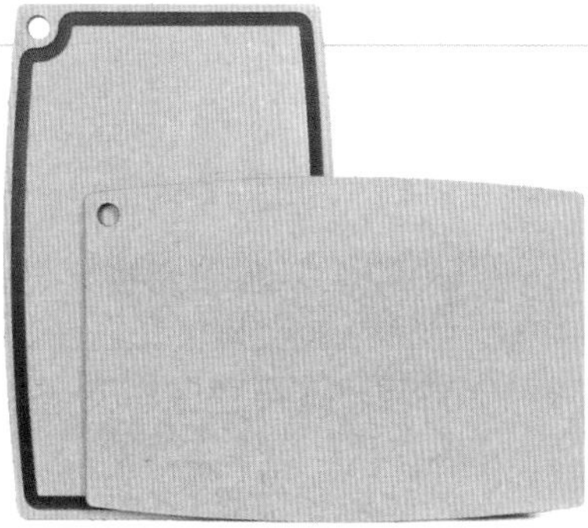

STEAK

1 (3- to 3½-pound) hanger steak (save trimmings)
Salt and pepper, to taste

MUSHROOM SAUCE

¼ cup shallots, minced
2 sprigs fresh thyme
2 cups merlot
Mushroom stems and steak trimmings (optional)
2 cups veal demi glace (Provimi Veal Demi-Glace, Regular or Mushroom, is good)
5 tablespoons butter, divided use
¾ cup assorted mushrooms
Salt and pepper, to taste

1. Cook the meat. Season the steak with salt and pepper. Cook on a hot grill to desired doneness. Because this is a thicker cut, cook the meat at a slightly lower heat so it will cook through without charring.

2. Make the sauce. In a small saucepan, combine the shallots, thyme, merlot, and steak trimmings. Bring to a simmer and cook until the liquid has reduced by half. Add the demi-glace and simmer for 10 to 15 minutes, until the sauce is the desired consistency. Strain the sauce into another pan and set aside. Discard shallots and trimmings.

3. In a sauté pan over medium-high heat, melt 3 tablespoons butter, and then add mushrooms. Season with salt and pepper, and sauté until tender. Add the mushrooms to the strained sauce. Taste and re-season. Depending on how much moisture is released by the mushrooms, you may need to simmer the sauce for a few more minutes to thicken. Remove the sauce from the heat and whisk in the remaining 2 tablespoons of butter.

4. Cook and serve. Cook the meat for 15 to 20 minutes, or until it reaches desired doneness. Let rest about 10 minutes, slice against the grain, and serve with the sauce.

RON'S TIP

Epicurean Cutting Surfaces

What do skateboarders and foodies have in common? They are both cutting it up on the same material. Epicurean created a line of home prep surfaces using the same material used in outdoor skate parks. That means this cutting board stands up to the hardest-working kitchens. Epicurean uses only premium materials for all of its innovative and highly functional surfaces — their cutting surfaces are made using eco-friendly materials that are dishwasher safe and made in the USA. Made of many layers of FSC-certified paper pressed together with a good, safe resin, Epicurean products will last for years of daily kitchen use.

Crown Roast of Pork with Roasted Red Potatoes and Leek-Wild Mushroom Ragout

Serves 12 to 16

PORK

1 (12-rib, about 10 pounds) crown roast of pork
Salt and pepper
1/4 cup garlic, minced
Olive oil, as needed

POTATOES

3 pounds red potatoes, quartered
1/4 cup garlic, minced
3 tablespoons rosemary, minced
1/4 cup olive oil
Salt and pepper, to taste

MUSHROOM RAGOUT

1/4 cup olive oil
2 pounds assorted mushrooms, cleaned and sliced
1/2 pound leeks, washed well and sliced
1/4 cup shallots, minced
1 tablespoon garlic, minced
1 cup white wine
2 cups heavy cream
1 tablespoon fresh thyme, chopped
1 tablespoon fresh parsley, chopped
Salt and pepper, to taste

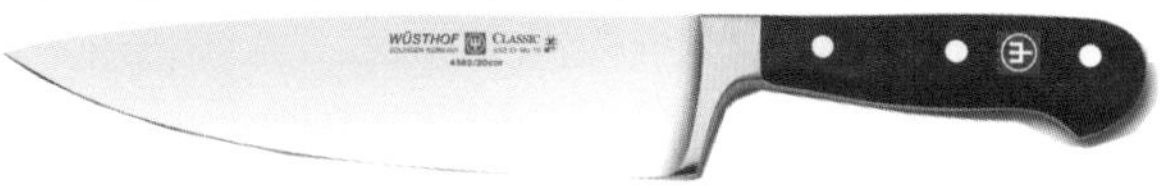

RON'S TIP

Wüsthof Knives

Any chef will tell you a good knife is one of the cook's most important tools, and Wüsthof knives are some of the best available. Made in the fine tradition of German swords, these knives are precision forged, each from one piece of high-carbon Solingen stainless steel. The blade is extremely sharp and will not stain, and the edge is easily maintained. A great variety of handle types is available, and all are seamless to ensure easy cleaning. With Wüsthof's wide range of products, there is a knife for every task — from small paring knives, to chef's knives of varying sizes, to bread knives, to slicer/carving knives, to boning and garnishing knives.

1. Cook the crown roast of pork. Preheat oven to 400°F. Season the roast with salt and pepper and garlic, and rub with a little olive oil. Place the pork in a roasting pan in the center of the oven and roast for 20 minutes, until golden brown. Reduce the oven to 350°F and cook to an internal temperature of 140°F to 145°F, about 1 to 1 1/2 hours longer. The potatoes can be added to the roasting pan during the last 30 to 40 minutes of cooking. Remove the pork from the oven and let rest for 20 minutes before carving.
2. Make the potatoes. Toss all ingredients together in a bowl. Place on a baking sheet or in the roasting pan with the pork roast. Roast in a 350°F oven until golden brown and tender, about 30 minutes.
3. Make the ragout. Heat the olive oil in large sauté pan over medium heat. Add the mushrooms, leeks, and shallots, and sauté until tender. Add the garlic and sauté for 1 more minute. Deglaze with the wine and cook until reduced by half. Add the cream and reduce until slightly thickened. Stir in the fresh herbs and season with salt and pepper.
4. Serve. Place the roast on a large serving platter. Spoon the potatoes into the center of the crown. Spoon the ragout onto the platter around the roast.

Vegetarian Entrées

ALLISON SHERWOOD MILLNER

Lettuce Wraps with Water Chestnuts and Saucy Baked Tofu
Moroccan Vegetable Tagine with Couscous
Zucchini Parmesan with Homemade Marinara Sauce
Spicy Spanish Paella with Saffron, Edamame, and Soyrizo

This menu was prepared and taught by Allison Sherwood Millner, our former cooking school director who is a practicing vegetarian. The bold flavors in the spicy lettuce wraps prove that veggie wraps can still be stunningly tasty without meat. The Moroccan tagine, which utilizes exotic spices and a tagine (cone-shaped cooking vessel) to braise the vegetables, makes the table look nice when you serve it, too. The paella features a spicy chorizo or sausage made from soy, with edamame (soybeans) and saffron. It is another beautiful stovetop-to-table recipe. And finally, who could resist a parmesan dish made with homemade marinara and zucchini? Even a confirmed carnivore will love these tasty recipes.

Lettuce Wraps with Water Chestnuts and Saucy Baked Tofu*

Serves 4 to 6

SAUCE

1/2 cup hoisin sauce
2 tablespoons plum sauce
3 tablespoons white vinegar
1 teaspoon Sriracha Thai hot sauce
3/4 teaspoon sesame oil
5 drops liquid smoke

LETTUCE WRAPS

2 tablespoons grapeseed oil
1 package baked tofu, diced small (Thai style from Trader Joe's is good)
1 head iceberg lettuce
1 cup shiitake mushrooms, diced small
1/2 cup red onion, diced small
1 (8-ounce) can water chestnuts, diced small
1/2 cup green onions, thinly sliced on a bias
1/2 cup fresh cilantro, chopped

1. Make the sauce. Mix all of the sauce ingredients in a bowl and set aside.
2. Make the lettuce wraps. Preheat a wok over medium-high heat and add the grapeseed oil. Add the tofu and stir-fry until brown on all sides and crisp on the outside, about 10 minutes.
3. While the tofu is cooking, remove the core of the iceberg lettuce and carefully break it apart into leaves large enough to be used as wrappers.
4. When the tofu is done, remove it from the pan and add in the shiitakes and red onion. Cook until soft, about 4 minutes. Add the water chestnuts and tofu back into the pan, cooking until warmed through. Slowly add the sauce until everything is coated. If you have extra sauce, it's great served on the side.
5. Garnish and serve. Pour the tofu mixture onto a platter, and serve with the green onions, cilantro, lettuce leaves, and extra sauce on the side.

Moroccan Vegetable Tagine with Couscous*

Serves 4 to 6

2 tablespoons olive oil, divided use
2 cups Japanese eggplant, halved lengthwise and cut into half moons
1 cup onion, diced
1 teaspoon cumin seed
1 teaspoon ground coriander
5 large cloves garlic, sliced
1 cup yellow crookneck squash, halved lengthwise and cut into half moons
1 cup red bell pepper, cut into 1x¼-inch strips
1 (15-ounce) can garbanzo beans, drained and rinsed
¼ cup pine nuts, toasted
⅓ cup golden raisins
1½ cups plain couscous
2 cups vegetable broth
Salt and pepper
Olive oil, for drizzling (Tibvrtini brand is good)
¼ cup fresh parsley, minced
¼ cup fresh mint, minced

Special Equipment Suggested: Moroccan tagine

1. In a tagine or deep sauté pan with a lid, heat 1 tablespoon of olive oil. Bring the temperature up to medium-high and cook the eggplant until brown on all sides and soft. Remove from the pan. Add the remaining oil, onion, cumin, and coriander, and cook until soft. Stir in the garlic, squash, and red pepper, cooking until slightly softened, about 3 minutes.
2. Place the eggplant back in the pan. Stir in the garbanzos, pine nuts, and raisins. Mix in the couscous and pour in the vegetable broth, leveling all the ingredients. Put the lid on the pan or tagine and turn off the heat. Let sit for 6 minutes. Fluff couscous and season with salt and pepper
3. Garnish and serve. Scoop out bowlfuls of the couscous and vegetables, top with a healthy drizzle of good-quality olive oil, and sprinkle with parsley and mint.

Zucchini Parmesan with Homemade Marinara Sauce*

Serves 6

MARINARA SAUCE *(Makes about 3 cups)*

1/4 cup olive oil
1 1/2 cups onion, chopped
3/4 cup carrot, finely diced
6 cloves garlic, sliced
2 (28-ounce) cans Italian whole tomatoes with basil in juice
1 (28-ounce) can tomato sauce
2 cups basil, chiffonade, divided use
Salt and pepper, to taste

ZUCCHINI

3 pounds zucchini, ends removed and sliced lengthwise 1/4 inch thick
Salt
Vegetable oil, for frying
2 cups flour, seasoned with salt and pepper
5 eggs, lightly beaten and seasoned with salt and pepper
2 cups Italian seasoned bread crumbs
3 cups whole-milk mozzarella, shredded
1 1/2 cups Parmesan cheese

1. Make the marinara sauce. In a large saucepan, heat the olive oil over medium heat, add the onion and carrot, and sauté until the carrot begins to soften. Add the garlic, tomatoes, tomato sauce, and 1 1/2 cups of basil. Stir to combine and bring the mixture to a simmer. Cover and turn the heat down to low. Cook until the tomatoes begin to fall apart and the flavors combine, about 30 minutes. Season with salt and pepper to taste.
2. With an immersion blender (or in a blender or food processor in batches), blend the sauce until smooth. Add the remaining basil and simmer an additional 5 minutes. If you like a chunkier sauce, replace the whole tomatoes with chopped and omit the blending. Set aside.
3. Make the zucchini. Preheat oven to 400°F. Slice the zucchini and lay them on a double layer of paper towels. Sprinkle salt onto the zucchini, flip and salt the other side, and let sit for 20 minutes. (The salt will draw out the extra water and make for better frying.) Dry the zucchini with extra paper towels, wiping off as much moisture as possible.
4. Heat a large frying pan over medium heat with 1/2 inch of vegetable oil. Work in an assembly line: Line up the flour, eggs, and bread crumbs in separate containers large enough to fit the zucchini slices. Coat both sides of each zucchini slice with flour, shake off the excess, then dip in the egg, again covering both sides. Remove each slice from the egg and coat with the bread crumbs. Gently slide the slices into the hot oil, frying until both sides are deep golden brown. Remove the slices and drain on paper towels. Continue until all the slices are fried.
5. Assemble the casserole. In a 13x9-inch baking dish, spread 1 cup of the marinara sauce. Fit the zucchini in snugly but without overlapping; sprinkle with mozzarella and Parmesan cheese. Repeat with another layer of sauce, zucchini, and cheese until you have 3 layers, ending with cheese.
6. Bake uncovered for 30 minutes, or until the cheese has melted and the zucchini is warmed through.

Spicy Spanish Paella with Saffron, Edamame, and Soyrizo*

Serves 4 to 6

2 tablespoons vegetable oil
1 package Soyrizo
$1^1/_4$ cups onion, chopped
2 cups shiitake mushrooms, thinly sliced
$1^1/_4$ cups red bell pepper, cut into $1^1/_2$x$^1/_4$-inch strips
$1^1/_4$ cups edamame beans
5 large cloves garlic, sliced
$^1/_3$ cup dry sherry
5 cups vegetable stock, plus extra as needed
2 large pinches saffron
$1^1/_2$ cups paella rice
Salt and pepper, to taste
$^1/_2$ cup parsley, chopped

1. In a paella pan, heat the oil over medium-high heat. Add the Soyrizo (removed from casing) and stir to break it up into pieces. Continue cooking until it is well-browned and in crumbles. Remove from the pan and drain on paper towels.
2. In the same pan, cook the onion and mushrooms until the mushrooms are soft, about 4 minutes. Stir in the bell pepper, edamame, and garlic cloves. Cook 2 minutes and then add the sherry.
3. Warm the vegetable stock and add the saffron. Let the saffron soak in the stock to allow it to "bloom" (to release its flavors).
4. Stir the paella rice into the onion and mushroom mixture, and cook for about 1 minute before adding the vegetable stock with the saffron. Level out all of the ingredients and turn down the heat to low. Your stock should be just bubbling; if the heat is too high, the rice will cook unevenly and burn on the bottom of the pan. Rotate the pan if necessary to even out the heat. Cook uncovered until the rice is tender but not mushy, adding more stock if needed. This will take about 20 to 30 minutes. It is not necessary to cover the paella pan, but if you want to, a piece of foil placed over the top will speed up the cooking time a little. Season with salt and pepper to taste.
5. Serve with the Soyrizo crumbles and a sprinkling of parsley.

Do-Ahead Easter Brunch

DIANE PHILLIPS

Field Greens Salad with Creamy Fresh Herb Dressing • Corn, Bacon, and Chive Strata
Pineapple Stuffing • Roasted Asparagus • Spicy Apple-Glazed Ham • Apple Slaw
Lemony Blueberry Bread Pudding with Quick Blueberry Sauce

An Easter meal is an absolute "must have" in a seasonal cookbook like this one. In this collection of recipes, Chef Diane, known as the "Do-Ahead Diva," provides the full dinner, start to finish, including glazed ham and all of the accompaniments. As a bonus, she includes time tables for shopping and preparing to make this holiday dinner your best one ever. Whether it is your first Easter celebration or one of many throughout the years, you will appreciate how well organized you will be using Diane's do-ahead methods. Included are tips for preparing and storing ahead, as well as serving on Easter day.

Field Greens Salad with Creamy Fresh Herb Dressing*

Serves 8 to 10 • Make dressing at least 2 hours ahead

HERB DRESSING *(Makes about 2 1/2 cups)*

2 cups regular or lowfat mayonnaise
1/2 cup whole or 2 percent milk
2 tablespoons fresh lemon juice
3 tablespoons fresh parsley, chopped
2 tablespoons fresh chives, snipped
1 tablespoon fresh oregano, chopped
2 teaspoons fresh tarragon, chopped
2 cloves garlic, mashed
1 teaspoon salt
1/2 teaspoon freshly ground black pepper
2 tablespoons lemon zest, finely grated

FIELD GREEN SALAD

3 (10-ounce) bags field greens, baby spinach or romaine leaves
1/2 cup red onion, sliced thinly and separated into rings
6 hard-cooked eggs, sliced
2 cups creamy fresh herb dressing
2 cups croutons (storebought or homemade)
12 strips bacon, cooked crisp, and crumbled (omit to make vegetarian)

1. Make the dressing. In a glass bowl, whisk together the ingredients until blended. Cover and refrigerate for at least 2 hours or up to 4 days.

2. Make the salad. In a large bowl, combine the greens, onions, and 3 eggs. When ready to serve, whisk the dressing to combine. Toss the mixture with about 1 cup of the dressing. Add the croutons and bacon, and toss with more dressing if desired. Sprinkle the top of the salad with the remaining sliced eggs for garnish, and serve any remaining dressing on the side.

RON'S TIP

Microplane Zesters

The Microplane Zester is one of the most versatile tools in the kitchen. Six unique designs all feature exactingly etched and spaced teeth for perfect grating every time. The fine grater can be used for zesting citrus, but also for fine grating of nutmeg, garlic, nuts, and Parmesan cheese. The coarse grater handles hard cheeses, as well as a wide range of fruits and vegetables. The ultra-coarse grater is optimal for cabbage, potatoes, and soft cheeses. There is a ribbon grater for carrots, and large and small shavers to shave chocolate and hard cheeses. The ergonomic handle is comfortable to use, and the curved nonslip end allows you to grate right over a bowl or on a flat surface. A sturdy stainless steel frame supports the nonrusting stainless steel grating surface on all models. The graters are a must-have and made in the USA.

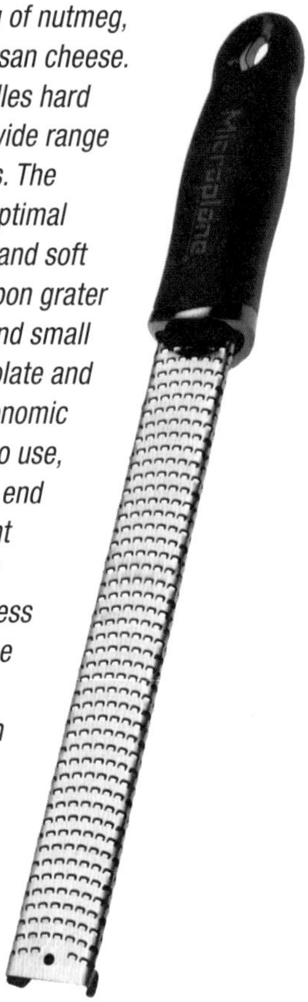

Corn, Bacon, and Chive Strata*

Serves 10 to 12 • Refrigerate for at least 8 hours before baking

2 tablespoons butter
4 green onions, white, and some of the light green parts, chopped
3 cups white corn, fresh, removed from cob, or frozen white corn kernels, defrosted
8 eggs
2 cups milk
1 teaspoon salt
6 shakes Tabasco
1 teaspoon dry mustard
1 (1-pound) loaf of good-quality white bread (remove the crusts if they are tough)
$^1/_4$ cup unsalted butter, melted
3 cups white cheddar cheese, grated
12 strips bacon, cooked crisp and crumbled (omit to make vegetarian)

1. Coat the inside of a 13x9-inch casserole dish with nonstick cooking spray.
2. In a large sauté pan, heat the butter, and sauté the corn and green onions together for 2 to 3 minutes to soften the green onions. Set aside in a bowl.
3. In another bowl, whisk together the eggs, milk, salt, Tabasco, and dry mustard until blended. Stir in the reserved corn mixture.
4. Arrange a layer of bread, wedging it in to fit into the bottom of the prepared baking dish. Brush the bread with some of the melted butter, and sprinkle with half of the cheese and half the bacon, and pour half of the egg mixture over the bread.
5. Arrange the remaining bread over the cheese, brush with butter, and pour the remaining egg mixture over the bread, tilting the pan to get the batter to the bottom of the casserole dish. Sprinkle with the remaining bacon and cheese. Cover and refrigerate for at least 8 hours or up to 4 days.
6. Remove the casserole from the refrigerator 45 minutes prior to baking to come to room temperature. Preheat oven to 350°F, and bake the casserole uncovered for 30 to 40 minutes, or until it is puffed and golden. If you want to freeze the baked casserole, bake it for 25 minutes, cool to room temperature, cover, and freeze for up to 1 month. Defrost in the refrigerator, cover, and bake at 325°F for 15 to 20 minutes, until warmed through. Serve warm or at room temperature.

VARIATION

For individual servings, coat the inside of 12 (4-ounce) ramekins or muffin cups with nonstick cooking spray. Tear the bread into small pieces and soak it in the egg/corn mixture. Scoop into the muffin tins and top with the cheese and bacon. Bake for 15 to 20 minutes, until the stratas are puffed and golden brown. Serve warm or at room temperature.

EASY ADD-INS

1. $1^1/_2$ cups diced smoked ham in the middle layer
2. Substitute $1^1/_2$ cups pepper Jack cheese for half of the cheddar cheese
3. 1 medium tomato, thinly sliced, in the middle layer
4. $1^1/_2$ cups diced cooked chicken in the middle layer
5. Substitute mozzarella for the cheddar and spread 1 cup prepared pesto over the middle layer

Pineapple Stuffing*

Serves 8 to 10 • Refrigerate for at least 4 hours before baking

1 cup unsalted butter
3/4 cup granulated sugar
6 eggs
1 (20-ounce) can pineapple chunks in syrup, drained
12 slices sturdy white bread, cubed

1. Coat the inside of a 13x9-inch baking dish with nonstick cooking spray.
2. In a large bowl, cream the butter and sugar until fluffy. Add eggs one at a time, beating well after each addition. Fold in the pineapple and bread cubes.
3. Pour the mixture into the prepared pan, cover and refrigerate for 4 hours or up to 3 days.
4. Preheat oven to 350°F.
5. Bring the casserole to room temperature, then bake for 45 to 50 minutes, until puffed and golden. Serve warm or at room temperature.

Roasted Asparagus*

Serves 6 to 8

2 pounds asparagus, trimmed of tough stem ends and peeled, if desired
1/4 cup olive oil
1 1/2 teaspoons salt
1 teaspoon freshly ground black pepper

1. Preheat oven to 400°F. Line a sheet tray with a silicone liner or foil.
2. Arrange the asparagus in a single layer on the prepared sheet. Sprinkle with the oil, salt, and pepper, and then roll the asparagus in the mixture until coated. Bake until crisp-tender, about 4 to 5 minutes (pencil-thin asparagus will take about 3 minutes, and thicker asparagus a bit longer). Remove from the oven.
3. Diva Do-Ahead. At this point, you can let sit at room temperature for up to 2 hours or let cool, cover, and refrigerate overnight. Return to room temperature before serving or heat in a skillet with 2 tablespoons of olive oil.
4. Serve warm or at room temperature.

Spicy Apple-Glazed Ham

Serves 10 to 12

CIDER GLAZE

4 cups apple cider
1 cup firmly packed dark brown sugar
2 teaspoons pumpkin pie spice
2 cups whole-grain mustard (Stonewall Kitchen Pub Mustard is good)

HAM

1 (6- to 8-pound) fully cooked, bone-in spiral-sliced or unsliced ham

1. **Make the glaze.** In a saucepan, combine the cider, sugar, and pumpkin pie spice.
2. Bring to a boil, and simmer for 1 hour, until the mixture is thickened.
3. Remove from the heat and cool. Add the mustard, and refrigerate for up to 2 weeks. Makes about 2 cups of glaze.
4. **Make the ham.** Preheat oven to 300°F. Line a large roasting pan with a silicone baking liner or foil.
5. Remove the packaging from the ham and drain off any juices. Place the ham in the prepared pan flat side down, making sure to remove the little plastic disk covering the bone. Cover the ham and pan completely with foil. Bake until an instant-read meat thermometer inserted in the center registers 120°F, about 2½ hours. (Since the meat is already cooked, you only need to warm it up.)
6. Increase the oven temperature to 400°F and remove the foil from the pan. Pour the glaze over the ham and bake uncovered, basting every 10 minutes with the pan juices, until the glaze is set, another 20 to 30 minutes.
7. Remove the ham from the oven; allow to rest for 15 minutes before carving, if necessary. Serve the ham drizzled with some remaining glaze.

Apple Slaw*

Serves 10 • Can be made up to 12 hours in advance

1 medium head green cabbage, finely sliced
4 large sweet, firm apples, like Gala or Jonathan, cored and thinly sliced (leave peel on)
1 cup celery, thinly sliced
1 cup seedless red grapes, cut in half
1/2 cup vegetable or canola oil
2 tablespoons fresh lime juice
2 tablespoons honey
2 tablespoons poppy seeds
1/8 teaspoon cayenne pepper
1 cup pecans, toasted and chopped

1. In a large bowl, combine the cabbage, apples, celery, and grapes.
2. In another bowl, whisk together the oil, lime juice, honey, poppy seeds, and cayenne. Pour the dressing over the cabbage mixture, and toss until combined. Cover and refrigerate the salad for up to 12 hours. When ready to serve, toss in 3/4 cup of the pecans, and toss again. Garnish with the remaining pecans and serve.

RON'S TIP

Kyocera Mandolines

A good slaw or au gratin recipe calls for evenly cut, consistently thin slices. This is simply impossible to do by hand. That's where the Kyocera Mandoline comes to the rescue. It makes quick, easy work of slicing through mounds of potatoes. The ceramic blade is sharp enough to glide through even tough-skinned fruits and vegetables and will stay razor sharp for years. It's small enough to store in a drawer, and it is also easily cleaned. The mandoline is adjustable — allowing you to choose from four different thicknesses, 0.5mm, 1.3mm, 2mm, or 3mm. A hand guard is included, and built-in notches allow you to rest the mandoline right on your bowl. Now you can adorn your salads with the thinnest of cucumber slices, shreds of cabbage, carrot rounds, and celery slices. Cut thicker eggplant or zucchini planks for grilling. For dessert, slice up some apples for a pie or an Easter apple slaw.

Lemony Blueberry Bread Pudding with Quick Blueberry Sauce

Serves 12 • Refrigerate for at least 12 hours before baking

BLUEBERRY SAUCE *(Makes about 3 1/2 cups)*

1 cup granulated sugar
2 tablespoons cornstarch
2 tablespoons water
2 tablespoons fresh lemon juice
2 cups blueberries

BREAD PUDDING

1 cup granulated sugar
1 lemon, zested
1/2 teaspoon lemon oil (or 1 teaspoon lemon extract)
1/8 teaspoon ground nutmeg
8 large eggs
1 1/2 cups heavy cream
9 cups torn bread, crusts removed
2 cups fresh blueberries, picked over for stems (or frozen blueberries, do not defrost)
1/4 cup granulated sugar
1/8 teaspoon ground cinnamon

1. Make the blueberry sauce. In a 3-quart saucepan over high heat, stir together the sugar, cornstarch, water, and lemon juice until blended. Add the blueberries and cook until the mixture begins to thicken and boil. Remove from the heat and allow to cool.

2. Diva Do-Ahead. At this point, the sauce can be refrigerated for up to 4 days or frozen for 1 month. Defrost in the refrigerator before serving at room temperature.

3. Prepare the bread pudding. Coat a 13x9-inch baking dish with nonstick cooking spray. In a large bowl, whisk together the sugar, lemon zest, lemon oil, nutmeg, eggs, and heavy cream until blended. Add the bread to the bowl, pushing it down into the mixture to absorb the liquid. Add the blueberries and stir to combine. Pour into the prepared dish.

4. Diva Do-Ahead. At this point, cover and refrigerate for at least 12 hours and up to 3 days. Bring to room temperature before continuing.

5. Bake the bread pudding. Preheat oven to 350°F. Combine the sugar and cinnamon, and sprinkle over the pudding. Bake until puffed and golden brown, 45 to 50 minutes. Remove from the oven and let rest for 10 minutes.

VARIATION

If you want to make muffin-size bread puddings, prepare the bread pudding but scoop into muffin tins that have been coated with nonstick cooking spray. Refrigerate 12 hours, sprinkle with the cinnamon-sugar mixture, and bake for 25 to 30 minutes, or until puffed, golden, and cooked through. Serve the muffin bread puddings warm.

Timpano from the Movie "Big Night"

CAROL BLOMSTROM, RESTAURATEUR

Timpano • Pizza Dough • Vodka Sauce • Creamy Pesto Sauce • Alfredo Sauce
Mixed Greens with Shallot Vinaigrette • Fruit Granita

Timpano was originally made in Calabria (the toe of Italy's boot) during Carnival time as a way to clean out the refrigerator of food that was not supposed to be eaten during Lent. This is why the recipe offers various options for some of the ingredients. Leftovers can certainly be substituted anywhere in the recipe. If you want to serve this on Friday, begin it on Wednesday. All ingredients must be cooked and cold before assembling. The Timpano is then cooked and cooled, and slices are reheated just prior to serving time. Feel free to experiment and enjoy!

Timpano

Serves 16 • Prepare, cook, and cool all ingredients before assembling

2 1/4 pounds fresh or 2 pounds dried penne
1 pound frozen spinach
7 (2-inch diameter) meatballs
1 1/2 pounds hot Italian sausages
2 cups rustico sauce or smooth tomato sauce
2 cups mushroom sauce or alfredo sauce with mushrooms added
2 cups grated mozzarella cheese, divided use
1 recipe Pizza Dough (see page 57)
6 tablespoons butter, softened
1/2 pan-size sheet spinach pasta, or substitute lasagna noodles
7 eggs, hard-boiled and cut in half lengthwise
1 cup fresco sauce or chunky tomato sauce
1 cup roasted red peppers, cut into strips
1/2 sheet semolina pasta
2 cups Vodka Sauce (see recipe page 58)
2 cups Creamy Pesto Sauce (see recipe page 58)
1 cup Alfredo Sauce (see recipe page 58)

1. Bring a large pot of water to a boil. Cook the penne for 3 minutes, drain, and put it in an ice bath to stop the cooking. Drain again and set aside.
2. Thaw the frozen spinach, chop, and squeeze dry.
3. Cook the meatballs and cut in half.
4. Cook the sausages and cut in half lengthwise.
5. Mix half the penne with the rustico or smooth tomato sauce.
6. Mix the remaining penne with the mushroom sauce and 1 cup of the mozzarella cheese.
7. Once steps 1 to 6 are completed and ingredients cooled or at room temperature, roll out the pizza dough. Use soft butter to grease a large pot. Line the pot with the pizza dough. Leave enough dough hanging over the edge of the pot to close the top of the Timpano.
8. Assemble the Timpano in this order: penne with rustico sauce; spinach; spinach pasta sheet; eggs (cut side down); sprinkling of mozzarella cheese >

to level the layer; meatballs (cut side down); fresco sauce to level the layer; sausages (cut side down); roasted red peppers as evenly as possible; semolina pasta sheet; and the penne, mushroom sauce, and mozzarella cheese mixture. Then fold the overhanging pizza dough over the top as evenly as possible and cut off the excess.

9. Bake in 375°F oven for 1 hour and 45 minutes. Remove, let it completely cool, and refrigerate before removing from pan (24 hours). To speed up cooling at room temperature, you can put the pan in an ice bath. Don't put it into the refrigerator while it is still hot. Store until ready to serve.

10. Slice into 16 wedges while cold. Reheat slices on a sheet tray at 350°F for 15 minutes before serving.

11. Serve with the vodka, creamy pesto, and alfredo sauces to represent the colors of the Italian flag.

Pizza Dough

Makes enough for 1 Timpano

1 cup water, heated to between 110°F and 115°F
1 tablespoon granulated sugar
1 tablespoon dry yeast
3 1/4 cups flour
1 teaspoon salt
1/4 cup oil, plus extra for oiling bowl
1/4 cup fresh herbs, chopped (any kind is fine)

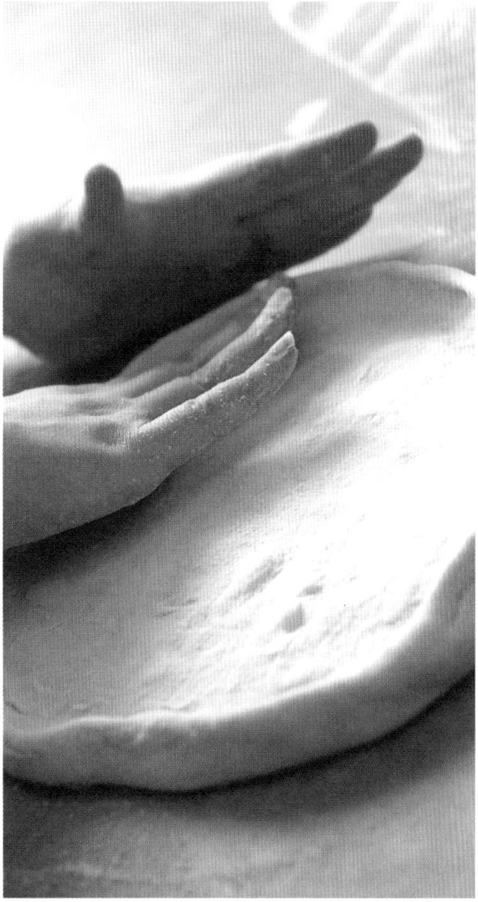

1. Prepare the hot water (and always have extra on hand).
2. Dissolve the sugar in the water. Stir in the yeast. Set aside.
3. In a mixer using the paddle attachment, combine the flour, salt, and oil.
4. If the yeast does not foam in about 5 minutes repeat step 2 with a new cup of water and package of yeast.
5. In a mixer on low speed using the hook attachment, add the yeast mixture to the flour mixture.
6. Add additional water or flour as needed.
7. Remove dough from mixer. Knead to form a ball. Place dough in a large oiled bowl and cover with plastic wrap. Place the bowl in a warm but not hot area and allow the dough to double in size.
8. After the dough rises, punch it down, add fresh herbs, and roll it into a large sheet. Now it is ready to use.

Vodka Sauce

Serves 16

1 tablespoon crushed red pepper
1 cup vodka
8 tablespoons butter
1 quart whipping cream
1 (28-ounce) can good-quality tomatoes, puréed in blender
3/4 cup Parmesan cheese, grated

1. In a pan, soak the crushed red pepper in the vodka for about 1 hour to infuse the flavor.
2. Bring the vodka to a boil. Boil for 5 minutes, or until alcohol is evaporated.
3. Stir in butter until melted, then add the cream and tomatoes and bring to a boil. Simmer for 5 minutes.
4. Whisk in Parmesan cheese.

Creamy Pesto Sauce

Serves 16

3/4 pound fresh basil, chiffonade
1 1/2 cups extra-virgin olive oil
1 1/2 cups pine nuts, lightly toasted
3/4 cup garlic cloves
1 1/2 cups Parmesan cheese, grated
3/4 cup Romano cheese, grated
3/4 teaspoon salt
Whipping cream

1. Bring a pot of water to a boil. Plunge basil into boiling water for 10 seconds. Immediately drain the basil and put it into an ice bath. This prevents the pesto from turning brown. Cool the basil, remove from the ice bath, and dry it off.
2. Purée blanched basil and remaining ingredients, except for the whipping cream, in a food processor.
3. When ready to use the sauce, mix 2 parts cream with 1 part pesto.

Alfredo Sauce

Serves 16

1/3 cup butter
1 1/3 tablespoons all-purpose flour
5 cups whipping cream
1 1/4 cups half & half
1 teaspoon ground nutmeg
4 cups Parmesan cheese, grated

1. Melt butter in a saucepan and whisk in flour to make a thin roux. Cook for 5 minutes on low heat.
2. Add cream and half & half, stirring constantly.
3. Allow mixture to come to a boil, stir well, and reduce heat. Add nutmeg and cheese, and stir until well incorporated.

Mixed Greens with Shallot Vinaigrette

Serves 16 • Make vinaigrette 12 to 24 hours before serving

2 cups shallots, minced
1 cup red wine vinegar
3 cups olive oil
1 cup bacon, cooked crisp, crumbled
4 bags mixed baby greens
2 cups hazelnuts, roasted and chopped
2 cups Gorgonzola cheese, crumbled

1. Mix the first 4 ingredients and let sit overnight to meld the flavors.
2. When ready to serve, toss the mixed greens with the vinaigrette, to taste. Divide the greens among salad plates and garnish with the hazelnuts and Gorgonzola cheese.

Fruit Granita

Serves 16

4 cups granulated sugar
4 cups water
3 cups grapefruit juice, freshly squeezed (reserve grapefruit halves)
2 cups pineapple juice, unsweetened
1 cup lime juice, freshly squeezed
3 limes, zested
1/2 cup lemon juice, freshly squeezed
1 lemon, zested
1/4 cup tequila, white
Garnish: Lime slices, lime leaves or mint

1. Bring the sugar and water to a boil in a large saucepan and simmer for 5 minutes, or until the mixture has a syrupy consistency. Add the juices and zests. Turn off the heat and allow to stand 10 minutes. Stir in the tequila and place the liquid in an ice cream freezer. Process according to the manufacturer's instructions. Transfer to a bowl and place in the freezer.
2. Once frozen, spoon into glasses or use the reserved grapefruit halves. Garnish with lime slices, lime leaves, or fresh mint.

Rice Bowls (Don Buri)

MINEKO TAKANE MORENO

Japanese White Rice • Chicken Curry Bowl • Salmon Teriyaki Bowl
Shrimp Tempura Bowl • Beef Fajita Bowl

The preparation of Gohan, or Japanese rice, is the essential foundation of all Japanese rice dishes. You can use either a heavy pot or a rice cooker machine, which is used by most households in Asia. Chef Mineko Takane Moreno hopes this menu collection will inspire love and respect for this simple ingredient. She offers four diverse dishes that are simple, yet complex. The salmon teriyaki and shrimp tempura bowls use classic Asian ingredients, while the chicken curry and beef fajita bowls feature bold flavors. You'll need to do a little extra shopping at Asian or specialty markets for some of the ingredients in this menu.

Japanese White Rice (Gohan)

Makes about 7½ to 9 cups cooked rice

3 cups short- or medium-grain Japanese white rice (4 rice cooker measuring cups)
3½ to 3⅔ cups water

1. Wash the rice with cold tap water in a large enough container so that the rice moves freely. Be gentle as you stir the rice with your hand. Do not break the rice grains. Then drain the rice and rinse again. The first 2 or 3 times, the water will become very milky. Never let the rice soak in the milky water; the dry rice grains will absorb water very quickly. Continue to wash and drain the rice until the water becomes almost clear. This will take approximately 2 to 3 additional rinses. From start to finish, it will take about 4 to 6 rinses until the water is almost clear.
2. Drain thoroughly and combine the washed rice with the 3½ cups of water in a rice cooker or a heavy pot. Let the rice soak for at least 1 hour. If you are using a rice cooker, simply start the rice cooker. If you are cooking the rice in a pot on the stove, bring the water to a boil over medium heat with the lid on. Once the water is boiling, without removing the lid, reduce the heat to low to prevent the water from boiling out. Cook the rice for about 15 minutes. Then reduce the heat to its lowest point and simmer for about 5 to 7 minutes. Before turning the heat off, raise the setting to high for about 7 seconds, then turn off the heat completely.
3. Let the rice rest for 12 to 15 minutes before removing the cover. Remove the lid and loosen the rice from the pot by inserting a moistened flat rice paddle between the inner edge of the pot and the rice. Slide the rice paddle all the way around. Fluff the rice by gently tossing with the rice paddle. Keep warm until ready to serve.

NOTES

- The measuring cup that comes with the rice cooker is the equivalent of three-quarters of a regular U.S. cup.
- If you are using a pot to cook the rice, pick one with a heavy bottom and a heavy, tight lid.
- When deciding how much rice to make, keep in mind that the rice will expand to approximately 2½ to 3 times its original volume.
- The ratio of water to rice varies according to how dry the rice is. However, usually you should add 15 to 20 percent more water than the quantity of rice.
- Do not open the cover when the rice is cooking.
- The best way to store leftover rice is to wrap one serving in plastic wrap, flatten for easy stacking, and place in the freezer. Microwave as you need it.

Chicken Curry Bowl

Serves 6

CHICKEN

2 tablespoons canola or grapeseed oil
1 pound boneless, skinless chicken thighs or breasts, cubed into bite-size pieces
1 large white or yellow onion, chopped into bite-size pieces
2 medium potatoes, cut into 3/4-inch cubes
2 medium carrots, cut into 3/4-inch cubes
4 cups water

YOGURT AND CUCUMBER GARNISH

1 Japanese cucumber
1/2 small red onion
1/2 teaspoon kosher or sea salt
2/3 cup plain yogurt
Pinch cumin
Pinch sugar

ASSEMBLY

3.5 ounces (100 grams) Japanese ready-made curry mix (such as House Kokumaro)
9 cups hot cooked Japanese rice

1. Cook the chicken. In a large pot, heat 2 tablespoons of oil and sauté the chicken for 2 to 3 minutes. Add the chopped onions and cook until the onions become translucent. Add the potatoes and carrots and sauté for a minute more. Add 4 cups of water and bring to a boil. Reduce the heat and simmer until the chicken and vegetables are almost cooked, approximately 15 minutes.
2. Make the garnish. Slice the Japanese cucumber and onion paper-thin with a vegetable slicer and sprinkle with the salt. Mix well and put aside for about 5 to 6 minutes. Squeeze the cucumber and onion to drain the liquid. Mix with the yogurt and add a pinch of cumin and sugar. Add salt if needed. Cover and refrigerate until serving.
3. Finish the chicken. When the chicken and vegetables are almost cooked, turn off the heat, slice the curry, break it apart, and add to the pot. Stir gently. Turn on the heat and simmer the curry gently for 5 to 8 minutes, or until the meat and vegetables are cooked and the sauce has thickened.
4. Assemble, garnish, and serve. Put about 1 1/2 cups of hot rice in a warm bowl. Place the hot curry carefully over the rice. Serve immediately with yogurt and cucumber garnish.

NOTES

- You can choose from mild, medium, and hot curry varieties.
- You may serve this curry with an assortment of Japanese pickles. *Rakkyo* and *fukujinzuke* are favorite condiments for curry dishes in Japan.

Salmon Teriyaki Bowl

Serves 4

TERIYAKI SAUCE

1/3 cup soy sauce
1/3 cup mirin (sweet rice wine)
2 tablespoons sake
1 tablespoon granulated sugar
Fresh ginger, a few slices

SALMON

1 pound fresh salmon filet (with or without skin)
8 to 12 green asparagus spears

ASSEMBLY AND GARNISH

6 cups freshly cooked hot short- or medium-grain Japanese rice
4 tablespoons scallions, thinly sliced
2 teaspoons roasted white sesame seeds

1. Make the teriyaki sauce. Combine all the ingredients in a small saucepot. Bring to a boil, reduce heat, and simmer for about 15 minutes, uncovered, or until the sauce becomes shiny and thick and it easily coats a spoon. Make sure not to burn the sauce.

2. Cook the salmon. Cut the salmon into 1/2-inch-thick slices. Broil or grill for about 4 to 5 minutes, or until light golden on both sides. Brush the fish with the prepared sauce, cook for a moment to brown the surface, and turn the fish over. Brush with the sauce again and broil or grill until the fish is golden on both sides.

3. Cook the asparagus. Peel the asparagus two-thirds of the way, cut into 1-inch long pieces, and steam or blanch. Set aside.

4. Prepare the garnishes. Place the thinly sliced scallions in a strainer and rinse with cold running water. Squeeze dry. Heat the sesame seeds in an ungreased frying pan for a few minutes to refresh their flavor.

5. Assemble, garnish, and serve. Place the hot rice in a warm bowl and sprinkle with some scallions. Slice the salmon into bite-size pieces and place over the rice and scallions. Add the cooked asparagus to the salmon. Heat up the remaining teriyaki sauce and pour over the salmon. Sprinkle with remaining scallions and sesame seeds. Serve immediately.

NOTES

- Teriyaki sauce bums easily. Watch carefully when preparing.
- Don't overcook the sauce, as it becomes bitter and too thick to pour over the fish.
- You can prepare chicken, beef, and other fatty fish in this same way to serve over rice.
- Broiled or grilled scallions or onions with teriyaki sauce can be added to the salmon.
- Broccoli, string beans, or snow peas can be used instead of asparagus.

Shrimp Tempura Bowl

Serves 4

TEMPURA SAUCE

1/2 cup mirin (sweet rice wine)
1/3 cup soy sauce
1 1/2 cups water
1/2 cup *katsuobushi* (dried bonito flakes)
3-inch square piece of *dashi kombu* (dried kelp)

SHRIMP

12 large shrimp (shelled, deveined, tails on)
4 shiitake mushrooms
8 *shishi-togarashi* peppers
1 1/2 quarts canola or corn oil for deep frying
1/4 cup dark sesame oil

TEMPURA BATTER

1 cup cold water
1 beaten egg
1 cup tempura mix or all-purpose flour
1/4 cup tempura mix to add to mixed batter during frying

ASSEMBLE AND GARNISH

1/2 cup tempura mix or flour for coating shrimp, mushrooms and peppers
6 cups freshly cooked hot short- or medium-grain white Japanese rice
1/2 cup *kaiware* (radish sprouts)

1. **Make the tempura sauce.** In a saucepan, cook all the ingredients together over medium heat. Bring to a boil, reduce heat, and simmer for a few minutes. Strain the sauce and return to the pan.
2. **Prepare the shrimp and mushrooms.** Cut the tip off each shrimp tail to allow water to escape and prevent oil splashes during frying. Make 4 to 5 slits on the underside of the shrimp to prevent curling when fried. Place the prepared shrimp on a paper towel-lined plate and keep refrigerated.
3. Clean the shiitake mushrooms with a damp cloth and cut off the stems. Cut in half if the mushrooms are large. Wash the *shishi-togarashi*, pat dry, and make a slit lengthwise along each pepper.
4. Heat the canola or corn oil to 350°F and add the dark sesame oil.
5. **Prepare the tempura batter.** Thoroughly combine the egg and cold water, then sift in the tempura mix. Mix gently to achieve a thin pancake batter consistency.
6. **Cook the shrimp, mushrooms and peppers.** Coat the prepared shrimp, shiitakes, and peppers with the tempura mix and dip in the batter. Deep-fry until crisp and drain on a wire rack.
7. **Assemble, garnish, and serve.** Heat the sauce to a boil, put the hot rice in the *donburi* (big rice bowl), and pour about 2 tablespoons of sauce over the rice. Dip the hot tempura in the remaining sauce one by one and place them on the hot rice. Garnish with *kaiware* and serve immediately.

Beef Fajita Bowl

Serves 4 • Marinates for 3 to 4 hours

MARINADE

1/4 cup lime juice (about 2 to 3 limes, zest limes before juicing for rice)
1/4 cup orange juice (1 small or 1/2 large orange)
2 cloves garlic, minced
1 teaspoon cumin
3 to 4 canned chipotle chiles in adobo, minced (add 1 to 2 teaspoons adobo sauce if desired)
1/4 cup cilantro, chopped
1/4 cup extra-virgin olive oil
Salt and pepper, to taste
1 pound skirt steak, silver skin removed

SALSA FRESCA

1 medium-size tomato, chopped
1/4 white onion, minced
1 avocado, diced small
1/4 cup cilantro leaves, chopped
1 serrano chile, minced, or to taste
1 tablespoon fresh lime juice, or to taste

FAJITA VEGETABLES

1 tablespoon olive oil
2 medium yellow or white onions, cut in half and sliced
2 red and/or yellow peppers, trimmed, seeds removed, and sliced lengthwise
Salt and freshly ground black pepper, to taste
1 lime, juiced

CILANTRO LIME-FLAVORED RICE

6 cups freshly cooked hot rice (cooked with a few sprigs of cilantro and a clove of garlic, remove before serving)
1 1/2 teaspoons lime zest (from limes used in marinade)

1. Make the beef marinade. Combine all the ingredients in a heavy plastic bag and mix well. Cut the steak in 2 to 3 pieces, place in the bag and marinate for about 3 to 4 hours in the refrigerator.
2. Make the salsa. Mix all the ingredients together. Set aside.
3. Cook the meat. When the meat is ready, heat a grill pan to medium-high and lightly oil the surface. Pat the marinated steak dry and grill until golden brown on both sides, about 4 to 6 minutes for medium-rare. Remove from the grill pan and set aside for a few minutes before slicing.
4. Cook the fajita vegetables. Heat up the same grill pan. In a bowl, combine the olive oil, onions, and peppers, and season with salt and pepper. Then sauté the vegetables on the grill pan for about 5 1/2 minutes, or until they reach desired doneness.
5. Assemble, garnish, and serve. When the vegetables are almost done, slice the steak thinly against the grain, and add to the vegetables. Season with freshly squeezed lime juice and toss together. Turn off the heat. Place the hot rice in warm bowls and sprinkle with some lime zest. Place the beef fajitas over the rice and garnish with some fresh salsa. Serve immediately.

Gluten-Free For All

KATHERINE EMMENEGGER

Gluten-Free Granola • Blueberry Pancakes with Maple Syrup • Pasta Alfredo
Southwestern Chicken Tortilla Lasagna • Chicken and Dumplings • Frozen Berry Nut Tart

Many people on restricted diets come to Great News! looking for delicious recipes to satisfy their taste buds and their doctors' orders. Intolerance of gluten (a protein found in wheat, barley, and rye) is just becoming better understood by physicians. Celiac disease is an autoimmune disease that requires a gluten-free diet. With this menu, Great News! Executive Chef Katherine shares many gluten-free options now available, including soy flour, rice flour, brown rice flour, almond flour, tapioca flour, sorghum (a millet-like grain) flour, gluten-free oats, gluten-free baking powder, and xanthan gum — all of which can be found at Trader Joe's, health-food stores, and many traditional grocery stores.

Gluten-Free Granola*

Makes about 10 cups

8 cups rolled oats, gluten-free
1 cup powered milk or flavored protein powder
1 cup soy flour
1 cup sliced almonds or your favorite nuts
1 cup sunflower seeds or your favorite seeds
2 teaspoons cinnamon or your favorite spice, optional
1 cup agave syrup or honey or maple syrup
1/2 cup grapeseed oil
2 teaspoons pure vanilla extract
Optional ingredients: Dried fruit, such as blueberries, cranberries, or cherries; crystallized ginger; other nuts; chocolate chips

1. Preheat oven to 300°F.
2. In a bowl, combine the first 6 (dry) ingredients.
3. In another bowl, combine the next 3 (liquid) ingredients. Combine the liquid and dry ingredients.
4. Prepare a few sheet trays by spraying the edges lightly with oil and lining with parchment paper.
5. Spread the mixture evenly over the sheet trays and place in the oven. Stir the mixture every 10 to 15 minutes during baking until the granola is evenly toasted. The granola becomes crisp when it has cooled. Do not over brown.
6. Remove from the oven and cool completely on the sheet trays. Transfer to a storage container.
7. Before serving, add any optional ingredients.

Blueberry Pancakes with Maple Syrup*

Makes about 12 medium pancakes

1 cup rolled oats, gluten-free
1 cup tapioca flour or rice flour
2 scoops protein powder, optional
1 tablespoon ground cinnamon
1 tablespoon baking powder, gluten-free
1/2 teaspoon salt
6 egg whites
1 cup water
2 tablespoons maple syrup, agave syrup, or honey
1 cup fresh blueberries, washed and drained well

1. In a blender, combine the first 6 (dry) ingredients until a fine powder is formed. Transfer to a bowl.
2. In a bowl, combine the next 3 (liquid) ingredients.
3. Combine the dry and liquid ingredients. Add the blueberries and combine well.
4. Heat a griddle to medium and lightly oil the surface. Ladle the pancake batter onto the griddle in half-cup portions. Cook for 1 to 1 1/2 minutes, flip, and cook 1 minute more, until just browned and cooked through. Transfer to plates and serve with your favorite syrup.

Pasta Alfredo*

Serves 4 to 6

1 pound brown-rice pasta or your favorite gluten-free pasta (Trader Joe's brand is good)
2 1/2 cups Mocha Mix original (or your favorite milk substitute)
2 cups cool water
6 tablespoons comstarch
1 tablespoon margarine or butter, optional
1/2 cup Parmesan cheese, shredded or grated
Salt and white pepper, to taste
Parmesan cheese, shredded
Italian parsley, minced

1. Prepare the pasta according to the package directions and drain well.
2. In a 2-quart saucepan over medium-high heat, bring the Mocha Mix to a simmer. In a bowl, combine the water and cornstarch; mix well to form a slurry. Add the slurry to the simmering Mocha Mix and stir with a wire whisk; the mixture will thicken fairly quickly. Lower the heat to medium and simmer the mixture for 1 to 2 minutes.
3. Remove from the heat. Whisk in the butter or margarine (if adding), the cheese, and salt and pepper. Combine with the pasta.
4. Top with more of the cheese and garnish with parsley.

Southwestern Chicken Tortilla Lasagna

Serves 8 to 10

HOMEMADE CORN TORTILLAS *(Makes 16 tortillas)*

2 cups Maseca masa harina
1 1/3 cups water
1/4 teaspoon salt

LASAGNA

Grapeseed oil, for the grill
4 (4-ounce) boneless, skinless chicken breasts
Salt and pepper, to taste
2 (16-ounce) jars Trader Joe's double roasted salsa (or your favorite salsa)
8 to 10 homemade corn tortillas (or store-bought gluten-free corn tortillas)
2 (15-ounce) cans low-sodium black beans, rinsed well and drained
1 pound fresh spinach, lightly steamed, or frozen spinach, thawed and squeezed to remove excess water
2 large roasted red peppers, cored, skinned and sliced into 1-inch-wide strips
2 large zucchini, washed, ends removed, sliced lengthwise 1/4-inch thick, and grilled until tender and well-marked
1/2 pound shredded pepper Jack cheese
1/2 pound shredded cheddar cheese

Special Equipment Needed: Tortilla press

1. Make the tortillas. Preheat oven to 350°F. In the bowl of an electric mixer fitted with the paddle attachment, or by hand, thoroughly combine masa harina, water, and salt. Mix for a few minutes.
2. Separate the dough into 16 balls. Place them in a large bowl and cover with a lightly damp towel.
3. Line the top and bottom of a tortilla press with plastic wrap. Place one ball of dough in the center and press to form a tortilla.
4. Transfer to a parchment-lined baking sheet and place a layer of parchment in between each layer of pressed tortillas.
5. In a cast-iron skillet or heavy sauté pan, cook each tortilla for about 40 seconds per side. Layer the cooked tortillas under a towel to keep them warm.
6. Cook the chicken. Preheat an indoor grill pan to medium-high heat. Generously brush with oil.
7. Season the chicken breasts with salt and pepper and grill until just done. Transfer to a platter, cool, and shred the chicken breast meat.
8. Assemble lasagna. In a 9x13-inch baking dish spread a thin layer of the salsa. Cut the tortillas in half and arrange them in a single layer over the salsa. You may need to quarter a tortilla to fill in the gaps. Top the tortilla layer with some of the black beans, spinach, and red peppers; finish with zucchini, chicken, and cheeses. Drizzle additional salsa over the cheese and repeat with another layer of tortilla. Repeat toppings and continue layering. The final layer should end with tortilla, salsa, and cheese. Bake for 35 to 45 minutes, or until the cheese is bubbly and browned. Let stand for 10 to 15 minutes before cutting.

Chicken and Dumplings

Serves 6

CHICKEN

6 bone-in, skinless chicken thighs
Salt and pepper, to taste
2 tablespoons vegetable oil
1 large yellow onion, peeled and diced small
4 medium carrots, peeled and cut into 1-inch slices
4 ribs celery, washed, tough strings removed, and cut into 1-inch slices
2 garlic cloves, minced
4 sprigs fresh thyme
1 bay leaf
3 quarts low-sodium, gluten-free chicken or vegetable broth
1 cup frozen peas
1/4 cup fresh Italian parsley, minced

DUMPLINGS

1/3 cup brown or white rice flour
1/3 cup sorghum flour
1/3 cup tapioca flour
1 tablespoon xanthan gum
1 1/2 teaspoons baking powder, gluten-free
2 teaspoons fresh thyme, minced
1/2 teaspoon salt
Black pepper, to taste
2 tablespoons olive oil
3 egg whites, beaten
1/4 cup water, soy milk, or almond milk

1. Season the chicken with salt and pepper.
2. In a large saucepan, heat oil on medium-high heat. Sauté the chicken until golden brown, about 3 minutes for each side.
3. Transfer the chicken from the pan to a platter. In the same pan, sauté the onion, carrots, celery, and garlic for 3 minutes; add the thyme and bay leaf.

4. Return the chicken to the pan, add the broth, cover, reduce the heat to low, and braise the chicken until tender, about 25 to 30 minutes.
5. With a slotted spoon, transfer the chicken to a platter and cover loosely with foil. When the chicken is cool enough to handle, remove the meat from the bones and cut into bite-size pieces; discard the bones. Return the meat to the pan and add the peas; simmer.
6. Make the dumplings. In a bowl, combine the rice, sorghum and tapioca flours, xanthan gum, baking powder, thyme, salt, and pepper.
7. Add the oil and mix well to form a coarse meal.
8. Add the egg whites and water, and mix well. The mixture should resemble a thick batter.
9. With a medium cookie scoop, drop some of the dumpling batter into the slowly simmering braising liquid; do not over crowd. Cover and steam for 10 to 15 minutes.
10. Serve. Ladle the chicken and dumplings into bowls; serve hot.

Frozen Berry Nut Tart

Makes 1 (10-inch) pie

PASTRY

1/2 cup buckwheat (Bob's buckwheat cereal is good)
1 cup brown rice flour
1/2 cup tapioca flour
1/2 cup almond flour or finely ground almonds
1 teaspoon xanthan gum
1/2 cup brown sugar
1/2 teaspoon salt
1 teaspoon baking powder, gluten-free
1 cup vegetable shortening or chilled butter or margarine, cut into 1/2-inch pieces
Ice water, as needed

FILLING

1 tablespoon unflavored gelatin (Knox brand is good)
1/4 cup water
4 egg whites
2 1/2 cups Cool Whip (or your favorite non-dairy whipped topping)
1/2 cup Chambord liqueur
1 cup mixed berries
1/2 cup sliced almonds, toasted

1. Preheat oven to 350°F.
2. Make the pastry. In the bowl of a food processor, combine the buckwheat, flours, xanthan gum, sugar, salt, and baking powder.
3. Add the butter and pulse until the mixture almost gathers together. If the dough seems too dry, with the processor running, add the water 1 tablespoon at a time until the mixture binds.
4. Wrap the dough in plastic wrap and refrigerate for 30 minutes.
5. Press the dough into a 10-inch deep ceramic pie dish or roll out the dough on a clean, dry work surface and then place in a pie dish. Bake until golden brown, about 30 to 40 minutes.
6. Cool completely before filling.
7. Prepare filling. Sprinkle the gelatin into the water and let stand to bloom, about 3 to 5 minutes.
8. In the bowl of an electric mixer fitted with the whisk attachment, whip the egg whites until soft peaks form. Transfer to a bowl.
9. In the same bowl of the electric mixer, combine the gelatin mixture, whipped topping, and Chambord on low speed, mixing just enough to combine.
10. Fold the egg whites and berries into the cream mixture by hand.
11. Assemble and serve. Pour the filling into the pie shell and garnish with toasted almonds. Place in the freezer. When ready to serve, slice the tart; let stand 10 minutes before serving.

Chef Katherine's Veggie Side Dishes

KATHERINE EMMENEGGER

Brussels Sprouts with Cranberries and Pecans • Mediterranean Stuffed Eggplant
Sauteéd Green Peas and Sun-Dried Tomatoes with Toasted Walnuts
Roasted Honey-Glazed Cipollini Onions • Szechuan Green Beans

Here Chef Katherine offers an assortment of side dishes to help round out any meal. The eggplant is stuffed with a crispy panko bread-crumb-and-herb mix that can be prepared year-round. Szechuan green beans reflect Chef Katherine's affinity for Asian flavors as well as her love for all things with a spicy kick. Roasted cipollini onions with a honey glaze are a great way to feature what are actually the bulbs of the grape hyacinth! Brussels sprouts with cranberries and pecans, and green peas with sun-dried tomatoes and toasted walnuts are two other wonderful dishes that are sure to win over even those who say they don't like veggies.

Brussels Sprouts with Cranberries and Pecans*

Serves 10

1 cup dried cranberries
2 cups off-dry riesling
3 tablespoons grapeseed oil or vegetable oil
2 large shallots, peeled and diced small
2½ pounds brussels sprouts, trimmed and halved lengthwise
Salt and freshly ground pepper, to taste
3 tablespoons unsalted butter
½ cup pecan pieces, toasted

1. In a microwave-safe bowl, heat the cranberries and wine at high power for 2 minutes. Let stand until the berries are slightly plumped, about 10 minutes.
2. In a large sauté pan, heat the oil over medium heat and sauté the shallots until softened, about 2 minutes. Add the brussels sprouts and cook until bright green, about 2 minutes. Add the wine and cranberries; season with salt and pepper.

3. Reduce the heat to medium, cover, and steam until the brussels sprouts are tender, about 12 minutes. Uncover and continue cooking until the liquid has evaporated, about 2 minutes more. Add the butter and toss to coat.
4. Transfer to a serving dish, top with the pecans, and serve.

Mediterranean Stuffed Eggplant*

Serves 6 as a side dish

FILLING

1/4 cup extra-virgin olive oil
3 large yellow onions, peeled and diced small
4 garlic cloves, minced
3/4 cup minced fresh Italian parsley leaves
1 1/2 cups panko bread crumbs
Salt and pepper, to taste

SAUCE

4 large Roma tomatoes, cored, seeded, and diced small
1/4 cup tomato paste
1/2 cup water
1 teaspoon granulated sugar
1 pinch cinnamon
Salt and pepper, to taste

EGGPLANT

6 small Japanese or Chinese eggplants, washed, slit lengthwise (about 1/2-inch deep)
3 tablespoons vegetable oil

1. Preheat oven to 350°F.
2. Make the filling. In a sauté pan over medium heat, sauté the onions, garlic, and parsley in the oil for about 5 minutes. Add bread crumbs and season with salt and pepper. Transfer from the heat and let cool.
3. Make the sauce. In the same sauté pan, combine all ingredients; simmer for 10 minutes.
4. Make the eggplant. Rub eggplant with oil and place on a baking sheet. Roast at 350°F for 20 minutes. Remove from the oven and let cool. Place in a baking dish.
5. Fill the slits in the eggplant with the filling, cover the dish with foil and place in the oven for 20 to 30 minutes. Remove the foil and roast an additional 10 minutes to brown. Top with the sauce and return to the oven for a final 10 minutes.

Sauteéd Green Peas and Sun-Dried Tomatoes with Toasted Walnuts*

Serves 8

1 medium yellow onion, peeled and julienned
2 tablespoons grapeseed oil
1 garlic clove, minced
1/2 cup oil-packed sun-dried tomatoes, drained and minced
6 cups frozen green peas, thawed
1 cup walnut halves, toasted
Salt and pepper, to taste

1. In a large sauté pan over medium heat, sauté the onion in oil until caramelized, about 5 to 10 minutes. Add the garlic and tomatoes; sauté 2 minutes more. Add the peas, stir to combine, and heat through. Mix in the walnut halves and season with salt and pepper.
2. Transfer to a serving dish.

Roasted Honey-Glazed Cipollini Onions*

Serves 8

GLAZE

2 tablespoons extra-virgin olive oil
1/4 cup honey
2 teaspoons dry mustard
1 tablespoon red wine vinegar
1/2 teaspoon paprika
1/4 teaspoon ground cloves
Salt and pepper, to taste

ONIONS

24 cipollini onions or other small mild onions, root ends sliced off, and onions peeled
1/4 cup water

1. Preheat oven to 350°F.
2. Make the glaze. In a bowl, combine all ingredients.
3. Prepare the onions. Arrange the cipollini in a glass or ceramic baking dish and add the water. Drizzle some of the glaze over each onion. Roast for 40 to 50 minutes or until tender, depending on the size of the onions. Baste with the remaining glaze every 15 to 20 minutes.

Szechuan Green Beans*

Serves 4

1/2 cup vegetable oil
1 pound Chinese long beans, ends trimmed, sliced diagonally into 2-inch-long pieces
2 garlic cloves, minced
1 tablespoon fresh ginger, minced
2 green onions, white part only, root ends removed, thinly sliced
1/2 teaspoon sambal chile paste, or to taste
1 tablespoon low-sodium soy sauce
1/2 teaspoon granulated sugar
1/4 teaspoon salt, or to taste
Szechuan pepper, to taste, optional

1. In a wok, heat the oil to 325°F over medium heat. Add the long beans and fry until they start to shrivel or "pucker" and turn brown, about 3 to 5 minutes.
2. Transfer beans to a paper towel-lined baking sheet. Remove all but 2 tablespoons of the oil. Return the wok to medium-high heat and add the garlic, ginger, and green onions; stir-fry for a few seconds. Add the remaining ingredients and the beans; stir to combine.
3. Transfer to a serving dish.

Sophisticated Cocktail Party

KATHERINE EMMENEGGER

Panko-Crusted Crabmeat Balls • Watermelon Martini • Citrus "Pomartini"
Stuffed Fingerling Potato Skins • Curried Turkey Salad Radicchio Wraps
Mushroom-Dusted Pork Canapés with Chile Crème Fraîche

"Designer" cocktails and martinis have become the rage at home parties, so Chef Katherine included two with this selection of appetizers, which can be served year-round. The stuffed fingerling potato skins are a riff on a classic. The crabmeat balls are given a chic spin with panko crust, and the turkey salad radicchio wraps bring some fresh crunch to the party. The pork tenderloin canapés dusted with mushrooms and topped with a dollop of chile crème fraîche add a touch of elegance to this tasty collection. Your guests be impressed with your style, and they certainly will not go home hungry.

Panko-Crusted Crabmeat Balls

Makes 20 to 24 pieces

1 pound lump crabmeat, cleaned and drained
4 green onions, green parts only, washed, drained, and thinly sliced
1 tablespoon Italian parsley leaves, minced
1/4 pound raw scallops, pureéd to a smooth paste (other raw fish will also work)
2 tablespoons mayonnaise
1 teaspoon Tabasco sauce
2 cups panko bread crumbs, or more if needed
1 tablespoon Old Bay seasoning
Vegetable oil, for frying
Cocktail sauce, for serving

1. In a bowl, combine the crabmeat, onions, parsley, pureéd scallops, mayonnaise, and Tabasco sauce.
2. With a small cookie scoop, portion out balls of the mixture and place on a parchment-lined baking sheet.

3. In a shallow dish, combine the panko crumbs and Old Bay seasoning. Dredge each of the crabmeat balls in the crumbs.
4. In a large, preferably nonstick, sauté pan, heat the oil over medium-high heat until hot but not smoking.
5. Brown the crabmeat balls, turning as they fry, until golden and crisp. Transfer to a baking sheet, and keep warm in a low-temperature oven, about 150°F, for up to 1 hour.
6. Serve with your favorite cocktail sauce.

Watermelon Martini

Serves 8

8 lime twists
Ice cubes
4 cups watermelon juice (press watermelon through a sieve or cheesecloth)
12 ounces premium vodka
4 limes, juiced
1 cup agave syrup or simple syrup, or to taste
8 watermelon wedges, for garnish

1. Rub the rims of 8 martini glasses with the lime twists, drop one into each of the glasses, and refrigerate to chill.
2. In a cocktail shaker, combine the ice, watermelon juice, vodka, lime juice, and agave syrup; shake well.
3. Pour the contents through a strainer into the chilled martini glasses. Garnish each with a wedge of watermelon and serve.

Citrus "Pomartini"

Serves 8

8 orange twists
Ice cubes
16 ounces pomegranate liqueur
8 ounces premium vodka, your favorite
4 ounces Cointreau liqueur

1. Rub the rims of 8 martini glasses with the orange twists, drop one into each of the glasses, and refrigerate to chill.
2. In a cocktail shaker, combine the ice, liqueur, vodka, and Cointreau; shake well.
3. Pour contents through a strainer into the chilled martini glasses. Serve.

Stuffed Fingerling Potato Skins*

Makes 20

10 fingerling potatoes, of similar size and a variety of colors, washed, and drained
2 tablespoons extra-virgin olive oil, or as needed
1/2 cup oil-packed sun-dried tomatoes, minced
1/2 cup pepper Jack cheese, shredded
1/2 cup sour cream
2 tablespoons chives, finely sliced

1. Preheat oven to broil.
2. In a pot of cold salted water over medium-high heat, bring the potatoes to a boil and cook until just tender. Transfer the potatoes from the water, drain, and let cool. Cut the potatoes in half lengthwise. With a melon baller, carefully scoop some of the potato from the center.
3. On a baking sheet, arrange the potatoes (scooped side up) and brush each with oil. Place under the broiler until golden brown and lightly crisp. Remove from the oven and let cool.
4. Make the filling. In a bowl, combine the minced tomatoes and cheese. Top the potatoes with the filling and return to the broiler.
5. Remove from the oven and place on a platter. Top each with sour cream and chives. Serve.

NOTE

- The potatoes can be made ahead up to the point of being filled. They can then be refrigerated until ready to broil, top, and serve.

Curried Turkey Salad Radicchio Wraps

Makes 16

1/2 cup white wine vinegar
2 tablespoons curry powder, or to taste
1 tablespoon fresh ginger, minced
2 tablespoons hot mustard, your favorite
Salt and pepper, to taste
1 cup extra-virgin olive oil
1 large crisp apple, peeled, cored, and diced small
3 green onions, washed, root ends removed, thinly sliced
2 pounds cooked turkey breast meat, julienned
1/2 cup slivered almonds, toasted
Radicchio leaves, washed and dried

1. Make the dressing. In a blender, combine the vinegar, curry powder, ginger, mustard, salt, and pepper. Add the oil in a slow, steady stream to emulsify. Refrigerate until needed.
2. Make turkey salad. In a bowl, combine apple, green onion and turkey. Add the dressing and toss to coat. Cover and refrigerate until needed.
3. Serve. Transfer the turkey salad to a serving dish and top with the almonds; set on a larger platter. Arrange the radicchio around the turkey salad. Allow guests to spoon the turkey salad into the raddichio cups as desired.

Mushroom-Dusted Pork Canapés with Chile Crème Fraîche

Makes 20 to 24 pieces

MUSHROOM DUST

1/2 teaspoon garlic powder
Salt and pepper, to taste
Enough dried porcini mushrooms to equal 3 tablespoons ground to a fine powder

PORK

1 teaspoon extra-virgin olive oil
1 (1-pound) pork tenderloin, trimmed
Vegetable oil for the pan

CHILE CRÈME FRAÎCHE

1/2 cup crème fraîche
Sriracha chile sauce, to taste
1 small garlic clove, minced
Salt and pepper, to taste

ASSEMBLY AND GARNISH

5 slices whole-grain bread, toasted
3 tablespoons butter, softened
1 small package or handful of microgreens or chives, finely sliced

1. Make the mushroom dust. Preheat oven to 425°F. In a bowl, combine all the dust ingredients.
2. Make the pork. Oil the tenderloin and coat with the mushroom dust. In a large oven-proof sauté pan, heat the vegetable oil over medium-high heat, and sear the pork on all sides to brown. Transfer the pan to the oven and roast for 15 minutes, or until a thermometer registers a minimum of 155°F. Transfer the pork to a platter, cover loosely with foil, and let stand 10 minutes. Slice the pork into 1/4-inch-thick slices.
3. Make the créme fraîche. In a bowl, combine all ingredients.
4. Assemble, garnish, and serve. Spread the butter on the toasted bread and cut each slice into 4 rounds using a small biscuit cutter. On a platter, place a slice of pork on each round, top with a dollop of the chile crème fraîche, and garnish with microgreens or chives.

Flavors From Around the World

KATHERINE EMMENEGGER

Chinese Veggie Spring Rolls • African Doro Wot with Injera Bread (Spicy Chicken Stew with Spongy Flat Bread)
Russian Pierogi (Potato-and-Cheese-Filled Dumplings) • Vietnamese Chuoi Chien (Fried Stuffed Bananas)

In this diverse menu, Chef Katherine has assembled an interesting collection of recipes from around the globe. The crispy spring rolls hail from China, the doro wat (chicken stew) with spongy injera bread is an African classic, pierogi (dumplings) are a staple in Russia, and chuoi chien (stuffed bananas) are a favorite from Vietnam.

Chinese Veggie Spring Rolls*

Serves 8

CHILE-HOISIN DIPPING SAUCE

1 1/2 cups hoisin sauce
1/2 cup sake
1 tablespoon Sambal Oelek (or your favorite hot sauce)
1 tablespoon fresh ginger, grated
2 garlic cloves, minced
1 tablespoon sesame oil
Salt and pepper, to taste

SPRING ROLLS

1 package (8 1/2-inch) rice spring roll wrappers
1 cup loosely packed fresh cilantro leaves
1 (6-ounce) package pea sprouts
1 cup carrots, finely julienned
1 cup daikon radish, finely julienned
1 cup cucumber, finely julienned
4 green onions, washed, root end removed, cut to 4-inch lengths and julienned
1 (5-ounce) package rice vermicelli, soaked in warm water to soften, drained well

1. **Make the dipping sauce.** In a bowl, combine all the sauce ingredients. Cover and refrigerate until ready to use.
2. **Make the spring rolls.** Fill a large, shallow dish with warm water. Soak the spring roll wrappers, one at a time, until pliable, about 5 to 10 seconds. Transfer from the water to a clean work surface.
3. Arrange some of the cilantro leaves, pea sprouts, carrots, radish, cucumbers, green onions, and rice noodles in the center of the wrapper.
4. Fold in the sides and roll the wrapper around the filling. Cut the roll in half at an angle and arrange on a platter.
5. Cover the rolls with a damp paper towel to keep them moist. Continue in the same manner with the remaining ingredients. Keep refrigerated for up to 3 hours before serving.
6. Serve with the dipping sauce.

African Doro Wot with Injera Bread (Spicy Chicken Stew with Spongy Flat Bread)

Serves 4 • Bread need to ferment for 24 hours or up to 3 days

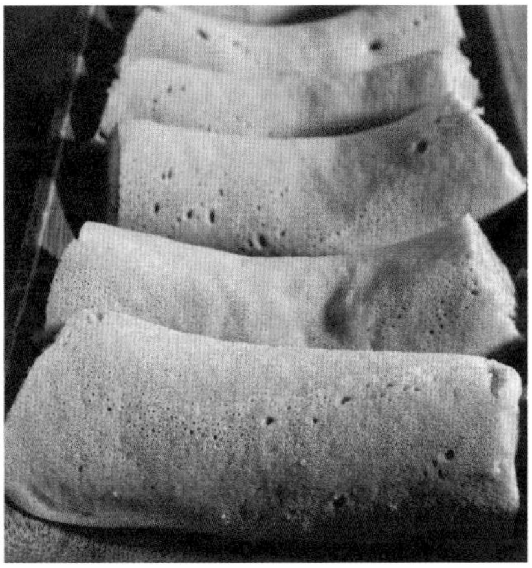

INJERA BREAD

1/4 cup teff flour, finely ground
3/4 cup all-purpose flour
1 cup water
Pinch salt
1 teaspoon dry yeast, if needed
Vegetable oil

DORO WAT

8 boneless, skinless chicken thighs
Salt and pepper
4 tablespoons unsalted butter
2 medium yellow onions, peeled and diced small
4 garlic cloves, minced
1 teaspoon fresh ginger, finely minced
1/2 teaspoon ground coriander
1/2 teaspoon ground fenugreek or ground fennel
1/8 teaspoon ground cloves
1 tablespoon paprika
1 teaspoon ground turmeric
1/2 teaspoon ground cardamom
1/2 teaspoon ground cinnamon
1/2 teaspoon ground nutmeg
Salt and cayenne pepper, to taste
4 Roma tomatoes, cored, seeded, and diced small
2 cups chicken stock
1 cup dry red wine
4 hard-boiled eggs, peeled and pierced 3 to 4 times

1. Make the bread. In a bowl, combine the teff flour and all-purpose flour. Slowly add the water, stirring to avoid lumps. Add the salt and stir to combine.

2. Cover and set the batter in a draft-free location for 24 hours or up to 3 days to ferment. The mixture will be slightly bubbly and develop a tangy flavor. If this has not occurred within 1 day, add 1 teaspoon of dry active yeast.

3. In a lightly oiled nonstick sauté pan over medium-high heat, coat the pan with a thin layer of the batter to form a flat bread that is thicker than a crêpe but not as thick as a traditional pancake; it will rise slightly when it heats. When holes appear on the surface of the bread and it begins to dry, remove the bread from the pan and let it cool.

4. Make the Doro Wat. Season the chicken with salt and pepper. In a Dutch oven over medium-high heat, melt the butter and sauté the chicken until browned, about 2 to 3 minutes per side. Transfer to a platter.

5. In the same pot, sauté the onions to soften, about 5 minutes. Add the garlic, ginger, coriander, fenugreek, cloves, paprika, turmeric, cardamom, cinnamon, nutmeg, salt, and cayenne pepper; sauté 1 minute more. Add the tomatoes, chicken stock, and wine; bring to a boil.

6. Return the chicken to the pot, reduce the heat to medium-low, cover, and simmer for 30 to 40 minutes.

7. Add the hard-boiled eggs for the last 15 minutes of cooking, pressing them gently into cooking liquid. Serve with the injera bread.

NOTE

• *Berbere* spice mix and *niter kibbeh*, a spiced butter, are traditionally used, but to achieve the same flavor and simplify the recipe, the stew can be made as above.

Russian Pierogi (Potato-and-Cheese-Filled Dumplings)*

Makes about 30

POTATO FILLING

$2^1/_2$ pounds red potatoes, washed, peeled, and cut into 2-inch pieces
1 tablespoon butter
1 pound yellow onions, peeled and finely diced
Salt and pepper, to taste
1 cup crumbled brinza or feta cheese

CARAMELIZED ONIONS

2 tablespoons vegetable oil
2 large yellow onions, peeled and julienned

PIEROGI DOUGH

$4^1/_2$ cups all-purpose flour, sifted, plus more for rolling out the dough
2 teaspoons salt
2 small eggs, lightly beaten
3 tablespoons sour cream, plus more for garnish
$^3/_4$ cup lukewarm water; or as needed

Special Equipment Needed:

$3^1/_2$-inch round cutter
Dumpling press

1. Make the potato filling. Put the potatoes in a large pot and add enough water to cover them. Season the water with salt and boil the potatoes until tender, about 10 minutes. Drain well and transfer to a large bowl. Mash the potatoes with no added liquid.
2. In a sauté pan over medium heat, melt the butter and sauté the onions. Season with salt and pepper.
3. Combine the onions and cheese with the potato. Do not over-mix. Adjust the seasoning. The filling can be made 1 to 2 days in advance and kept refrigerated.
4. Make the caramelized onions. In a large sauté pan over medium heat, sauté the onions in oil until softened and amber in color, about 30 minutes. Refrigerate until ready to use.
5. Make the pierogi dough. In a bowl, combine the flour and salt. Make a well in the center of the flour and add the eggs, sour cream, and water. Work the mixture together with a fork; do not overwork the dough — it should be sticky and not very smooth. Let stand for 30 minutes.
6. On a clean, dry work surface well dusted with flour, turn the dough out from the bowl and lightly work in a bit more flour. Divide the dough in half. Roll out the dough on the well-floured surface until it is $^1/_{16}$-inch thick.
7. Assemble the pierogi. Cut the rolled dough into circles with a well-floured cutter. Place a heaping scoop of the filling into the center of each dough circle. Fold the dough over so that the edges meet. Place the dumpling into the press and press to seal the pierogi; you can also press with your fingers or the tines of a fork.
8. Transfer the dumplings to a lightly floured parchment-lined baking sheet. The pierogi can be frozen at this stage, then transferred to an airtight container and stored for up to 6 months.
9. Cook the pierogi. Carefully place the pierogi in a large pot of boiling water with a perforated insert. Boil from a fresh or frozen state for a total of 10 to 12 minutes, or until the pierogi float to the surface. Carefully stir the pierogi periodically during the cooking process.
10. Garnish and serve. Drain and transfer to serving plates. Serve with the caramelized onions and additional sour cream.

NOTE

- Wonton wrappers can be used for making the pierogi, though they are thinner than the traditional dough.

Vietnamese Chuoi Chien (Fried Stuffed Bananas)

Serves 8

BATTER

2/3 cup all-purpose flour, sifted
1/4 cup cornstarch, sifted
2 tablespoons granulated sugar
1 teaspoon salt
1 teaspoon baking powder
2/3 cup plus 2 tablespoons water
1 tablespoon vegetable oil

BANANAS

4 large ripe but firm bananas, peeled, cut in half crosswise, and then in half lengthwise
3/4 cup pecans, chopped
3/4 cup sweetened coconut flakes
1 tablespoon pure vanilla extract
1 tablespoon water
Vegetable oil, for deep frying
Cornstarch, for coating
1/2 cup rum
Powdered sugar

1. Make the batter. In a bowl, combine the flour, cornstarch, sugar, salt, and baking powder. Add the water and oil; mix until smooth.
2. Prepare the bananas, keeping each set of two long halves together.
3. In a food processor fitted with the steel blade, combine the pecans, coconut, vanilla extract, and water; process until smooth.
4. Place 1/2 tablespoon of the filling between each of the sets of banana pieces. Lightly dredge the bananas in comstarch and shake off the excess. In a large saucepan, heat about 2 inches of oil to 375°F.

5. Coat the bananas in the batter, letting the excess drain off. Place in the hot oil and fry until golden brown, about 1 to 2 minutes for each side.
6. Transfer to a paper towel-lined baking sheet.
7. Place the bananas in a stainless steel sauté pan, over medium heat. Pour the rum over the bananas and bring to a simmer. Carefully light the rum and let the fire burn until it goes out.
8. Transfer the bananas to a serving plate and dust with powdered sugar.

summer

summer menus

NOTE: Recipes highlighted with an asterisk (*) are vegetarian or can easily be adapted to be vegetarian.

Cooking with Beer

PHILLIS CAREY

Cheesy Beer Fondue with Smoked Sausage, Broccoli, and Bread Dippers
Orange Ginger Beer Flank Steak • Borracha Chipotle BBQ White Beans • Beer and Bacon Kale
Cheddar and Chile Beer Muffins • Guinness Chocolate Brownies

San Diego has been called the "Napa Valley of Beer" because it's home to more than 40 microbreweries that brew some amazing, award-winning craft beers. That's what inspired Chef Phillis to create an entire menu focused on beer. Start the celebration with some potentially messy fun with cheesy beer fondue. Then move to the grill for beer-marinated flank steak. The side dishes have beer, too: borracha (Spanish for "drunken") BBQ white beans, kale with beer and bacon, and chile and cheddar muffins with, of course, beer. Finish your meal appropriately with Guinness chocolate brownies. Why not make it a BYOG (bring your own growler) tasting party so everyone can sample a variety of craft beers? (A growler is a refillable 64-ounce bottle you bring to a brewery for beer fresh from the tap.)

Cheesy Beer Fondue with Smoked Sausage, Broccoli, and Bread Dippers

Serves 6 to 8

1/2 pound fully cooked kielbasa sausage, cut into 1-inch-thick slices
2 cups beer, divided use
2 cups grated sharp cheddar cheese
2 cups grated Emmentaler cheese
2 tablespoons flour
1/2 teaspoon dry mustard
1/4 teaspoon freshly ground pepper
1 clove garlic, cut in half lengthwise
1/8 teaspoon hot pepper sauce
1/2 loaf French bread, cut into 1-inch cubes
2 to 3 cups broccoli florets, raw

1. Place sausage and 1/2 cup beer in a medium saucepan and bring to a boil. Reduce heat and simmer for 8 minutes; drain and set sausage aside.
2. Toss cheeses, flour, dry mustard, and pepper in a large bowl until cheese is coated with flour. Rub bottom and sides of a 3-quart saucepan with cut clove of garlic. Add remaining beer to saucepan and bring just to a simmer over medium-low heat. Add cheese, a handful at a time, to the beer, stirring after each addition until cheese is melted and smooth. Stir in hot pepper sauce.
3. Transfer fondue to a fondue pot to keep warm. Serve with sausage, bread cubes, and broccoli for dipping.

Orange Ginger Beer Flank Steak

Serves 6 to 8 • Marinate 1 to 36 hours

2 (1 1/2- to 2-pounds each) flank steaks
1 1/2 cups beer
1/2 cup olive oil
2 tablespoons fresh ginger, finely chopped
2 cloves garlic, minced
1 (1x3-inch piece) orange peel

1. Place the meat in a casserole dish. In a medium bowl, stir together the beer, olive oil, ginger, garlic, and orange peel. Pour over the flank steak, cover, and let stand at room temperature 1 hour or refrigerate up to 36 hours, turning occasionally to evenly distribute flavors.
2. Strain the marinade into a small saucepan, bring to a simmer, and then cook 2 minutes. Set aside to use as a basting sauce.
3. Grill the flank steak 7 to 9 minutes per side or to desired doneness, basting once or twice with the cooked marinade. Let steak stand at least 5 minutes before slicing across the grain into thin strips. You may serve any remaining basting sauce over the sliced meat.

Borracha Chipotle BBQ White Beans

Serves 8

3 slices bacon, diced
1 1/2 cups onions, chopped
1 1/4 cup barbecue sauce (your favorite)
3/4 cup dark beer
1/4 cup molasses
3 tablespoons Dijon mustard
3 tablespoons dark brown sugar
2 tablespoons Worcestershire sauce
1 tablespoon soy sauce
2 to 4 teaspoons canned chipotle chiles in adobo sauce, minced
6 (15-ounce) cans Great Northern beans, drained
Fresh parsley, chopped

1. Preheat oven to 350°F. Cook bacon in a large skillet over medium-high heat until crispy; remove to paper towels to drain. Drain off all but 2 tablespoons bacon fat and sauté onions until tender, about 6 minutes.
2. Transfer onions to a large bowl and stir in bacon and all the remaining ingredients except the parsley. Pour into a 13x9-inch baking dish and bake, covered, until liquid bubbles and thickens slightly, 45 to 60 minutes. Cool 10 minutes, sprinkle with parsley, and serve.

Beer and Bacon Kale

Serves 8

$^1/_2$ pound bacon, chopped
3 cups onions, sliced
Salt and pepper, to taste
Pinch cayenne
1 tablespoon garlic, minced
1 (12-ounce) can or bottle beer
$^1/_4$ cup rice vinegar
1 tablespoon molasses
6 pounds kale, thick stalks removed and leaves cut into wide strips

1. Cook bacon in a large Dutch oven over medium-high heat until crispy, about 5 minutes. Add the onions and cook for 6 to 7 minutes, or until wilted. Season with salt, pepper, and cayenne. Add the garlic and cook 1 minute longer.

2. Stir in beer, vinegar, and molasses, and bring to a simmer. Stir in kale, a third at a time, pressing down as greens start to wilt. Cook the kale, uncovered, stirring often, for 30 minutes, or until very tender. Serve with a slotted spoon.

Cheddar and Chile Beer Muffins*

Makes 8 to 12

3 cups self-rising flour
2 tablespoons white sugar
1 (12-ounce) bottle beer
1/2 cup grated cheddar cheese
1 (4-ounce) can diced green chiles
6 tablespoons butter, melted

1. Preheat oven to 375°F. Coat a muffin pan with nonstick spray.
2. In a large bowl, stir together flour, sugar, beer, cheese, and chiles. Spoon into muffin cups and brush tops with melted butter. Bake for 20 to 30 minutes, or until a toothpick inserted into center of muffins comes out clean. Turn out onto a rack to cool slightly before serving.

Guinness Chocolate Brownies

Makes 16

1 cup flour
3/4 cup unsweetened cocoa powder
1/4 teaspoon salt
6 tablespoons unsalted butter, cut into cubes
8 ounces bittersweet chocolate, chopped
5 ounces white chocolate, chopped
4 large eggs, at room temperature
1 cup sugar
1/4 cup Guinness stout, room temperature
1 cup semisweet chocolate chips
Powdered sugar, for dusting
Vanilla ice cream

1. Preheat oven to 375°F. Line a 9x13-inch pan with aluminum foil and butter the foil.
2. In a medium bowl, whisk together flour, cocoa powder, and salt to combine; set aside. Melt butter with bittersweet chocolate and white chocolate in a glass bowl in the microwave on high power for 1 minute; stir and microwave 30 seconds longer; stir until smooth.
3. With a mixer, beat eggs and sugar on high speed until light and fluffy, about 3 minutes. Add melted chocolate mixture, beating on medium-low speed until combined. Beat in flour mixture alternately with stout beer; the batter will seem a bit thin.
4. Pour batter into prepared pan and sprinkle with semisweet chocolate chips — some will sink. Bake 25 to 30 minutes, or until a tester inserted in the middle comes out almost clean. Cool on a rack.
5. Serve. Sprinkle with powdered sugar and serve with ice cream.

Vacation in Mexico

DEBORAH SCHNEIDER

Secret Sauce • Avocado Sauce • Pico de Gallo • Salsa de Chiles de Arbol
Fish Tacos "La Bufadora" • Churros

Chef Deborah Schneider is THE expert when it comes to Mexican cuisine. She has traveled, researched, and written about food in Mexico, and has authored several cookbooks, including one with Rancho La Puerta Spa, just south of the border in Tecate. In this menu, she shares secrets for preparing the best fish tacos you'll ever have. The fish taco is one of San Diego's favorite comfort foods, made popular by surfers bringing it back from their visits to Mexican fishing villages. The tasty creation is a battered fried piece of freshly caught white fish served up with avocado sauce, pico de gallo, salsa de chiles de arbol, and, of course, a "secret" sauce. The fillings are served in fresh corn tortillas with shredded cabbage and a squeeze of lime. Crispy, cinnamon sugar-covered churros end the meal on a sweet note.

Secret Sauce

Enough for 24 tacos

1/2 cup mayonnaise or lime-flavored mayonnaise
1 to 2 teaspoons white vinegar
1 1/2 tablespoons water or milk

1. There is no secret, of course. With a fork, slowly add the vinegar to the mayonnaise. Add water until it loosens up; it should be the consistency of thick cream.

Avocado Sauce

Enough for 24 tacos

This is not guacamole, but a creamy, thin sauce used at many street stands to lend a little moisture and flavor to fish or carne asada tacos. Recipe can easily be doubled, if desired.

1/4 avocado, peeled
Pinch salt
Few drops lime juice
1 to 2 tablespoons water or milk
2 sprigs cilantro, stemmed and chopped (optional)

1. Place the avocado, salt, and lime juice in a blender jar. Add 1 tablespoon of the water or milk and pulse. Add more liquid as necessary to make a sauce the consistency of thick cream. Add the cilantro last, and pulse again just to blend. Taste for seasoning; it should be a little bland.

Pico de Gallo

Makes 2½ cups

5 large ripe Roma tomatoes
6 cilantro sprigs, stemmed
1 small white onion
2 serrano chiles (optional)
2 teaspoons kosher salt, or to taste
1 lime, juiced

1. On a large cutting board, core the tomatoes and slice thinly. Push to one side. Roughly chop the cilantro and push it beside the tomatoes. Cut the onion into the smallest dice you can manage and push aside. Chop the serranos.
2. Use the side of your knife to push the onions and chiles back into the middle of the board. Chop by holding the tip of your knife down with one hand and pivoting the blade back and forth, occasionally sweeping the pile back into the center with the edge of your knife. Chop until the onions are a little more finely diced.
3. Scoop up the tomatoes and cilantro, put them on top of the onions, and keep chopping back and forth — sweeping into a pile — until all the ingredients are finely chopped and blended together.
4. When the salsa is a rosy, juicy heap, scoop everything, including the juices, into a serving bowl. Season with the salt and lime juice. Let the flavors blend for at least 30 minutes before serving.

Salsa de Chiles de Arbol

Makes ½ cup

Chiles de Arbol are a Mexican red chile pepper. They are small in size but strong in heat.

1 garlic clove, unpeeled
1 cup (about 30) chiles de arbol, stemmed
¾ cup water
½ teaspoon kosher salt, or to taste
1 teaspoon vinegar, or to taste

1. Heat a heavy frying pan or comal over high heat, in a well-ventilated area. Add the garlic and roast until soft and brown (about 7 minutes). Remove the peel.
2. Seed the chiles and place in a blender. Process until well pulverized. Add the garlic, water, and salt, and pureé until as smooth as possible. Scrape into a bowl and add the vinegar. Let stand 30 minutes. Taste for seasoning. The sauce should be hot and highly seasoned; add more vinegar and salt, if necessary. If desired, the salsa may be thinned with a little water.

NOTE

- This sauce may be strained before serving, but don't bother. If you want it hotter, leave the seeds in.

Fish Tacos "La Bufadora"

Enough for 24 tacos

THE FISH

2 cups all-purpose flour
1 1/2 teaspoons baking powder
1/2 teaspoon granulated garlic
1/4 teaspoon cayenne
1/2 teaspoon dry mustard
1/2 teaspoon whole Mexican oregano, rubbed to a powder
1 teaspoon kosher salt
1/2 teaspoon ground black pepper
12 ounces (1 bottle) cold beer, plus more to thin the batter if necessary
2 pounds fresh, firm, meaty fish
1/2 lime, juiced
Kosher salt
Vegetable oil, for deep frying

ASSEMBLY AND GARNISH

24 corn tortillas
Secret Sauce (see recipe page 90)
Avocado Sauce (see recipe page 90)
Salsa de Chiles de Arbol (see recipe page 91)
Pico de Gallo (see recipe page 91)
Finely shredded green cabbage (not lettuce!)
Lime wedges
Cilantro leaves
White onions, chopped (optional)

1. Make the batter: In a bowl, whisk together the flour, baking powder, garlic, cayenne, mustard, oregano, salt, and pepper until well blended. Stir in the beer until there are no lumps. (Batter may be made several hours ahead and refrigerated.)
2. Trim the fish of all blood lines and skin. Cut into pieces the size and shape of your index finger. Sprinkle with a few drops of lime juice and a little salt. (If not using immediately, wrap and refrigerate.)
3. Pour the oil into a deep, wide pan to a depth of 2 inches and heat over medium-high heat to 350°F. (A deep-fry thermometer is best, but also test the heat by dropping a little of the batter into the oil. It should bounce to the surface almost immediately and be surrounded by little bubbles.)
4. Pat the fish dry with paper towels. Check the thickness of the batter by dipping one piece of fish. The batter should be the consistency of medium-thick pancake batter, coating the fish easily and dripping very little. Add a little beer if the batter seems too thick.
5. Add the fish to the batter. Using tongs, thoroughly coat each piece of fish, then lift it out of the batter, let it drip once, and lay the fish gently into the hot oil. Cook a few pieces at a time until they float and the batter is set but still very light in color. If a piece sticks to the bottom, leave it alone — it will release itself.
6. Remove the fish to a rack to drain; reserve the frying oil. (The fish can be prepared ahead to this point, cooled on a rack, and refrigerated uncovered. Cool the oil and reserve.)
7. When you are ready to serve, reheat the oil to 350°F to 360°F and refry the fish a few pieces at a time until crisp and golden brown. While you fry the fish, quickly heat the tortillas on a hot griddle until they soften; wrap in foil to keep warm.
8. Assemble, garnish, and serve. Hold a tortilla in your hand and add a spoonful of avocado sauce. Top with fish and a squeeze of lime. Then drizzle a little secret sauce and a few drops of chiles de arbol sauce. Top with pico de gallo and shredded cabbage. Add a cilantro leaf or some extra white onions, if desired.

Churros

Makes about 20 (5-inch) churros

2 cups water
1 tablespoon granulated sugar
1 teaspoon salt
2 tablespoons vegetable oil
2 cups all-purpose flour, sifted
4 large eggs
1 lime, zested
2 teaspoons pure vanilla extract
3 to 4 cups vegetable oil, for frying
1/2 cup granulated sugar
1 tablespoon ground cinnamon

1. Combine the water, sugar, salt, and oil in a 2-quart saucepan. Bring to a boil quickly and immediately remove from the heat. Add all the flour at once and beat with a wooden spoon until well combined.
2. Transfer to the bowl of a standing mixer fitted with a paddle. Beat the dough until smooth and no longer steaming hot but still warm. Add the eggs, one at a time, beating well after each addition and scraping the sides of the bowl several times. (After each egg, the dough will break into lumps, but as you mix, it will come back together.) Add lime zest and vanilla.
3. Fit a small star tip (No. 5 or No. 7) in a pastry bag or cookie press. Transfer the dough to the pastry bag, filling the bag no more than halfway.
4. Pour the oil into a 12-inch sauté pan to a depth of 1 inch and heat over medium-high heat to 360°F

RON'S TIP

CDN Deep Fry Thermometers

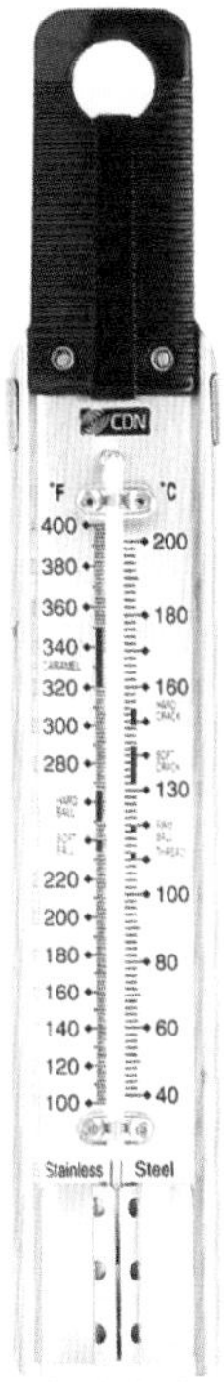

With a good deep-fry thermometer, you can avoid soggy, greasy fried food, or foods that burn to a crisp on the outside while remaining uncooked on the inside. For deep frying, candy and jelly making, the CDN thermometer is a handy tool. It is easy to read and has a plastic handle that remains cool to the touch. A sliding clip allows it to fit any size pot and to hold onto the pot edge securely. A color-coded scale shows temperature ranges for each stage of candy making, and there is a dual Fahrenheit or Celsius scale that ranges from 100°F (38°C) to 400°F (204°C).

(measured on a deep-fry thermometer).
5. Pipe the dough in straight lines about 5 inches long directly into the hot oil. Use a sharp knife or kitchen scissors to "cut" the dough off at the tip.
6. Fry on both sides until the churros are a deep golden brown and very crisp, 3 to 5 minutes. Drain well on paper towels.
7. Garnish and serve. Combine the sugar and cinnamon. Dust the warm churros with the cinnamon-sugar and serve immediately.

Ribbin' It

STAN GLENN AND CHRIS BRILL, IOWA MEAT FARMS AND SIESEL'S MEATS

French Country-Style Lamb Ribs with Mustard Bread-Crumb Crust • Asian-Style Baby-Back Ribs
Barbecued St. Louis-Style Ribs with BBQ Sauce • Country-Style Ribs with Smoky Beans

In San Diego people eat ribs year-round, but in summer grilling ribs is practically a requirement. Our friends and expert butchers at Siesel's and Iowa Meat Farms share with us not only their great-quality meats, but also their recipes and tips on how best to prepare them. These recipes feature both pork and lamb ribs, but they can also be used for beef ribs. They include a classic St. Louis-style rib with dry rub, finished with barbecue sauce; French country-style lamb ribs with mustard-bread-crumb crust, and two styles of marinated ribs — smoky country style and zesty Asian. These last two are best when left overnight to marinate. The extra time is worth it!

French Country-Style Lamb Ribs with Mustard Bread-Crumb Crust

Serves 4 • Marinate for several hours or overnight

MARINADE

1/4 cup olive oil
1/4 cup red wine
2 tablespoons whole-grain Dijon mustard
3 cloves garlic, minced
1 teaspoon fresh rosemary, minced
1 teaspoon fresh mint, minced
Salt and pepper, to taste

RIBS

2 racks lamb ribs
1/2 cup red wine
1/2 cup water

HERB CRUST

1/2 cup panko bread crumbs
Fresh or dried herbs, to taste
2 tablespoons butter, melted
Salt and pepper, to taste

HONEY MUSTARD

2 tablespoons Dijon mustard
2 tablespoons whole-grain Dijon mustard
1/4 cup honey

1. Make the marinade. Combine all the marinade ingredients.
2. Prepare the ribs. Brush ribs with marinade and marinate in the refrigerator for several hours or overnight.
3. Cook the ribs. Preheat oven to 350°F. Place ribs in a baking dish or baking sheet. Add wine and water to the bottom of the pan. Cover with foil, sealing well. Bake for 60 to 75 minutes.
4. Make the herb crust. Combine bread crumbs, herbs, and butter. Mix well and season with salt and pepper.

RON'S TIP

Rösle Garlic Presses

The clever German-designed lever system of the Rösle makes pressing garlic effortless. You don't even have to peel the clove of garlic to achieve excellent mincing results. Pressed clove pieces always come out in a uniform size and texture. The oversized basket holds larger elephant garlic cloves or several smaller cloves. Best of all, this tool is simple to clean. There are no loose pieces, just a pivoting sieve component that completely opens up for simple rinsing. Storage is also easy; there is a locking handle that keeps the press closed and a ring on the end in case you want to hang it on a hook.

5. Make the honey mustard mixture. Combine the mustards and honey.
6. Remove the foil from the ribs. Brush the racks with the mustard mixture and sprinkle with herb crumbs. Return the ribs to the oven.
7. Bake for 15 minutes, or until crumbs are golden brown, and serve.

Asian-Style Baby-Back Ribs

Serves 4 • Marinate for several hours or overnight

MARINADE AND SAUCE

$^3/_4$ cup ketchup
$^1/_2$ cup hoisin sauce
$^1/_2$ cup honey
$^1/_4$ cup sesame oil
$^1/_4$ cup soy sauce
2 teaspoons granulated garlic
1 teaspoon freshly ground black pepper
1 teaspoon salt

SPICE MIXTURE

1 tablespoon five-spice powder
1 tablespoon granulated garlic
1 teaspoon black pepper
1 teaspoon white pepper
2 teaspoons salt

RIBS

2 racks baby-back ribs
1 cup pineapple juice
1 cup water
Sesame seeds

1. Make the marinade and sauce. Combine all the ingredients and mix well.
2. Make the spice mixture. Combine all the dry spices and mix well.
3. Prepare the ribs. Sprinkle ribs with dry spice mixture and massage into meat. Brush ribs with $^3/_4$ cup of the sauce (reserve the rest of the sauce for Step 4) and marinate for several hours or overnight in the refrigerator.
4. Cook the ribs. Preheat oven to 325°F. Place ribs in a baking dish and pour the juice and water over the top. Cover with foil and seal well. Bake for $1^1/_2$ hours, or until the ribs are tender. Remove the foil and baste ribs twice with the reserved sauce, baking 10 minutes in between basting, or until ribs are sticky and glazed.
5. Garnish and serve. Garnish with sesame seeds and serve.

Barbecued St. Louis Style Ribs with BBQ Sauce

Serves 6 to 8

RIBS

2 racks baby-back ribs
$^1/_4$ cup dry rub (your favorite kind)
12 ounces (1 bottle) beer
Barbecue sauce, as needed

1. Season ribs generously with dry rub and massage.
2. Place ribs in a baking dish and pour the beer over the top.
3. Cover tightly with foil and bake in a 350°F oven for 60 to 90 minutes, or until tender.
4. Remove ribs and finish on a grill, basting often with sauce.

Country-Style Ribs with Smoky Beans

Serves 6 • Requires overnight soaking of beans and marinating of ribs

SMOKY MARINADE

2 1/2 pounds country-style pork ribs
1/3 cup storebought barbecue sauce

BEANS

2 tablespoons olive oil
1 cup onion, diced
2 cloves garlic, minced
1 jalapeño pepper, minced
1 pound dried pinto beans, soaked overnight
7 cups water or stock
1 bay leaf
3/4 cup ketchup
1/4 cup brown sugar
2 tablespoons molasses
1/3 cup yellow mustard
1 teaspoon paprika
1 teaspoon dried thyme
1 teaspoon chili powder
1 teaspoon garlic powder
Salt and pepper, to taste

1. Prepare the meat. Coat the pork with the barbecue sauce, cover, and marinate overnight in the refrigerator.
2. Cook the meat. Cook the ribs on a grill for 15 minutes (low heat) or in a 350°F oven for 20 minutes.
3. Make the beans. Heat oil in a large pot, add onions, and sauté until soft and translucent, about 5 minutes. Add the garlic and jalapeño, and sauté for 1 minute. Add soaked beans, stock or water, and bay leaf, and bring to a boil. Reduce to a simmer and cook for 15 minutes. Add pork ribs and simmer for 1 hour, until beans and pork are tender. (The beans and pork can also be transferred to the oven and baked at 325°F until tender.) Combine the remaining ingredients, stir into beans, and cook for another 30 minutes, until flavors have come together. Taste and adjust seasoning with salt and pepper.

Sensational Summer Salads

DIANE PHILLIPS

Sugar Snap Pea, Corn, and Bacon Salad • Arugula, Blood Orange, and Red Onion Salad
Orzo, Corn, and Tomato Salad
Roasted Marinated Baby Artichokes and Baby Shiitakes on Mixed Greens with Lemon Dill Aioli
Sesame Noodle Salad with Pulled Pork Shoulder

This collection of salads is not your ordinary plate of greens. Serve these up for a cool summer dinner or brunch. Either way they satisfy the craving for something fresh and delicious. These salads use amazing ingredients grown in San Diego County, where dozens of boutique farms provide the freshest greens and produce available. The final recipe is sesame noodle salad with pulled pork shoulder. It uses a slow cooker for the pork, so plan ahead for this salad. You will be happy to have the extra pulled pork to use for other meals!

Sugar Snap Pea, Corn, and Bacon Salad

Serves 10 to 12 • Make at least 4 hours in advance

SALAD

1/4 cup (1/2 stick) butter
1 cup onion, finely chopped
1 1/2 pounds sugar snap peas
4 cups fresh or defrosted frozen corn kernels

SWEET MUSTARD VINAIGRETTE

3/4 cup vegetable oil
1/2 cup rice vinegar
3 tablespoons firmly packed light brown sugar
2 tablespoons Dijon mustard
1 teaspoon salt
1 teaspoon freshly ground black pepper
12 strips bacon, cooked until crisp, drained on paper towels, and crumbled
1/4 cup fresh chives, snipped

1. **Make the salad.** In a large skillet over medium heat, melt the butter. Cook the onion, stirring, until it begins to caramelize, 10 to 15 minutes.
2. Add the peas and cook for another 2 minutes, tossing the peas in the butter-and-onion mixture. Transfer the mixture to a large salad bowl and let the peas cool.
3. Add the corn to the bowl and stir to blend.
4. **Make the vinaigrette.** In a medium bowl, whisk together the oil, vinegar, brown sugar, mustard, salt, and pepper until thickened. Pour over the salad and toss to blend well.
5. **Diva Do-Ahead:** Cover and refrigerate for at least 4 hours or overnight.
6. Remove from the refrigerator 30 minutes before serving and toss with the bacon and chives.

Arugula, Blood Orange, and Red Onion Salad*

Serves 6 • Make 8 to 24 hours in advance

MARINATED RED ONIONS

2 large red onions, cut in half and thinly sliced into half-moons (about 3 cups)
3/4 cup red wine vinegar
1/2 cup granulated sugar
1/2 cup vegetable oil
Pinch red pepper flakes
1 teaspoon dried oregano
1 teaspoon salt
1/2 teaspoon freshly ground black pepper

SALAD

2 bunches arugula, washed and spun dry
2 blood oranges, sectioned
Marinated red onions
1/3 cup blood orange juice
2 teaspoons balsamic vinegar
3/4 cup extra-virgin olive oil
1 teaspoon salt
1/2 teaspoon freshly ground black pepper
1 cup crumbled goat cheese

1. Make the red onions. Place the onions in a glass bowl. In another bowl, whisk together the vinegar, sugar, oil, pepper flakes, oregano, salt, and pepper. Pour over the onions.

2. Diva Do-Ahead: At this point, cover and refrigerate the onions for at least 8 hours and up to 24 hours.

3. Drain the onions. You can cover and refrigerate for up to 3 to 4 days at this point.

4. Assemble salad. Arrange the arugula on salad plates. Top with orange sections and red onion.

5. In a small bowl, whisk together the orange juice, vinegar, olive oil, salt, and pepper.

6. Drizzle the dressing over the salad and garnish with the crumbled goat cheese. Serve immediately.

7. The dressing can be made 4 days ahead and refrigerated until you are ready to use it.

Orzo, Corn, and Tomato Salad*

Serves 8

1 (16-ounce) box orzo pasta
1/4 cup extra-virgin olive oil
2 tablespoons red wine vinegar
1 teaspoon oregano, finely chopped
2 teaspoons thyme, finely chopped
2 tablespoons chives, finely chopped
1 teaspoon salt
1/2 teaspoon freshly ground black pepper
1 1/2 cups corn, either cut from the cob or frozen and defrosted
2 cups heirloom tomatoes, chopped
1/4 cup Italian parsley, finely chopped

1. Cook the pasta. Cook the orzo in boiling salted water for 8 to 10 minutes, until *al dente*. Drain thoroughly and transfer to a large bowl.
2. Make the dressing. In a small bowl, whisk together the oil, vinegar, oregano, thyme, and chives. Stir in the salt and pepper, and toss half of the dressing with the warm orzo. Add the corn, tomatoes, and parsley, and toss together.
3. Diva Do-Ahead. At this point, the salad can be covered with plastic wrap and refrigerated for up to 2 days.
4. Serve. Bring the salad to room temperature and toss with additional dressing before serving.

RON'S TIP

Trudeau Graviti Pepper Mill

This pepper mill is as much fun to use as it is functional. Powered by six AAA batteries, it can be operated with one hand. Simply turn the mill upside down to begin the grinding process. Turning it back upright stops the grinding, and as a bonus, there's no leaking pepper to mess up the table. Use the dial on top to adjust the coarseness of the grind. The ceramic blade is super sharp and will never rust, even when used over steaming pots. The Graviti mill comes filled with pepper, but you can also fill it with coarse sea salt. The acrylic window lets you know when it is time for a refill. Nothing compares to the flavor of freshly ground salt or pepper.

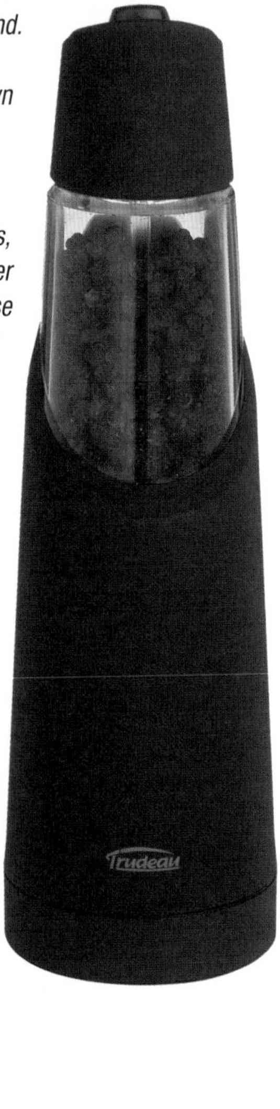

Roasted Marinated Baby Artichokes and Baby Shiitakes on Mixed Greens with Lemon Dill Aioli*

Serves 4

ARTICHOKES

8 baby artichokes
1 quart water
1/4 cup lemon juice

MARINADE

2 teaspoons fresh dill, chopped
2 teaspoons fresh parsley, chopped
2 teaspoons fresh tarragon, chopped
2 teaspoons fresh thyme, chopped
2 teaspoons fresh chives, chopped
2 teaspoons fresh basil, chopped
2 cloves garlic, minced
1/4 teaspoon fresh ground black pepper
1/2 cup brown sugar
1 cup balsamic vinegar
1 1/2 cups olive oil

BABY SHIITAKES

1/2 pound baby shiitake mushrooms, cleaned

LEMON DILL AIOLI

1 1/2 cups mayonnaise
2 tablespoons fresh lemon juice
1 lemon, zested
4 cloves garlic, minced
2 tablespoons fresh dill, chopped
6 drops Tabasco sauce
Salt, to taste

ASSEMBLY AND GARNISH

8 cups mixed greens
1 1/2 cups extra-virgin olive oil
Salt and pepper, to taste
Roasted baby artichokes and shiitakes
Lemon dill aioli
Chives

1. Prepare the artichokes. Peel back the outer leaves, snapping them off at the stem. Trim off the stem and cut the artichokes in half lengthwise.

2. Combine the water and lemon juice in a large bowl, and drop each cleaned artichoke into the water.

3. Make the marinade. In a blender, combine the herbs, garlic, pepper, brown sugar, and vinegar. Blend for about 10 seconds at medium speed. Slowly add the olive oil in a thin stream. Transfer the marinade to a 9-inch glass or ceramic baking dish. Drain the artichokes from the lemon water, and add them to the marinade, turning them to coat. Add the shiitakes, and turn in the marinade.

4. Line a baking sheet with a silicone baking liner or foil. Preheat the oven to 350°F.

5. Drain the artichokes and mushrooms, and transfer them to the baking sheet. Bake for 8 to 10 minutes. The artichokes should be easily pierced with the tip of a sharp knife, and the shiitakes should be golden brown. Remove from the oven and allow to cool slightly, or you can cool them completely and refrigerate them until ready to serve.

6. Make the aioli. In a large bowl, whisk together the mayonnaise, lemon juice, zest, garlic, dill, and Tabasco. Season the aioli to taste with salt, cover with plastic wrap, and refrigerate for up to 4 days.

7. Assemble, garnish, and serve. Place the greens in a large salad bowl, and toss with the oil, salt, and pepper. Arrange some of the greens on each salad plate, sprinkle some shiitakes over the greens, and top with 4 artichoke halves. Dollop the aioli onto each artichoke half and arrange some chives over each salad. Serve immediately.

Sesame Noodle Salad with Pulled Pork Shoulder

Serves 6 • Make 10 to 24 hours in advance

PULLED PORK

3 sweet yellow onions, coarsely chopped
6 cloves garlic, minced
1 tablespoon dried oregano
1/4 cup olive oil
1 tablespoon salt
2 teaspoons freshly ground black pepper
1 (5-pound) boneless pork shoulder roast

NOODLE SALAD

1 pound linguine, cooked in boiling salted water until al dente and drained
1/4 cup toasted sesame oil
2 tablespoons vegetable oil
2 cloves garlic, minced
2 teaspoons fresh ginger, peeled and grated
1/4 cup soy sauce
1/4 cup creamy peanut butter (don't use natural)
1/4 cup rice vinegar
1 tablespoon brown sugar
1 cup snow peas, strings removed
3 scallions (white and tender green parts), thinly sliced on the diagonal
2 medium-size carrots (about 1cup), cut into matchsticks
2 cups cooked pulled pork
2 tablespoons sesame seeds

1. Make the pulled pork. Place onions in a 6- to 7-quart slow cooker. In a small bowl, combine the garlic, oregano, oil, salt, and pepper. Rub the mixture on the roast and set on top of the onions.
2. Cover and cook on low for 10 hours, or until the pork is fork-tender. Remove the pork from the insert and allow to rest for 15 minutes covered with foil.
3. Remove the fat from the liquid in the cooker.
4. Shred the meat and add half of it back into the sauce. The remaining meat can be stored in the refrigerator for up to 5 days or frozen for six weeks.
5. Make the salad. Toss the pasta with 1 or 2 tablespoons of the sesame oil.
6. In a blender or food processor, process together the remaining sesame oil, vegetable oil, garlic, ginger, soy sauce, peanut butter, vinegar, and brown sugar until smooth. Taste and add more soy sauce and sugar, if needed
7. Diva Do-Ahead: At this point, you can cover and refrigerate for up to 3 days. Return dressing to room temperature and whisk to blend before continuing.
8. Microwave the snow peas on high or plunge them into boiling water for 1 minute. Shock in ice water, pat dry, and cut in half on the diagonal.
9. Add the peas, scallions, carrots, pork, and half of the sesame seeds to the linguine. Pour half of the dressing over the salad and toss to coat.
10. Diva Do-Ahead: At this point, cover and refrigerate the salad and remaining dressing for at least 6 hours and up to 24 hours.
11. Garnish and serve. One hour before serving, remove the salad from the refrigerator and toss with more dressing if needed. Garnish with remaining sesame seeds.

Wine Country Cooking

PHILLIS CAREY

Arugula Salad with Grilled Prosciutto-Wrapped Fresh Mozzarella and Sun-Dried Tomato Balsamic Dressing
Fresh Fig and Ricotta Flatbread with Balsamic Onions and Walnuts
Rosemary-Rubbed Pork Tenderloin with Blackberry Wine Sauce and Boursin Polenta
Angel Food Cake with Raspberry Filling, Lemon Curd Frosting, and Lemon Crunch Candy

Products from the California Wine Country are both the inspiration for this menu and the elements that make it so delicious. Chef Phillis uses California zinfandel and blackberries to make the reduction sauce for her rosemary-rubbed pork tenderloin. The flatbread starts with fresh summer figs, California blue cheese, California walnuts, and balsamic-glazed onions. An arugula salad is topped with grilled prosciutto-wrapped mozzarella and sun-dried tomato balsamic dressing. A light, filled angel food cake topped with lemon curd and lemon candies completes this delightful menu.

Arugula Salad with Grilled Prosciutto-Wrapped Fresh Mozzarella and Sun-Dried Tomato Balsamic Dressing

Serves 4

6 slices prosciutto
12 small balls fresh mozzarella
Olive oil
Freshly ground pepper

DRESSING
6 tablespoons extra-virgin olive oil
2 tablespoons balsamic vinegar
Pinch dry mustard
3 tablespoons sun-dried tomatoes in oil, drained and chopped
1 clove garlic, minced
Salt and pepper, to taste
1 (5-ounce) bag arugula

1. Cut the prosciutto slices across in half. Wrap each mozzarella ball in a piece of prosciutto and skewer closed. Brush with olive oil and season with pepper. Grill over medium heat for 2 to 3 minutes or until cheese softens.

2. Make the dressing. Whisk together the olive oil, vinegar, and dry mustard. Stir in the sun-dried tomatoes and garlic. Season with salt and pepper.

3. Serve. Toss arugula with dressing and divide among 4 plates. Top with grilled cheese and serve immediately.

Fresh Fig and Ricotta Flatbread with Balsamic Onions and Walnuts*

Makes 4 (16 appetizer-size servings)

2 tablespoons olive oil
3 red onions, thinly sliced lengthwise
2 tablespoons balsamic vinegar
1/2 teaspoon salt
1/4 teaspoon freshly ground black pepper
2 packages fresh pizza dough (Trader Joe's is good)
1 (15-ounce) container whole-milk ricotta cheese
1 pound firm-ripe figs, rinsed, stem ends trimmed and halved lengthwise
1/2 cup walnuts, chopped
1 cup Danish blue cheese, crumbled (optional)
8 ounces (about 2 cups) arugula leaves

1. Heat olive oil in a large skillet over medium-high heat. Stir in the onions and cook 2 to 3 minutes. Lower heat and cook another 20 minutes, or until onions are very tender and lightly colored. Stir in balsamic vinegar, salt, and pepper, and cook until liquid is cooked out. Set aside to cool.

2. Divide each package of pizza dough in half and form each into a ball. Let dough rest for 10 minutes. Shape each ball into an oval on a Silpat- or parchment-lined baking sheet — you will need 2 baking sheets with 2 pizza balls on each. Cover and let rest if necessary before stretching again.

3. Preheat oven to 450°F. Divide cooled onions evenly over pizza-dough ovals. Drop 1/2-tablespoon portions of ricotta over onions. Arrange figs, cut side up, around cheese. Sprinkle with walnuts and optional blue cheese. Bake for 15 minutes or until crust is crispy and brown. Top with arugula and cut lengthwise and then across to make 16 pieces.

Rosemary-Rubbed Pork Tenderloin with Blackberry Wine Sauce and Boursin Polenta

Serves 4 to 5

TENDERLOIN

2 pork tenderloins
3 cloves garlic, minced
1 tablespoon fresh rosemary, minced
1/4 cup olive oil
Salt and pepper, to taste

POLENTA

1 1/2 cups whole milk
1 1/2 cups chicken broth
1 tablespoon unsalted butter
Salt and pepper, to taste
3/4 cup yellow cornmeal
1 (5-ounce) package Boursin cheese

SAUCE

2 cups fresh or frozen blackberries
2 cups California zinfandel
1/4 cup granulated sugar
1/4 cup unsalted butter, cut into 4 pieces and chilled

GARNISH

Rosemary sprigs

1. Prepare tenderloin. Trim pork of all fat and silverskin. Combine garlic, rosemary, and olive oil. Rub all over the pork and let stand 30 minutes. Season to taste with salt and pepper.

2. Cook tenderloin. Preheat oven to 400°F. Heat a large skillet over medium-high heat, add the pork, and brown well on all sides, about 6 to 8 minutes. Transfer to a parchment-lined baking sheet and roast for 25 to 30 minutes, or until the internal temperature reaches 155°F. Let stand 8 minutes before slicing on the diagonal into 1/2-inch slices.

3. Make polenta. Place milk, broth, and butter in a medium saucepan over medium heat and bring to a gentle boil, seasoning with salt and pepper. Slowly whisk in cornmeal. Lower heat and cook, stirring often, until thick and smooth and cornmeal is tender, about 5 to 7 minutes. Remove from heat and stir in Boursin cheese.

4. Make sauce. Place berries (still frozen if using frozen berries), wine, and sugar in a medium saucepan and bring to a boil, stirring until sugar dissolves. Reduce heat and simmer until reduced by half. Strain sauce, pressing on berries to extract as much juice as possible. Return to saucepan and bring to a boil. Whisk in butter, a piece at a time, until melted. Season to taste with salt and pepper.

5. Assemble, garnish, and serve. Spoon polenta onto the center of each plate and arrange pork slices overlapping each other and the polenta. Drizzle sauce over and around the pork. Garnish with rosemary sprigs.

Angel Food Cake with Raspberry Filling, Lemon Curd Frosting, and Lemon Crunch Candy

Serves 8 • Make 3 to 4 hours ahead

CANDY

1 1/2 cups granulated sugar
1/4 cup water
1/4 cup light corn syrup
1 tablespoon baking soda
2 teaspoons lemon extract

CAKE

1 (10-inch) purchased angel food cake
3/4 cup seedless raspberry jam

LEMON-CURD CREAM

2 cups heavy whipping cream
3/4 cup prepared lemon curd (found at Great News! and other specialty stores)

GARNISH

2 baskets fresh raspberries, tossed with 1/3 cup granulated sugar

1. Make the candy. Cover a baking sheet with parchment paper and set aside. Combine sugar, water, and corn syrup in a heavy 4-quart saucepan. Cook over medium-high heat, without stirring, until sugar dissolves. Continue cooking, again without stirring, until syrup reaches the hard-crack stage (300°F on a candy thermometer).

2. Remove pan from heat and immediately stir in baking soda and lemon extract. Stir until blended; it will be very foamy. Quickly pour candy on prepared baking sheet and spread as thin as possible. Let cool completely, 20 to 30 minutes. Break and crush candy into tiny pieces. (You probably won't need it all for the cake).

3. Prepare the cake. Using a serrated knife, split cake into 3 layers. Place the bottom layer on a cake plate and spread half the raspberry jam on the cake layer. Top with the second layer and repeat with jam. Set top layer on cake.

4. Make the lemon-curd cream. Whip the heavy cream to stiff peaks and fold in the lemon curd.

5. Frost the cake and serve. Frost the cake with lemon cream and press crushed candy into the sides of the cake to coat well. Refrigerate for 3 to 4 hours to set cream into a mousse-like texture before serving. Cut cake into wedges and garnish with sugared berries spooned next to the cake.

Summer Pies & Tarts

KATHERINE EMMENEGGER

Chocolate Dulce de Leche Ice Cream Pie
Lattice-Topped Ginger Peach Pie • Classic Lemon Meringue Pie • Chambord Berry Tart

This menu of summer dessert pies and tarts features the bounty of summer. You won't have trouble finding someone to share a bite of the peach pie, with its homemade crust and a lattice design on top. Lemon meringue pie is a favorite in San Diego, where lemon trees are abundant. The Chambord berry tart provides the ideal canvas for summer berries, and the chocolate dulce de leche ice cream pie (its Spanish name means "confection of sugar and cream") is the perfect cold, refreshing treat for a warm summer nights.

Chocolate Dulce de Leche Ice Cream Pie

Serves 8 • Freeze a minimum of 4 hours or overnight

CRUST

1/2 cup pecan pieces
2 tablespoons granulated sugar
40 vanilla wafer cookies
5 tablespoons unsalted butter, melted

FILLING

1 jar chocolate sauce (Stonewall Kitchen or Fran's is good)
2 pints premium dulce de leche or caramel ice cream, softened
1 cup whipped cream, homemade, or ready-whipped toppping
2 tablespoons pecan pieces, toasted

1. Preheat oven to 350°F.
2. Make the crust. In a food processor fitted with a steel blade, combine the pecan pieces, sugar, and cookies until finely ground. Add the butter and blend until the crumbs become moist and will bind when pressed into the palm of your hand.
3. Press the crust onto the bottom and sides of a 9-inch deep pie dish.
4. Bake for about 10 minutes, until the crust is golden brown and firm. Transfer from the oven and cool completely on a cooling rack.
5. Make the filling. Drizzle one-quarter of the jar of chocolate sauce over the bottom of the pie crust and place the crust in the freezer to firm, about 10 minutes.
6. Press the softened dulce de leche ice cream into the pie crust, cover with plastic wrap, and freeze for a minimum of 4 hours, or overnight, if possible.
7. Serve. Slice the pie. Top with the whipped cream and garnish with the pecan pieces and remaining chocolate sauce.

Lattice-Topped Ginger Peach Pie

Serves 8

CRUST

3 cups unbleached all-purpose flour
2 tablespoons granulated sugar
1 teaspoon salt
7 tablespoons vegetable shortening, chilled
10 tablespoons (1 1/4 sticks) unsalted butter, chilled, cut into 1/4-inch pieces
3/4 cup cup ice water, as needed

FILLING

6 to 7 medium-sized, ripe peaches
2 tablespoons crystallized ginger, minced
1 lemon, juiced
1 cup granulated sugar
Pinch ground cinnamon
Pinch ground nutmeg
Pinch table salt
3 tablespoons potato starch or 2 tablespoons cornstarch
1 tablespoon granulated sugar, for sprinkling

1. Make the crust. Position a rack in the center of the oven and preheat it to 425°F.

2. In a food processor fitted a the steel blade, pulse the flour, sugar, and salt. Add the shortening and process until mixture has the texture of coarse >

sand, about 10 seconds. Add the butter pieces and pulse until the mixture resembles coarse crumbs.

3. Turn mixture into a medium bowl and sprinkle with about 5 tablespoons of ice water. Combine in a folding motion with a silicone spatula. Sprinkle 5 more tablespoons of ice water over the mixture and continue to combine until the dough begins to hold together. Add the remaining water only if needed.

4. Turn the dough onto a clean, dry work surface. Gather and gently press into a ball; divide into 2 pieces, one slightly larger than the other. Flatten the larger piece into a 5-inch square and the smaller piece into a 4-inch disk; wrap each with plastic wrap and refrigerate for 30 minutes.

5. Remove the dough from the refrigerator and let stand for 5 minutes. Line a clean, dry work surface with plastic wrap and dust lightly with flour. Unwrap the larger piece of dough and place on the work surface. Lightly dust with flour and cover loosely with plastic wrap.

6. With a rolling pin, roll the dough to an 11x15-inch rectangle about 1/8-inch thick. As you roll the dough, you may need to lift the top sheet of plastic wrap to loosen it from the dough.

7. Transfer the dough rectangle to a parchment-lined baking sheet. With a pizza wheel, fluted pastry wheel, or paring knife, trim to even out long sides of rectangle, then cut rectangle lengthwise into eight strips, 1 1/4-inches wide by 15-inches long. Cover and refrigerate the strips for 30 minutes.

8. Roll the smaller dough piece in the same manner to a 13-inch round. Transfer the dough to a 9-inch pie plate. Ease dough into pan corners by gently lifting the dough edges with one hand while pressing around the pan bottom with the other hand. Cover and refrigerate for half an hour.

9. Make the filling. Peel the peaches with a serrated peeler. Cut them in half and remove the pit. Slice the peaches into 1/4-inch-thick wedges.
In a bowl, combine the peach slices with the ginger, lemon juice, sugar, cinnamon, nutmeg, salt, and potato starch.

RON'S TIP

Vic Firth Classic Rolling Pins

Vic Firth made a name for himself as a great timpanist for the Boston Symphony Orchestra, and he's recognized as one of the most famous drumstick makers in the world. When he turned his attention to the kitchen, he became renowned for his fabulous peppermills and rolling pins. Vic Firth Gourmet rolling pins are crafted from solid rock maple and are fitted with steel ball bearings to ensure a lifetime of effortless rolling — the perfect tool for both the home baker and the professional chef! The Vic Firth company is also committed to eco-friendly practices. They purchase FSC-certified wood when possible, the sawdust and scrap wood that are generated are burned to heat the factory, and the rolling pins are 100 percent made in the USA.

10. Fill the pie shell with the peach filling. Remove the dough strips from the refrigerator; let stand at room temperature until just soft enough to handle. Weave the strips into a loose lattice and place over the pie. Crimp the pie dough and lattice top to form the classic pie edge. Lightly brush the lattice top with water and sprinkle with the remaining sugar. Place the pie on a baking sheet and bake until crust is set and begins to brown, about 25 minutes.

11. Reduce oven temperature to 375°F and continue to bake as needed until the crust is deep golden brown and the filling is bubbly, 25 to 30 minutes.

12. Serve. Cool on wire rack for 2 hours before serving.

Classic Lemon Meringue Pie

Serves 8

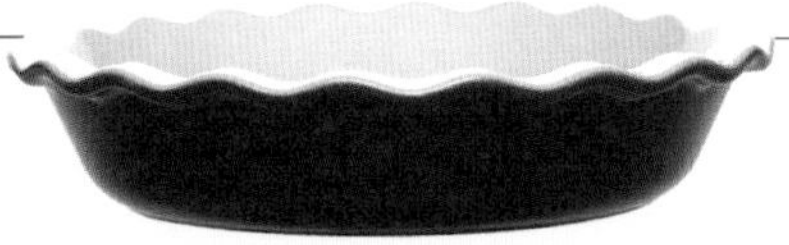

PIE SHELL

2 cups unbleached all-purpose flour
1 tablespoon granulated sugar
1 teaspoon salt
4 tablespoons vegetable shortening, chilled
6 tablespoons unsalted butter, chilled and cut into 1/4-inch pieces
3 to 4 tablespoons cold water

LEMON FILLING

1 cup granulated sugar
1/4 cup cornstarch
1/8 teaspoon salt
1 1/2 cups cold water
6 large egg yolks, room temperature
1 lemon, zested
1/2 cup lemon juice
2 tablespoons unsalted butter

MERINGUE TOPPING

1 tablespoon cornstarch
1/4 teaspoon cream of tartar
1/2 cup granulated sugar
4 large egg whites
1/2 teaspoon pure vanilla extract

1. Make the pie shell. Preheat oven to 325°F.
2. In a food processor fitted with a steel blade, pulse the flour, sugar, and salt. Add the shortening and process until mixture has the texture of coarse sand, about 10 seconds. Add the butter pieces and pulse until the mixture resembles coarse crumbs.
3. Turn mixture into a medium bowl and sprinkle with about 3 tablespoons of ice water. Combine in a folding motion with a silicone spatula. Sprinkle 1 more tablespoon of ice water over the mixture and continue to combine until the dough begins to hold together. Add more water if needed.
4. Turn the dough onto a clean, dry work surface. Gather and gently press into a ball. Flatten the dough into a 4-inch disk; wrap with plastic wrap; and refrigerate for 30 minutes. Remove the dough from the refrigerator and let stand for 5 minutes. Line a clean, dry work surface with plastic wrap and dust lightly with flour. Unwrap the dough and place on the work surface. Lightly dust with flour and cover loosely with plastic wrap. >

RON'S TIP

Emile Henry Pie Pans

French Burgundy clay fired at extremely high temperatures is the proprietary Ceradon manufacturing process that gives the Emile Henry pie dish the ability to slowly and evenly distribute heat. This allows for even browning of pie crusts and perfect cooking of pies. The bakeware is crack and chip-resistant and can go directly from freezer to oven without cracking or breaking. These pans are suitable for use in the microwave or under the broiler, and they're nice enough to use as a beautiful serving piece for vegetables, fruit crisps, au gratin potatoes, and dips. The pan comes in a large variety of colors, and the glazes will not crack, discolor, or fade over time. You can even cut on the surface without scratching or damaging it, and as a bonus, it is also stick-resistant. Cleanup is "as easy as pie!"

5. With a rolling pin, roll the dough to 1/8-inch thick, about 13 inches in diameter. As you roll the dough, you may need to lift the top sheet of plastic wrap to loosen it from the dough. In a 9-inch pie plate, ease the dough into the pan corners by gently lifting the dough edges with one hand while pressing around the pan bottom with the other hand.

6. Trim the overhang to 1 inch and fold under. Crimp the edge. Wrap the dough with plastic wrap and refrigerate for 30 minutes.

7. With a fork, prick the base of the pie shell evenly, about 6 times. Press a 12-inch square of foil into the shell and fill with pie weights.

8. Bake at 400°F for 15 minutes. Then reduce temperature to 350°F, remove the foil, and let the pie shell bake for 10 minutes more, or until crisp and golden brown.

9. **Make the filling.** In a saucepan over medium heat, combine the sugar, cornstarch, salt, and water; bring to a simmer, whisking occasionally.

10. When mixture starts to simmer and turn translucent, whisk in egg yolks, two at a time.

11. Whisk in zest, then lemon juice, and finally butter. Bring mixture to a brisk simmer, whisking constantly.

12. Remove from the heat and create a false skin by placing plastic wrap directly on the surface of the filling.

13. **Make the meringue.** In a small saucepan over medium heat, combine the cornstarch with 1/3 cup of water. Whisking constantly, bring the mixture to a simmer and cook until translucent. Transfer from the heat and cool to room temperature.

14. In a bowl, combine the cream of tartar and sugar. In the bowl of an electric mixer fitted with the whisk attachment, whisk the egg whites and vanilla until frothy. Add the sugar mixture, 1 tablespoon at a time, until it is incorporated and the mixture forms soft peaks.

15. Add the cornstarch mixture, 1 tablespoon at a time; continue to beat meringue to stiff peaks.

16. **Assemble.** Preheat oven to 325°F.

17. Remove the plastic wrap from the filling and pour the filling into the pie shell.

18. Using a silicone spatula, distribute the meringue evenly around the edge and then the center of the pie. Make sure the meringue is spread all the way to the crust to prevent it from shrinking. Using the back of a spoon, create peaks over meringue.

19. Bake the pie until meringue is golden brown, about 20 minutes. Transfer to a wire rack and cool to room temperature. Serve.

Chambord Berry Tart

Serves 8

PASTRY

2 cups all-purpose flour
2 tablespoons granulated sugar
1 teaspoon salt
1/4 pound chilled unsalted butter, cut into small pieces, or 1/2 cup vegetable shortening
3 tablespoons Chambord liqueur, or more as needed, ice cold

FILLING

6 cups fresh berries, a combination of blackberries, raspberries, sliced strawberries
1/4 cup granulated sugar
1/4 cup all-purpose flour
2 tablespoons Chambord liqueur

1. Preheat oven to 375°F and place the rack in the center.
2. Make the pastry. In a food processor fitted with a steel blade, combine flour, sugar, and salt. Add the butter a few pieces at a time and pulse until the mixture resembles a coarse meal. Slowly add the Chambord while pulsing until the dough just binds together. Transfer the pastry dough to a sheet of plastic wrap, form it into a disk, and refrigerate for 1 hour. On a clean, dry work surface, roll the pastry dough to a 10-inch round. Transfer the pastry dough to a parchment-lined baking sheet.
3. Make the filling. In a bowl, combine all ingredients. Cover and let stand for 15 minutes. Spoon the berries into the center of the pastry dough, leaving a 2-inch border around the edge. Using the parchment as an aid, fold the outer edge of pastry dough over the filling, leaving the center of the tart open.
4. Bake until the berries are tender and the pastry is golden brown, about 40 minutes.
5. Serve. Cut the tart into wedges, place on individual dessert plates, and serve with a scoop of your favorite vanilla ice cream.

Fast & Fabulous Chicken

PHILLIS CAREY

Chicken Provencal • Hawaiian Grilled Shoyu Chicken with Five-Spice Sauce
Chicken Pesto Saltimbocca Bundles with Creamy Roasted Tomato Sauce
Chicken Florentine Risotto with Saffron and Parmesan Cheese
Hazelnut-Crusted Honey Mustard Chicken with Balsamic Glaze • Italian Chicken Cordon Bleu

Chicken is one of those ingredients that is so versatile, you can do almost anything with it! It's easy to prepare and not very expensive. In this menu, Chef Phillis shares four flavorful chicken dishes with ingredients that you probably already have in your kitchen (or ingredients that can be easily found in any grocery store). Phillis has authored many cookbooks, and she has prepared chicken literally hundreds of ways. We love all of her recipes!

Chicken Provencal

Serves 4

4 boneless, skinless chicken breasts
Salt and pepper, to taste
1/4 cup all-purpose flour
2 tablespoons olive oil
1 teaspoon garlic, minced
1 1/2 tablespoons capers, rinsed and drained
1/2 cup dry white wine
1 pound ripe plum tomatoes, peeled, seeded, and diced
3/4 cup chicken broth
10 pitted Kalamata olives, thinly sliced lengthwise
2 tablespoons unsalted butter, softened
1 tablespoon basil, finely shredded

1. Trim chicken and pound to an even 1/2-inch thickness. Season with salt and pepper to taste; dredge in flour, shaking off excess.
2. Heat oil in a large, heavy skillet over medium-high heat. Add chicken and cook 2 minutes per side. Remove chicken to a plate.

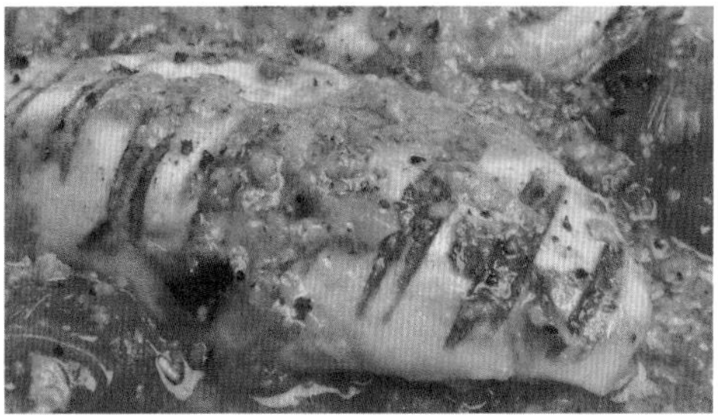

3. Add garlic and capers to skillet and cook over medium heat, stirring, until fragrant, about 30 seconds. Add wine and bring to a boil, scraping up brown bits. Stir in tomatoes, broth, and olives; simmer, uncovered, stirring occasionally, until mixture has thickened into a sauce, 8 to 10 minutes.
4. Return chicken to skillet, adding any juices from plate and turn to coat with sauce. Cover and simmer 6 to 8 minutes, or until chicken is cooked through. Remove chicken to serving plates and whisk in butter and basil. Serve chicken topped with sauce.

Hawaiian Grilled Shoyu Chicken with Five-Spice Sauce

Serves 6 • Marinate for 3 hours

MARINADE

1 cup soy sauce
1/2 cup fresh orange juice
1/2 cup mirin (Japanese rice wine)
1/2 cup water
1/4 cup brown sugar
1 1/2 teaspoons garlic, minced
1 1/2 teaspoons fresh ginger, minced
1 tablespoon fresh cilantro, minced
1/4 teaspoon Chinese five-spice powder
1 tablespoon cornstarch
2 tablespoons water

CHICKEN

6 to 8 boneless, skinless chicken breasts
3 tablespoons vegetable oil
3 tablespoons green onion tops, chopped

1. Make the marinade. Combine the first 7 ingredients in a medium bowl. Transfer 1 1/2 cups to a small saucepan and whisk in the cilantro and five-spice powder; bring to a boil and then simmer for 10 minutes or until reduced to 1 cup. Combine the cornstarch and water; whisk into sauce and bring to a simmer, stirring constantly, until mixture thickens. Set aside or refrigerate until ready to use. Reserve remaining marinade for basting during grilling.

2. Prepare the chicken. Trim and pound the chicken to 1/2-inch thickness. Place in a shallow casserole dish and pour marinade over the top, turning to coat the chicken well. Cover and refrigerate for 3 hours.

3. Remove chicken from marinade and pat dry. Discard marinade. Brush chicken with oil and grill 2 minutes; turn over and cook 2 minutes. Brush with some of the thickened sauce, turn over, and cook 2 minutes. Brush with more sauce, turn over, and grill 2 minutes, or until chicken is cooked through.

4. Garnish and serve. Arrange chicken on a platter and top with remaining sauce and with green onion.

Chicken Pesto Saltimbocca Bundles with Creamy Roasted Tomato Sauce

Serves 4

SAUCE

8 plum tomatoes, cut in half lengthwise
2 tablespoons shallots, chopped
2 tablespoons olive oil
Salt and pepper, to taste
1/4 cup melted unsalted butter
2 tablespoons heavy whipping cream
2 tablespoons fresh basil, chopped

CHICKEN

4 boneless, skinless chicken breasts
Freshly ground black pepper, to taste
4 basil leaves
4 slices prosciutto
4 slices provolone cheese
2 eggs
1/4 cup prepared basil pesto
1 cup plain dry bread crumbs
1/4 cup freshly grated Parmesan cheese
1/4 cup olive oil

1. Make the sauce. Preheat oven to 400°F. Arrange tomatoes skin side up on a parchment-lined baking sheet. Sprinkle with shallots and drizzle with olive oil; season with salt and pepper. Roast for 20 minutes, or until soft and browned. Transfer to a blender; add the melted butter and whipping cream, and purée until smooth. Set aside. Increase oven temperature to 425°F.

2. Prepare the chicken. Trim chicken and pound between 2 sheets of plastic wrap to an even 1/4-inch thickness. Season with pepper and top each chicken breast with a basil leaf, then a slice of prosciutto, and finally a slice of cheese. Fold chicken in half and press the edges together to seal. Chicken may be refrigerated at this point for several hours or overnight.

3. Cook the chicken. Whisk eggs with pesto sauce in a pie plate. Combine bread crumbs with Parmesan cheese in another pie plate. Coat chicken bundles well with egg mixture and dredge in bread crumbs to coat well. Pour olive oil on a baking sheet and heat in the oven for 4 minutes, or until very hot but not smoking. Set chicken in hot oil and roast for 8 minutes. Turn chicken over and roast for 7 to 9 minutes, or until chicken is cooked through.

4. Serve. Transfer sauce to a small saucepan and warm without boiling. Season to taste with salt and pepper; stir in basil. Spoon sauce onto serving plates and set the chicken bundles in the sauce to serve.

Chicken Florentine Risotto with Saffron and Parmesan Cheese

Serves 6

6 cups chicken broth
3 tablespoons olive oil, divided use
4 boneless, skinless chicken breasts, cut into 1/2-inch cubes
Salt and pepper
1 1/2 cups sauvignon blanc wine, divided use
1 teaspoon plus 2 tablespoons unsalted butter, divided use
1 small onion, diced
5 cloves plus 2 teaspoons minced garlic, divided use
2 cups arborio rice
1/2 teaspoon saffron threads
12 ounces baby spinach leaves
1/3 cup freshly grated Parmesan cheese
1/3 cup heavy whipping cream
Chives, chopped

1. Place chicken broth in a saucepan and bring to a simmer. Heat 2 tablespoons olive oil in a large Dutch oven or pot. Season chicken with salt and pepper, and sauté in oil over medium heat. When chicken is brown, add 1/2 cup wine. Simmer until wine evaporates and cook for 5 more minutes, or until chicken is just done. Remove chicken and set aside.
2. Heat remaining 1 tablespoon olive oil and 1 teaspoon butter in pot and sauté onions for 2 minutes. Add the 5 cloves of garlic. Sauté until onions are translucent, about 5 more minutes.
3. Add rice and cook, stirring constantly until glistening, 1 to 2 minutes. Add saffron and remainder of the wine. Stir until wine is completely absorbed. Add 2 cups broth and stir until absorbed completely. Add remaining broth, 1 cup at a time, stirring until completely absorbed before adding more.
4. Cooking time will be approximately 25 minutes for *al dente*. After the first 20 minutes of cooking, add the cooked chicken and spinach and 2 teaspoons of garlic to the rice; stir until spinach wilts. After 22 minutes, stir in the remaining 2 tablespoons of butter, Parmesan, and cream. Check seasoning, adding salt and pepper if needed. Remove from heat, transfer to a serving dish, and garnish with chives.

Hazelnut-Crusted Honey Mustard Chicken with Balsamic Glaze

Serves 4

GLAZE

2 cups balsamic vinegar
2 tablespoons granulated sugar

CRUST

1 cup finely toasted hazelnuts, chopped
1 cup panko bread crumbs
1 1/2 teaspoons coarse kosher salt, divided use
1 teaspoon freshly ground black pepper, divided use
1/3 cup honey mustard
1/4 cup Italian parsley, finely chopped
1 teaspoon fresh thyme leaves
1/4 cup mayonnaise
1 tablespoon Dijon mustard

CHICKEN

4 boneless, skinless chicken breasts
4 tablespoons unsalted butter
3 tablespoons vegetable oil

1. Make the glaze. Bring the balsamic vinegar and sugar to a boil in a small pan, stirring until sugar dissolves. Lower heat and simmer until reduced to 1/2 cup, about 20 to 30 minutes. Cool.

2. Make the crust. Preheat oven to 375°F. Mix hazelnuts, panko, 1 teaspoon salt, and 1/2 teaspoon pepper in a shallow bowl. Mix honey mustard, parsley, thyme, mayonnaise, Dijon mustard, remaining 1/2 teaspoon salt, and remaining 1/2 teaspoon pepper in another shallow bowl.

3. Prepare the chicken. Trim chicken and pound to an even 1/4-inch thickness. Dip chicken into mustard mixture to coat well. Then dip chicken into crumb-nut mixture, coating both sides and pressing to adhere. Transfer coated chicken pieces to a baking sheet.

4. Cook the chicken. Melt half the butter with half the oil in a large nonstick skillet over medium-high heat. Add 2 chicken pieces to skillet and cook until chicken is lightly brown, about 2 minutes per side. Remove chicken to a rack set over a baking sheet; repeat with remaining butter and oil and chicken. Transfer pan to oven and roast chicken until cooked through, 7 to 9 minutes.

5. Serve. Plate chicken and drizzle with the glaze.

Italian Chicken Cordon Bleu

Serves 4

CHICKEN

4 boneless, skinless chicken breasts
4 slices prosciutto
4 slices Fontina cheese
1/2 cup flour
2 eggs, beaten with 2 tablespoons milk
3/4 cup Italian-seasoned bread crumbs
1 teaspoon paprika
1/4 cup olive oil

SAUCE

3 tablespoons unsalted butter
1 prosciutto slice, chopped
3 tablespoons flour
1 cup chicken broth
1 cup whole milk
Salt and white pepper, to taste
Pinch grated nutmeg
1/2 cup freshly grated Parmesan cheese
1 cup tiny frozen peas, thawed

1. Prepare the chicken. Preheat oven to 450°F. Slice each breast horizontally into two thin scallops. Lightly pound. Place prosciutto and cheese on half of the chicken scallops and top with the remaining scallops. Press edges to seal. Get three plates: place flour on first; whisk eggs and milk on a second; toss bread crumbs with paprika on third. Dredge chicken in flour and eggs, and coat well with bread crumbs.
2. Cook the chicken. Pour oil onto a baking sheet with sides. Heat pan in oven for 4 minutes, or until oil is very hot but not smoking. Set the chicken in the oil and bake for 6 minutes. Turn over and bake for 5 to 7 minutes more, or until cooked through and crispy.
3. Make the sauce. Melt butter in a saucepan over medium heat. Cook prosciutto for 30 seconds. Add flour and cook 1 minute, stirring constantly. Slowly whisk in broth and milk. Season with salt, pepper, and nutmeg, and bring to a boil, stirring constantly. Simmer for 1 more minute. Stir in cheese and peas; heat to warm through.
4. Serve. Plate the chicken with sauce on top.

Grillin' & Chillin' Seafood

KATHERINE EMMENEGGER

Tea-Smoked Scallops Nested in Vegetable Noodles • Alder-Planked Salmon with Roasted Peach Chimichurri
Lobster Tails with Basil-Infused Brown Butter Drizzle
Whole Striped Bass with Chardonnay-Caper Beurre Blanc • Lemon-Thyme Semifreddo

Nothing says summer like food cooked on the grill. At Great News! Cooking School, we offer ways for cooks of all skill levels to create great grilled fare. This summer menu features simple but sublime seafood choices like scallops smoked over tea leaves, sea bass stuffed with fennel and served with a chardonnay sauce, and salmon cooked on an alder plank for a special smoky sensation. And the classic grilled lobster tails with basil-infused brown butter will take any summer party up a notch!

Tea-Smoked Scallops Nested in Vegetable Noodles

Serves 4

WASABI VINAIGRETTE

1 tablespoon wasabi powder, or to taste
1/2 cup rice vinegar
1/3 cup grapeseed oil
1 tablespoon sesame oil, or to taste

SMOKING MIX

1 cup long-grain rice
1 cup granulated sugar
1 cup oolong or black tea leaves

SCALLOPS

2 pounds large sea scallops, tendon/foot removed
2 tablespoons unsalted butter, melted
Salt and pepper, to taste

VEGETABLE NOODLES

2 large carrots, washed, ends removed, and peeled
1/2 small butternut squash, peeled
1 medium zucchini, washed and ends removed
1 medium yellow squash, washed and ends removed

1. Make the vinaigrette. Combine all ingredients.

2. Make the smoking mix. Combine all ingredients.

3. Prepare the scallops. Coat scallops with butter; season with salt and pepper. Thread the scallops onto doubled, preferably flat metal skewers.

4. Prepare the grill and wok for smoking. Preheat grill to medium high. In a grill wok lined with foil, sprinkle the smoking mix evenly over the bottom; place the wok on the grill. When mixture starts to smolder, set a perforated grill rack over the top. Close the grill lid and let the smoke build, about 3 minutes. Place scallops on the rack and cover loosely with foil.

5. Cook the scallops. Smoke for 15 minutes. Turn off the grill and smoke 15 minutes more.

6. Make the noodles. With a spiral slicer or a serrated peeler, cut all the vegetables into ribbons. Steam them for 3 to 4 minutes, or until tender, just before serving.

7. Serve. Remove the scallops from the grill and transfer to warmed plates with the vegetables. Drizzle with the wasabi vinaigrette.

Alder-Planked Salmon with Roasted Peach Chimichurri

Serves 4

MARINADE

2 limes, juiced
2 tablespoons grapeseed oil
1 teaspoon garlic powder
Salt and pepper, to taste

ROASTED PEACH CHIMICHURRI

1/2 cup extra-virgin olive oil
1/4 cup red wine vinegar
1 small bunch Italian parsley leaves, coarsely chopped, about 1/2 cup
1 small yellow onion, peeled and coarsely chopped
2 large garlic cloves
2 roasted medium yellow bell peppers, seeded and peeled
6 roasted ripe peach halves (3 peaches), pitted and peeled
2 teaspoons minced fresh rosemary leaves
1 teaspoon paprika, or to taste
Salt and pepper, to taste
Red chile flakes, to taste

SALMON

2 untreated alder planks
4 (6-ounce) skinless, center-cut salmon fillets

1. Make the marinade. In a bowl, combine all the ingredients.
2. Prepare the salmon. Marinate the salmon for 30 minutes before grilling.
3. Make the chimichurri. In a food processor, combine all ingredients. Can be stored, refrigerated in an air-tight container, for up to 1 week.
4. Prepare the grill and planks. Preheat the grill to medium. Preheat the planks over indirect heat for 5 minutes before use.
5. Grill the salmon. Arrange the salmon on the hot planks, skin side down. Close the grill lid and roast for 20 minutes, or until the salmon is just slightly underdone in the center. Transfer from the grill and cover loosely with foil. Let stand for 10 minutes.
6. Serve. Plate the salmon and serve with the roasted peach chimichurri.

Lobster Tails with Basil-Infused Brown Butter Drizzle

Serves 4

LOBSTER

4 (8-ounce) lobster tails
1/4 cup melted butter
1 lemon, cut into wedges, for garnish

DRIZZLE

1/2 cup unsalted butter
2 shallots, peeled and finely diced
2 tablespoons fresh basil leaves, chiffonade
1 tablespoon fresh lemon juice
Salt and pepper, to taste
Lemon wedges

1. Prepare the lobster. Preheat the grill to medium or preheat the broiler with the oven rack placed in the center of the oven.

2. Place the lobster tails back side down on a cutting surface. Cut into the tail at the last segment, slicing the tail in half, leaving it attached at the fins. Gently loosen the meat from the shells, leaving it attached. Rinse the meat and shell under cool running water, drain, and pat dry with paper towels.

3. Brush the lobster tails with the melted butter. Oil the grill. With the meat exposed and the shells curled to the sides, place the lobster tails on the grill over direct heat. Grill for 1 minute, turn, and grill 1 minute more. Move the tails to indirect heat, baste with more melted butter, lower the lid, and grill 2 to 4 minutes more, until the meat is just opaque.

4. Make the drizzle. In a sauté pan over medium-heat, melt the butter, add the shallots and basil; simmer until the butter is a light brown color. Add the lemon juice, salt, and pepper; cook until the butter is amber in color.

5. Serve. Plate each lobster, serve with lemon wedges, and drizzle with basil-infused brown butter.

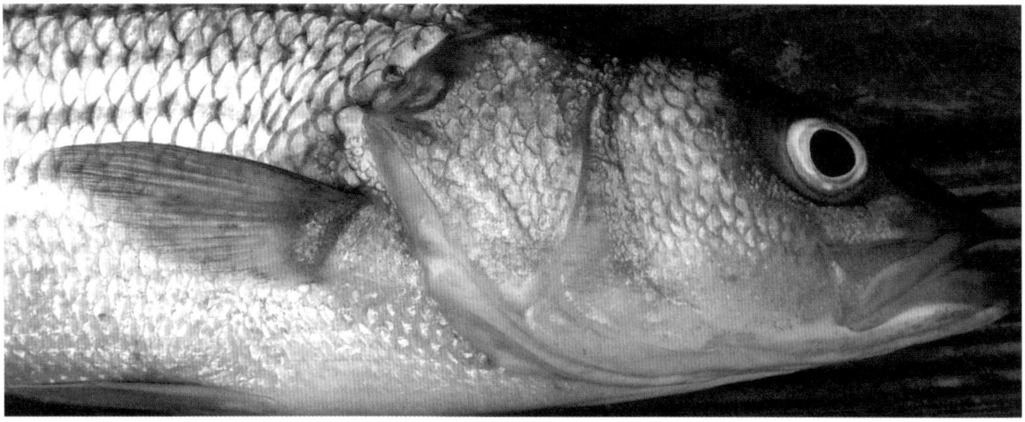

Whole Striped Bass with Chardonnay-Caper Beurre Blanc

Serves 4

BASS

2 ($1^1/_2$ pounds) whole striped bass
3 tablespoons grapeseed oil
Salt and pepper, to taste
1 tablespoon fennel pollen (found at Great News! and other specialty stores)
2 garlic cloves, sliced
2 green onions, sliced 1-inch long
1 lemon, thinly sliced
Grapeseed oil, for grilling

BEURRE BLANC

1 shallot, peeled and minced
1 cup chardonnay
1 lemon, juiced
1 tablespoon capers, rinsed, drained, and chopped
10 ounces unsalted butter, cut into 1-ounce cubes
Salt and white pepper, to taste

GARNISH

1 lemon, cut into wedges

1. Prepare the fish. Using a sharp knife, scale and gut fish. Make shallow diagonal slashes, about 2 inches apart, on both sides of the fish.
2. Rub the fish with grapeseed oil inside and out; season with salt, pepper, and fennel pollen. Arrange the garlic, onion, and lemon slices in the fish cavities and rest on a baking sheet until ready to grill.
3. Prepare the grill. Preheat the grill to medium high. Prepare a sheet of heavy-duty foil large enough for each fish by brushing the surface with oil.
4. Cook the fish. Place the fish on the foil and place it on the grill over direct heat for 6 to 7 minutes. Gently turn the fish, using the foil as an aid, and grill until the flesh is no longer translucent and the skin is crisp; about 5 minutes more.
5. Make the sauce. In a small saucepan over medium heat, combine the shallots and wine; simmer to reduce the wine to 2 tablespoons.
6. Add juice and capers; reduce for about 1 minute more. Incorporate a few pieces of butter at a time while constantly whisking and adding more as it melts. If the sauce starts to separate on the edges and gets thin, add butter faster and transfer the pan from the heat.
7. If you want to make the sauce ahead, try to maintain a temperature between 100°F to 130°F.
8. Serve. Plate fish topped with the chardonnay caper beurre blanc. Garnish with lemon wedges.

Lemon-Thyme Semifreddo

Serves 4 • Freeze for 4 hours before serving

LEMON CURD *(Makes about 1 1/2 cups)*
2 large eggs
2 large egg yolks
1/2 cup granulated sugar
2 teaspoons lemon zest
6 tablespoons fresh lemon juice
1/2 cup unsalted butter, chilled and cut into 8 pieces

SEMIFREDDO
1 pint heavy cream, whipped to firm peaks
1 1/2 cups lemon curd (or 10- to 11-ounce jar)
1 tablespoon fresh thyme leaves, minced, or to taste

GARNISH
Crisp cookies
Fresh berries
4 fresh thyme sprigs

1. Make the lemon curd. In a saucepan over low heat, combine the eggs, egg yolks, sugar, lemon zest, and juice; whisk to combine. Add the butter and stir constantly until melted and the mixture begins to thicken. The curd is thick enough when it holds the marks of the whisk and bubbles begin to appear on the surface, about 10 minutes. Immediately pour the curd through a fine sieve over a bowl. Cover the curd with plastic wrap and press the wrap on the curd to form a skin. Cool and refrigerate for up to 5 days.

2. Make the semifreddo. In a bowl, fold the whipped heavy cream into the lemon curd. Add the thyme and stir to combine.

3. Arrange 4 (6-ounce) ramekins on a baking sheet. Fill the ramekins to the top with the semifreddo and smooth with a spatula.

4. Place in the freezer for a minimum of 4 hours or until frozen. Before serving, let stand at room temperature for 5 minutes.

5. Garnish and serve. Place on a doily-lined plate for service. Serve with a crisp cookie and garnish with fresh berries and a sprig of thyme.

autumn

autumn menus

NOTE: Recipes highlighted with an asterisk (*) are vegetarian or can easily be adapted to be vegetarian.

Ron and Devora's Tuscan Adventure

RON EISENBERG AND DEVORA SAFRAN EISENBERG

Bellini Cocktail • Ron's Ravin' Saffron Pressure Cooker Risotto
Duck Porchetta Antipasti • Zucchini Alla Menta • Tiramisu

Tasty adventures in food and travel were our focus when we partnered with La Cucina de Castello, an Italian cooking school in Tuscany. We lived and cooked in a beautifully renovated 1,000-year-old castello. Many of our students took amazing trips that combined hands-on cooking lessons with unique travel experiences. In addition to the fabulous garden, the wood-fired oven, and the local markets, the experience included pressing olive oil, hunting wild boar at night, and truffle hunting with trained dogs. Ron and Devora learned most of the recipes in this menu from Chef John Carlo of the Castello. The risotto recipe was adapted to use a pressure cooker because it comes out so delicious in only 7 minutes. Even Vittorio Cambria, owner of the Italian cooking school, was impressed.

Bellini Cocktail

Serves 8

8 ounces white peach purée, nectar, or Kern's Peach Nectar
32 ounces Prosecco

1. Prepare white peach purée. Peel and slice a very ripe and fragrant white peach and purée in a food processor or blender. Add simple syrup or bartender's sugar to adjust sweetness. Chill until very cold.
2. Serve. Spoon 1 ounce of the purée into a shaker, add the Prosecco, and gently stir. Pour into a champagne flute and serve at once. Repeat.

Ron's Ravin' Saffron Pressure Cooker Risotto*

Serves 8 to 10 as a side dish

1/2 teaspoon saffron threads
1/2 cup dry white wine
2 tablespoons olive oil
1 small onion or 3 shallots, finely chopped
2 cups arborio rice
3 1/2 cups chicken or vegetable broth
1/2 cup Parmesan cheese, grated
3 tablespoons unsalted butter
Salt and pepper, to taste
3 tablespoons Italian parsley, chopped

1. Place the saffron threads in a bowl with the wine and allow them to bloom at least 30 minutes, or until wine is a bright saffron color.
2. In a 2-quart or larger pressure fry pan, heat oil over medium heat until hot but not smoking. Add the onion. Sauté until just tender. Add the rice and stir to coat.
3. Add the saffron wine and broth, stirring to combine. Increase heat to high and bring to a boil, stirring often. Place the lid on the pressure cooker and bring to first red ring. Lower heat to stabilize pressure and cook for 7 minutes. Remove pan from heat and use cold-water release method by cooling the hot pressure cooker under running water until pressure drops and pan cools. Remove lid carefully.
4. Stir in cheese and butter, and cook 1 minute more. Adjust the seasoning. Top with parsley and serve.

Duck Porchetta Antipasti

Serves 8

DRY MARINADE

2 tablespoons fresh rosemary, minced
2 tablespoons fresh sage, minced
2 tablespoons garlic, minced
Salt and pepper

DUCK

2 whole skin-on, boneless duck breasts
4 thick slices pancetta
2 duck livers, sliced thin (optional)
3 teaspoons fennel seeds
2 tablespoons olive oil

SAUCE

1 cup rosé wine or other light, fruity red wine
1 3/4 cups seedless red grapes, cut in half (or pomegranate seeds)
Salt and pepper, to taste

1. Preheat oven to 400°F.
2. Make the marinade. Combine all ingredients in a small bowl.
3. Coat the duck breasts with the dry marinade.
4. Lay each duck breast flat on a cutting board with the flesh side up. Place two slices of pancetta side by side on each breast, top with liver, if desired, and sprinkle with fennel seeds. Roll the duck into a cylinder and secure it tightly with kitchen twine. Cut small slits in the duck skin to allow the fat to render during cooking.
5. Cook the duck. Heat the oil in an oven-ready sauté pan and brown the duck breasts. Place the pan in the oven and roast for 25 to 30 minutes, until duck reaches an internal temperature of 150°F.
6. Remove the duck to a platter, cover loosely with foil, and let stand for 10 minutes before slicing into rounds. Reserve the pan juices for the sauce.
7. Prepare the sauce. Drain off the duck fat, leaving the pan juices. Add the wine and deglaze by stirring up the browned bits, or "fond," in the bottom of the pan. Simmer until the sauce has reduced by half. Add the grapes. Continue to simmer for 1 or 2 more minutes. Season with salt and pepper.
8. Serve duck slices with wine sauce.

Zucchini Alla Menta*

Serves 8

2 tablespoons vegetable or peanut oil, for frying
4 pounds zucchini, thinly sliced lengthwise
6 garlic cloves, peeled and minced
1 1/2 tablespoons fresh mint, minced
1 tablespoon dried oregano
1/4 cup red wine vinegar, or more to taste
Salt and pepper, to taste

1. In a large nonstick frying pan, heat the oil until hot but not smoking. In batches, fry the zucchini until golden on both sides. Drain on paper towels.
2. Place the zucchini in a large baking dish and add the garlic, mint, oregano, vinegar, salt, and pepper. Refrigerate until ready to serve. Zucchini can be made up to 2 days ahead.

Tiramisu

Serves 12 • Chill for 2 hours

2 pounds mascarpone cheese, softened
10 tablespoons granulated sugar
10 large eggs, separated
2 packages ladyfinger cookies
2 cups strong coffee, cooled
2 tablespoons unsweetened cocoa powder

1. In the bowl of an electric mixer, cream the mascarpone and sugar until light and fluffy. Add the egg yolks and combine until smooth.

2. Beat the egg whites until they form stiff peaks; gently fold into the mascarpone mixture.

3. Dip each ladyfinger quickly into the coffee and place them side-by-side in the bottom of a 9x13-inch baking dish. When the layer is complete, add half of the cheese mixture. Top with another layer of dipped lady fingers and spread on the remaining mascarpone mixture.

4. Chill the tiramisu for 2 hours.

5. Dust with cocoa powder and serve.

Filipino Favorites

AISSA SHELBURN

Lumpiang Shanghai (Pork Spring Rolls) • Chicken Adobo • Pancit Bihon (Stir-Fry Noodles)
Bistek (Steak) with Garlic Rice • Bananas with Brown Sugar Syrup

San Diego boasts a highly diverse international community that adds an exciting blend of flavors and techniques to the cooking community. In this menu, Chef Aissa highlights her Filipino heritage and some of her favorite dishes — including lumpia (fried pork spring rolls) and an amazing chicken adobo that uses imported soy and vinegar. Bistek is marinated sirloin strips with the sweet juice of the calamansi fruit — a hybrid of a mandarin orange and a kumquat. Bananas are paired with a brown sugar syrup, crushed ice, and evaporated milk for a sweet ending to this great Filipino feast. You can find Filipino soy sauce and some of the other special ingredients at Asian markets.

Lumpiang Shanghai (Pork Spring Rolls)

Makes 28 to 32 pieces

1 pound ground pork
3 tablespoons carrots, finely chopped
1½ tablespoons scallions, finely chopped
1½ tablespoons water chestnuts, finely chopped
1 egg white
½ teaspoon salt
¼ teaspoon freshly ground black pepper
1 package round lumpia wrappers
Vegetable oil, for frying

1. In a bowl, combine pork, carrots, scallions, water chestnuts, egg white, salt, and pepper. Mix well.
2. Place 2 to 3 teaspoons of the filling on each wrapper, spreading to about a ½-inch cylinder, to fill the length of the wrapper, leaving about a ½-inch border on each side. Roll up the wrapper around the filling. Brush a little water on the wrapper to seal the end. At this point, the rolls can be frozen before frying.
3. In a deep-fryer, heat oil to 375°F. Fry lumpia until crisp and golden. Drain off excess fat. If the lumpias are too long, they can be sliced in half on a diagonal. Serve hot.
• **NOTE:** Frozen lumpia can be fried without thawing.

Chicken Adobo

Serves 4

¼ cup Filipino vinegar or distilled white vinegar
¼ cup Filipino soy sauce
6 cloves garlic, crushed
2 pounds chicken pieces
½ cup water, if needed
10 whole black peppercorns
1 bay leaf
¼ cup vegetable oil, optional
2 to 3 cups steamed rice

1. Place vinegar, soy sauce, and garlic in a non-reactive pot. Stir to combine. Add chicken and marinate for about 20 to 30 minutes, turning the pieces after 10 to 15 minutes.

2. Cover pot and cook chicken over high heat until liquid comes to a rolling boil. Do not stir chicken. Turn heat down to medium-low and cook chicken until tender, about 40 minutes. Turn chicken halfway though the cooking time.

3. If the sauce is too thick or if there's not enough liquid in the pot, add ½ cup of water.

4. Add peppercorns and bay leaf, and cook for another 10 to 15 minutes.

5. Transfer chicken and sauce to a platter. Add oil to the pot. When the oil is hot, fry chicken pieces until the outsides are crisp and brown. Return chicken to the platter and serve with the sauce and steamed rice.

Pancit Bihon (Stir-Fry Noodles)

Serves 4 to 6

3 tablespoons vegetable oil, divided use
2 cloves garlic, coarsely chopped
1 small onion, diced large
12 ounces pork tenderloin, sliced into thin strips
3 tablespoons Filipino soy sauce, divided use
1/2 pound small shrimp, peeled
1 cup snow peas, strings removed, cut in half on a diagonal
3 stalks celery, sliced on a diagonal into 1/2-inch-thick pieces
1/2 cup carrots, julienned
1 cup cabbage, shredded
4 cups chicken broth
1 small package Bihon noodles (Pancit Bihon)
Salt and pepper, to taste
Sweet lemon (calamansi) halves or lemon wedges

1. Place 2 tablespoons oil and garlic in a wok over medium-high heat. Sauté garlic until fragrant and a golden color. Add onion and sauté until soft.
2. Stir in pork and 2 tablespoons soy sauce. Cook until the pork is done. Add shrimp and sauté until they turn pink and are just done. Transfer pork and shrimp to a platter.
3. Add the remaining oil to the wok. Sauté snow peas, celery, and carrots until vegetables are crisp-tender. Add cabbage and cook until tender. Transfer vegetables to the platter with the pork.
4. Place broth in the wok and bring to a boil. Add Bihon noodles and stir to soften and soak noodles. The noodles will absorb the broth. Add more broth if the noodles need more cooking time. Stir in the remaining soy sauce when the noodles are translucent and cooked.
5. Add half of the pork and vegetable mixture to the noodles and stir to combine. Season to taste with salt and pepper. Transfer noodles to a platter then top with remaining pork mixture. Serve with calamansi halves or lemon wedges.

Bistek (Steak) with Garlic Rice

Serves 3 to 4 • Marinate 4 hours or overnight

BISTEK

1/4 cup Filipino soy sauce
3 to 4 tablespoons sweet lemon juice (from about 8 calamansi fruits) or lemon juice
1 pound sirloin steak, sliced into 1 1/2 x 1/2-inch strips
2 tablespoons vegetable oil
1 medium red or white onion, sliced into 1/2-inch-thick rings

GARLIC RICE

1 tablespoon butter
1 tablespoon garlic, finely chopped
2 cups cooked jasmine rice
Salt and ground black pepper

1. Prepare the bistek. Mix soy sauce and juice in a non-reactive dish. Taste for salt and tartness, and adjust if needed. Add beef strips and stir to coat with soy sauce mixture. Refrigerate at least 4 hours or overnight.
2. Heat 1 tablespoon oil in a nonstick pan. Sauté beef strips in batches and transfer cooked beef to a platter. Add more oil as needed between batches. Sauté onion rings until they begin to soften. Place cooked onions on top of beef strips.
3. Make the sauce. Place marinade in the pan and bring mixture to a boil. Reduce heat to a simmer and cook for about 5 minutes.
4. Make the rice. Melt butter in a wok or shallow, wide pan over medium-low heat. Add garlic and sauté until garlic is fragrant and begins to turn golden brown. Add cooked rice and sauté until warmed through. Season with salt and pepper.
5. Serve. Pour sauce over beef and onions. Serve with the garlic rice.

Bananas with Brown Sugar Syrup

Serves 4

1 cup brown sugar
1 1/2 cups water
4 large, ripe bananas, sliced into 1/2-inch-thick pieces
1 to 2 cups crushed ice
1/2 cup evaporated milk (or half & half)

1. Make the syrup. Place sugar and water in a pan over medium heat. Stir until sugar melts.
2. Cook the bananas. Add the bananas and cook, stirring occasionally, until the syrup begins to thicken and bananas are soft. Remove from heat and cool.

3. Serve. Divide cooled bananas into 4 bowls. Drizzle with some syrup, then top with crushed ice and 2 tablespoons milk.

First Thanksgiving

KATHERINE EMMENEGGER

Herb-Roasted Turkey with Pan Gravy • Green Beans Amandine
Mashed Potatoes • Cranberry Relish • Sage-Scented Mixed Bread Dressing
Roasted Sweet Potatoes and Shallots • Pumpkin Pie

This menu provides the perfect guide for preparing your first Thanksgiving dinner. Chef Katherine includes not only classic, tasty recipes, but also a timetable of how to prepare the dishes ahead so you can actually enjoy the occasion and not be a frazzled mess the whole day. This menu serves 8 to 10 people, depending on how much your guests eat and if you want to make extras for leftovers. Make sure you have a good roasting pan, a gravy separator, and an internal temperature thermometer with a probe. The right tools always make the job easier. So jump right in and enjoy making your Thanksgiving dinner!

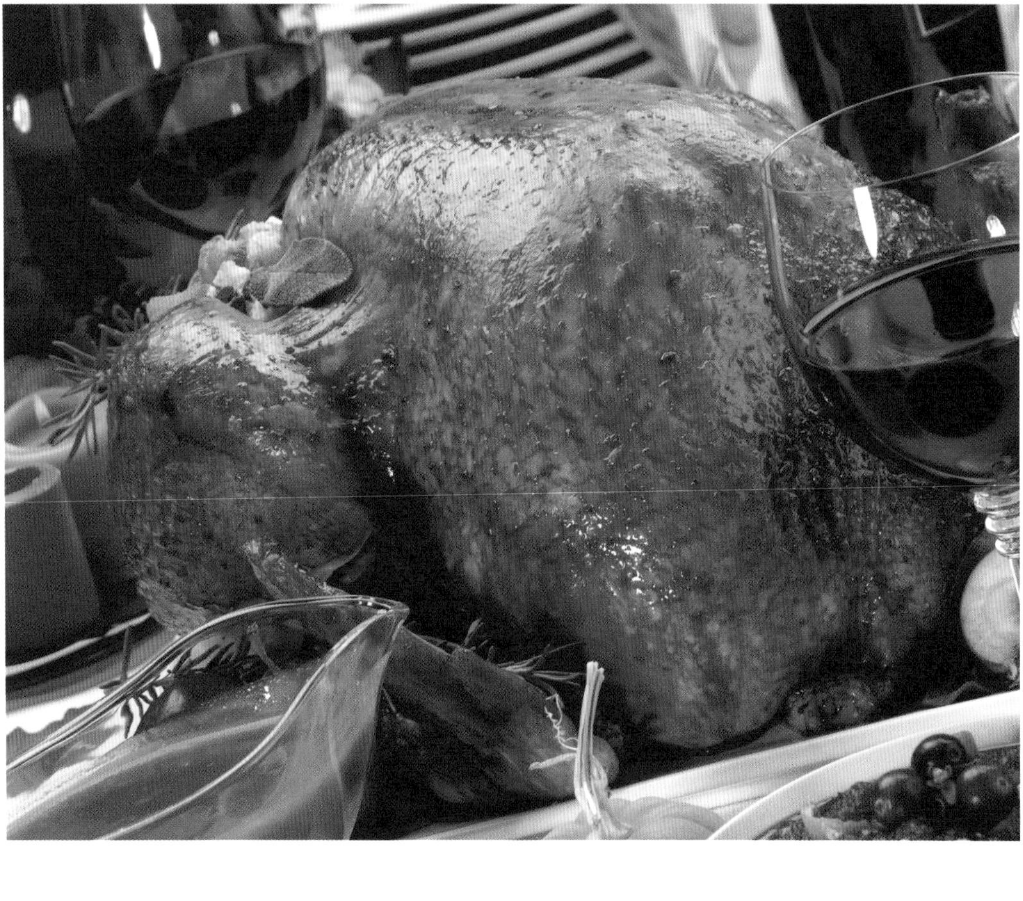

Do-Ahead Planning

TWO WEEKS AHEAD
- Determine how you will serve the meal — family-style, plated, or buffet
- Prepare a list of dishes and serving utensils needed for the chosen style of service
- Order fresh turkey
- Shop for nonperishable items

ONE WEEK AHEAD
- Make pie dough from scratch and freeze

5 DAYS AHEAD
- Shop for the remaining menu items including turkey, if frozen

3 DAYS AHEAD
- Pick up fresh turkey, if ordered
- Move frozen turkey to refrigerator to thaw
- Make cranberry relish

2 DAYS AHEAD
- Prepare the bread for the dressing but do not add the eggs or stock
- Peel potatoes and hold in cold water in refrigerator

DAY BEFORE
- Make pie filling and bake pie
- Prepare sweet potato ingredients, wrap and refrigerate
- Wash and trim green beans; toast almonds
- Set table

THANKSGIVING DAY
- Preheat the oven and, 1 hour before roasting, remove turkey from the refrigerator and prepare for roasting
- Put turkey in the oven and plan to roast 20 minutes per pound

2 HOURS BEFORE SERVING
- Roast sweet potatoes and dressing in the oven
- Remove cranberry relish from refrigerator

1 HOUR BEFORE SERVING
- Make mashed potatoes, place in serving dish, cover, and set aside to keep warm
- Steam the green beans

45 MINUTES BEFORE SERVING
- Remove turkey from the oven
- Make gravy

SERVING TIME
- Carve turkey and place on a platter
- Gather for dinner

Equipment List

- Sharp carving knife
- Kitchen twine
- 1 large platter for turkey
- 4-6 large casserole dishes
- 1-2 sheet trays
- 1 gravy boat
- 4 large serving spoons
- 2 small serving spoons
- Kitchen timer
- Meat thermometer
- Oven thermometer
- Heavy-duty roasting pan
- Cooling rack
- Potato ricer or masher
- Bowl for cranberry sauce
- Pie weights
- Parchment paper
- 9-inch pie pan
- Gravy separator
- Measuring cups and spoons
- Nutmeg grater
- Food processor
- Stand mixer

Herb-Roasted Turkey with Pan Gravy

Serves 8 to 10

TURKEY

1 (12 - to 16-pound) turkey

1/2 pound butter, softened

Fresh rosemary sprigs

Fresh sage sprigs

Fresh parsley sprigs

Salt and pepper

2 ribs celery, washed, cut into 1-inch pieces

2 carrots, washed, peeled, cut into 1-inch pieces

1 onion, peeled and cut into large dice

2 onions, peeled and cut into 1/2-inch thick slices

4 cups hot poultry stock

GRAVY *(Makes about 4 cups)*

1/2 cup butter

1/2 cup all-purpose flour

4 cups combined reserved pan juices and hot poultry stock

Salt and pepper, to taste

1. Make the turkey. Preheat oven to 350°F.
2. Remove the giblets and neck, and set aside for the stuffing. Rinse the turkey under cold running water and pat dry. Trim the excess fat.
3. Beginning at the tail end, loosen the skin over the breast meat. Insert one hand under the skin, taking care not to tear it. Loosen the skin at the drumstick from the same direction. Spread the butter evenly over the turkey meat under the skin.
4. Arrange the herb sprigs beneath the skin on each leg and breast. Press the skin to secure.
5. Rub the inside of the turkey with salt and pepper. Stuff the celery, carrots and diced onions into the turkey cavity. Pull the wings up and behind the back so that the turkey rests on them. Tie or truss the turkey with cotton twine.
6. Line the bottom of a roasting pan with the sliced onions and rest the turkey on top, or use a roasting rack. Either method will keep the turkey from sticking to the pan. Pour the hot stock into the pan.
7. Cover the turkey with a foil tent. (The foil should not touch the turkey.) Place in the oven.
8. Roast the turkey for 20 minutes per pound and baste every 30 minutes with the pan juices. The turkey is ready when an instant-read thermometer placed in the thickest part of the thigh registers a minimum of 165°F. Be careful not to hit the bone with the thermometer, as the temperature will not be accurate. Remove the foil and place the turkey on a parchment-lined baking sheet for the last 20 to 30 minutes of roasting to brown. Reserve the pan juices.
9. Remove the turkey from the oven and place on a platter. Cover loosely with foil and let stand for 20 minutes before carving.
10. Make the gravy. In a medium saucepan over medium heat, melt the butter. Add the flour and cook, whisking constantly, for 3 minutes. Add the reserved pan juices and stock in a steady stream, whisking constantly.

RON'S TIP

Cuisipro Roast and Serve Racks

Turkey lifters and wobbly roasting racks can be real headaches — especially on stress-filled holidays. This gadget from Cuisipro is a removable rack that lets you easily transport meat from the roasting pan to the serving tray in one motion — without lifters. A removable pin allows the rack to separate into two pieces. The nonstick surface makes cleanup quick, and the rack folds up for easy storage. The rack holds up to a 25-pound bird or roast and fits any 16x13-inch rectangular roasting pan.

11. Simmer until lightly thickened. Season to taste with salt and pepper. Transfer to a gravy boat for serving.
12. Serve. Arrange turkey slices on a platter and serve with gravy.

Green Beans Amandine*

Serves 8

¼ cup unsalted butter
3 pounds steamed green beans, trimmed
Salt, pepper, and fresh lemon juice, to taste
½ cup sliced almonds, lightly toasted

1. In a large sauté pan, melt and brown the butter. Add the beans and stir to coat; season to taste with salt, pepper, and lemon juice.
2. Place in a serving bowl and top with the almonds.

Mashed Potatoes*

Serves 8

10 large russet potatoes, washed, peeled, and cubed
1 cup (or more as needed) heavy cream, half & half or milk, heated
4 tablespoons butter, softened, or more to taste
Salt and pepper, to taste
Freshly ground nutmeg, to taste

1. Place the potatoes in a large pot and cover with cold water. Add 2 teaspoons of salt and bring to a boil. Cook potatoes until fork-tender, drain, and return them to the pot. Place the pot over low heat for 1 minute to slightly dry the potatoes.
2. Mash the potatoes using a ricer, electric mixer, or manual potato masher. Add the butter and then pour in the heated cream, a little at a time, until potatoes are light and fluffy. Season with salt, pepper, and nutmeg.
3. Serve.

Cranberry Relish*

Serves 8

1 large, seedless orange, washed, peel on, ends removed, and quartered
1 pound fresh cranberries, washed and drained
¼ cup brown sugar
1½ cups chopped California dried figs, stems removed
¼ cup apricot preserves
1 cup fresh, ripe, pineapple, diced (optional)
2 tablespoons fresh lemon juice

1. In a food processor, chop the orange.
In a saucepan over medium heat, combine the cranberries and brown sugar. Cook until the cranberries just begin to pop, stirring occasionally. Add the figs and simmer for 3 minutes. Add the preserves, chopped orange, pineapple, and lemon juice. Cool to room temperature and transfer to a storage container; cover and refrigerate to cool before serving.

Sage-Scented Mixed Bread Dressing*

Serves 8

$1^{3}/_{4}$ pounds bread, cut into cubes and toasted (whole wheat, white, or a blend)
2 tablespoons butter
2 large onions, peeled and diced small
6 celery stalks, washed and diced small
3 tablespoons fresh parsley, minced
2 tablespoons fresh sage, minced
3 garlic cloves, minced
Turkey giblets, boiled, chopped (optional)
3 eggs, beaten
2 cups chicken or vegetable stock, or more for desired consistency
Butter, for the baking dish
Salt and pepper, to taste

1. Preheat oven to 350°F.
2. In a sauté pan over medium heat, melt the butter and sauté the onions, celery, herbs, and garlic; let cool. Combine the giblets and the cooled vegetables with the toasted bread cubes. Combine the eggs and stock; add to the dressing and season with salt and pepper. Place in a buttered baking dish and cover with foil. Bake for 30 minutes.
3. If you prefer a moister dressing, add more stock.

Roasted Sweet Potatoes and Shallots*

Serves 6

$^{1}/_{4}$ cup low-sodium chicken broth or vegetable broth
3 tablespoons olive oil
2 tablespoons balsamic vinegar
2 pounds red-skinned sweet potatoes (yams), peeled, cut into 1-inch chunks
10 large shallots, peeled, halved through root end
4 bay leaves
2 tablespoons fresh marjoram, minced
Salt and pepper, to taste
3 tablespoons fresh Italian parsley, minced

1. Preheat oven to 400°F.
2. Line a baking sheet with parchment paper.
3. In a large bowl, combine broth, olive oil, and balsamic vinegar. Add the sweet potatoes, shallots, bay leaves, and marjoram, and toss to coat; season with salt and pepper.
4. Arrange the sweet potato mixture on the baking sheet. Roast about 1 hour, or until the potatoes soften and brown, stirring regularly as they roast.
5. Transfer to a serving dish and garnish with the parsley.

Pumpkin Pie

Makes 1 (9-inch) pie / Serves 8 • Chill pie shell 1 hour before baking

PIE SHELL *(Makes 2 shells or pastry for 1 pie, top and bottom)*
2 cups all-purpose flour
1 1/2 teaspoons salt
2/3 cup unsalted butter or Crisco
4 to 6 tablespoons ice water

FILLING
1 tablespoon cornstarch
1/2 teaspoon salt
1 teaspoon ground ginger
1 teaspoon ground cinnamon
1/8 teaspoon ground cloves
1 1/2 cups fresh or canned pumpkin purée
(Kabocha squash is great for fresh purée)
1 teaspoon pure vanilla extract
3 large eggs, lightly beaten
1 1/2 cups sweetened condensed milk

WHIPPED CREAM
1 cup heavy whipping cream
3 tablespoons granulated sugar
2 teaspoons pure vanilla extract

1. Make the pie shell. In a bowl, combine the flour and salt. Add the butter or Crisco and work into the flour with your fingers or a pastry cutter.
2. Continue to work the flour mixture until it resembles a course meal, about the size of peas. (This can also be done in a food processor or mixer.)
3. Make three indentations into the dough and add 4 tablespoons of the ice water. Toss together with your hands. Work quickly; do not overwork the dough. If the dough is too dry and crumbly, add remaining water 1 tablespoon at a time until dough tightens up.
4. Divide dough in half and flatten into disks. Wrap tightly in plastic wrap and place in the refrigerator for 1 hour before rolling.
5. Between two pieces of plastic wrap, roll one of the disks into a 10-inch circle. Put dough into a 9-inch glass pie plate and trim evenly along edge, leaving about a 1/2-inch overhang. Pinch to form a decorative the edge. If the dough begins to soften, chill for 15 minutes.
6. Make the filling. Preheat oven to 425°F.
7. Line a baking sheet with parchment paper and set aside.
8. In a large bowl, combine all filling ingredients. Pour filling into the prepared pie shell. Transfer to the prepared baking sheet.
9. Bake for 10 minutes. Reduce the heat to 350°F. and continue baking for 30 minutes more. Remove from the oven and cool on a wire rack at room temperature.
10. Make the whipped cream. With an electric mixer fitted with the whisk attachment, combine the cream, sugar, and vanilla. Whip to firm peaks.
11. Serve pie with fresh whipped cream.

Party in a Pot
(for slow cookers and crock pots)

DIANE PHILLIPS

Cinnamon Red Wine-Poached Apples with Goat Cheese • Slow-Cooker Brisket with Fruits
Turkey Breast Roulade Braised in Pinot Grigio with Prosciutto, Golden Raisins, and Corn Bread Stuffing

Slow cookers or crock pots have been a household favorite of busy families for many years. With slow cookers, you put ingredients inside a removable insert (the "crock"), turn it on, and forget it for most of the day. Coming home to a house filled with the great aromas of a slow-cooked dish is made even better by the simplicity of it all. Slow cookers are made by top-brand appliance manufacturers. Many have advanced heat settings, timers, and digital readouts, and are available in new materials and finishes like brushed chrome. This menu from Chef Diane highlights the diversity of this appliance with hearty recipes that range from brisket to turkey breast to a gourmet dessert.

Cinnamon Red Wine-Poached Apples with Goat Cheese*

Serves 8

2 cups red wine
1½ cups firmly packed light brown sugar
2 (4-inch) cinnamon sticks
1 vanilla bean, cut in half and scraped
4 medium Granny Smith apples, peeled, cored, and cut into wedges
2 cups crumbled goat cheese

1. Combine the red wine, sugar, cinnamon, and vanilla in the insert of a 5- to 7-quart slow cooker.
2. Add the apples and coat them with the liquid. Cover and cook on high for 1½ to 2 hours, until the apples are tender.
3. Uncover the slow cooker and allow the apples to cool. Carefully remove the apples from the slow cooker with a slotted spoon and transfer to a platter.
4. Strain the poaching liquid into a saucepan, discarding any solids. Bring the liquid to a boil and boil for 5 to 10 minutes, until the liquid is syrupy.
5. Spoon some of the syrup over the apples and sprinkle with crumbled goat cheese. Serve at room temperature.

Slow-Cooker Brisket with Fruits

Serves 8

2 teaspoons salt
1 teaspoon freshly ground black pepper
1/4 cup Dijon mustard
1/2 cup firmly packed light brown sugar
1 (3- to 4-pound) beef brisket (first cut or flat cut), trimmed of as much fat as possible
3 tablespoons olive oil
3 large sweet yellow onions, thinly sliced
2 teaspoons dried thyme
1/2 cup red wine
1/2 cup beef broth
1 cup dried figs, cut in half
1/4 cup dried plums, cut in half
1/2 cup dried apricots, cut in half
2 tablespoons cornstarch

1. In a small bowl, combine the salt, pepper, mustard, and brown sugar. Pat the mixture onto the brisket.
2. In a large skillet, heat the oil over medium-high heat, and brown the brisket on each side.
3. Remove the brisket from the pan. Add the onions and thyme, and sauté for 2 to 3 minutes, until softened.
4. Deglaze the pan with the wine and broth, swirling the pan and bringing the liquid to a boil.
5. Pour the mixture into the slow-cooker insert, and top with the dried fruits and the brisket. Cover and cook on low for 8 to 10 hours or on high for 4 to 5 hours, until the meat is fork-tender.
6. Remove the brisket and fruits from the insert and cover. Pour the liquid into a saucepan or saucier. Remove any excess fat from the top of the sauce.
7. Bring the liquid to a boil, and add the cornstarch stirring until it returns to a boil. Taste the sauce for seasoning and adjust if necessary.
8. Remove any fat from the brisket, and slice thinly against the grain. Serve the brisket surrounded with the fruit and topped with some of the sauce. Serve additional sauce on the side.

RON'S TIP

Breville Slow Cookers

Slow cookers enable you to make healthy, delicious home-cooked meals without spending hours in the kitchen. Breville's 7-quart cooker even has a tough titanium nonstick insert that can go right on the stovetop to sauté, sear, and brown your food (no need to dirty a separate pan). Keeping all the ingredients in one pan means you will retain all the delicious caramelizations and nutrients, and also have less cleanup. The silicone handles remain cool to the touch, so you can safely and easily transfer the insert from the stovetop to the cooker. Start your meal before you go to work by choosing the slow setting, and fabulous aromas and a nutritious, home-cooked dinner will await you when you come home. The cooker also has a high and dual setting for grains and vegetables and better cuts of meat.

Turkey Breast Roulade Braised in Pinot Grigio with Prosciutto, Golden Raisins, and Corn Bread Stuffing

Serves 8 • Needs 3 to 4 hours cooking time

STUFFING

2 tablespoons unsalted butter
1 medium onion, finely chopped
6 thin slices prosciutto, julienned
1 teaspoon dried thyme
1 teaspoon dried sage
3 cups crumbled corn bread or packaged unseasoned corn bread crumbs
1/2 cup golden raisins
1 cup chicken broth, or more as needed
1 egg, beaten

ASSEMBLY

1 (3- to 4-pound) boneless turkey breast
2 teaspoons salt
1 teaspoon freshly ground black pepper
2 medium onions, quartered
2 medium carrots, cut into 1-inch pieces
3 ribs celery, cut into 1-inch pieces
1 cup pinot grigio wine
1 cup chicken broth
2 tablespoons unsalted butter mixed with 2 tablespoons all-purpose flour

1. Make stuffing. In a small sauté pan, melt the butter and sauté the onion, prosciutto, thyme and sage until the onion is softened and the prosciutto begins to curl in the pan, about 3 minutes.
2. Transfer to a mixing bowl, and add the corn bread, raisins, broth, and egg, stirring to distribute the ingredients. Set aside.
3. Prepare the turkey. Lay the turkey breast on a flat surface, skin side down. Lay a piece of plastic wrap over the turkey, and pound until the meat is an even thickness, about 1/2 to 3/4 inch.
4. Sprinkle with salt and pepper and spread the stuffing over the turkey breast in a 1/2-inch layer.
5. Roll up the breast from the short side and secure using kitchen string or silicone bands.
6. Arrange the vegetables in the slow cooker, pour in the wine and broth, and top with the turkey breast.
7. Cover and cook on high for 3 1/2 to 4 hours, until the turkey registers 170°F on an instant-read meat thermometer.
8. Remove the turkey from the cooker, cover with aluminum foil, and allow to rest for 15 minutes.
9. Make the sauce. Strain the sauce into a saucepan, discarding the vegetables, and bring to a boil. Continue boiling for 5 minutes.
10. Whisk in the butter and flour paste, and bring back to a boil. Taste for seasoning and adjust using salt and pepper, if needed.
11. Remove the string or silicone loops from the turkey breast and cut into 1/2-inch slices. Serve the sauce on the side.

International Curries

PHILLIS CAREY

Chicken Tikka Masala • Thai Fresh Green Curry Shrimp with Snow Peas and Red Peppers
Singapore Curry Noodles with Shrimp, Chicken, and Pork
Thai Braised Fresh Ginger Pork Curry

Curry dishes originate from many countries and cultures around the world. They are primarily savory dishes served with rice. Curries may be created with the addition of dry spice powders, fresh spices, curry pastes, or a combination of these ingredients. All are available at your local store, but a trip to an ethnic market or specialty store is a rewarding experience for the adventurous cook. If you have a mortar and pestle and a little time on your hands, you can easily make the curry pastes at home. In this collection of recipes, Chef Phillis takes you on an exotic global taste tour — featuring a range of curries that go from mild to spicy. We highly recommend setting your table with some internationally themed linens or serveware to enhance the travel experience.

Chicken Tikka Masala

Serves 4

Garam Masala is a ground spice mixture often used in Indian dishes. It includes — but is not limited to — garlic, ginger, chiles, turmeric, coriander, mustard, fennel seeds, star anise, and sesame seeds. It loses its potency on the shelf because the ingredients are pre-ground, so buy it in small quantities.

2 tablespoons vegetable oil
1 cup onion, chopped
2 tablespoons fresh ginger, minced
1 jalapeño pepper, seeded and chopped
2 teaspoons garam masala spice blend
1 (6-ounce) can tomato paste
1 1/2 cups chicken broth
1/2 cup heavy whipping cream
4 boneless chicken breast halves
Salt and pepper, to taste
1/4 cup unsalted butter, divided use
1 tablespoon cilantro, chopped
2 to 3 cups cooked basmati rice

1. Heat oil in a 3-quart saucepan over medium heat. Add onion, ginger, and pepper, and stir until tender and lightly browned, about 4 minutes. Stir in the garam masala and transfer to a blender. Add the tomato paste and broth. Blend until smooth. Return to saucepan and add the cream. Bring to a simmer and cook until sauce reduces to 2 1/2 cups, about 5 minutes. Set aside. (Can be made the day before.)

2. Trim chicken and cut into 1-inch cubes. Season with salt and pepper. Heat 1 tablespoon butter in a large skillet over medium-high heat. Add the chicken and cook 3 to 4 minutes to brown lightly. Pour in the reserved sauce and simmer, uncovered, 5 to 7 minutes, or until chicken is cooked through. Sprinkle with cilantro and serve with basmati rice.

Thai Fresh Green Curry Shrimp with Snow Peas and Red Peppers

Serves 6

Fish sauce is a potent and intensely flavored liquid created from fermenting fish. Galangal is a ginger relative that has a very distinctive spicy, citrusy, flowery flavor. Both are used extensively in Southeast Asian cuisine.

GREEN CURRY PASTE *(Makes 3/4 cup)*

1 tablespoon ground coriander
1 teaspoon ground cumin
1 teaspoon freshly ground black pepper
15 fresh Thai or serrano peppers
2 shallots, coarsely chopped
4 cloves garlic, mashed
1 bunch cilantro, stemmed
1 (2-inch) piece galangal, peeled and coarsely chopped
2 stalks lemongrass, white part only, chopped
2 Thai lime leaves, torn up
1 teaspoon salt
1/2 cup water

SHRIMP, SAUCE, AND ASSEMBLY

2 1/2 cups canned coconut milk, divided use
4 tablespoons homemade green curry paste (or 3 tablespoons purchased green curry paste)
1 onion, coarsely chopped
18 pea pods, strings removed
1/2 red bell pepper, cut into 2x1/2-inch strips
8 Thai lime leaves
1/2 to 1 cup chicken broth
2 tablespoons fish sauce
2 tablespoons palm sugar or light brown sugar
1 tablespoon fresh lime juice
1 pound large raw shrimp, cleaned
10 fresh Thai basil leaves, slivered
2 tablespoons cilantro, minced
3 to 4 cups cooked jasmine rice

1. Make the curry paste. Place coriander and cumin in a small dry skillet over medium-low heat. Cook until fragrant, about 2 minutes. Toss with black pepper. Set aside. Put remaining ingredients except for the water in food processor with spices and pulse. Add water and grind into a paste. Keeps refrigerated 5 days and freezes 3 months.

2. Make the sauce. Remove 1/2 cup coconut milk from the top of the can and place in a large pot. Boil until most of the water has evaporated and what is left is coconut oil. Add the curry paste and mash, and cook it into the oil for 1 minute. Add the onion and sauté until tender, about 3 minutes.

3. Add the pea pods and red peppers, and toss for 2 minutes. Add the lime leaves, chicken broth (use more to thin sauce, less for a richer sauce), remaining coconut milk, fish sauce, palm sugar or brown sugar, and lime juice. Bring to a simmer and cook 5 minutes to blend flavors.

4. Cook the shrimp. Add shrimp and cook about 2 to 3 more minutes, or until shrimp are pink and cooked through. Taste and correct seasonings with more fish sauce, sugar, and/or lime juice. Stir in the basil and cilantro, and serve immediately with jasmine rice.

Singapore Curry Noodles with Shrimp, Chicken, and Pork

Serves 6 • Rice noodles need to soak for 1 hour before cooking

Madras curry powder is a mixture of ground dried ingredients, typically somewhat hot and spicy. It orginates in Southern India and contains chiles, turmeric, cumin, coriander, ginger, and paprika.

1/4 cup dry sherry
2 tablespoons light or thin soy sauce
1 teaspoon Asian sesame oil
1 tablespoon cornstarch
1/2 teaspoon ground white pepper
1 pound uncooked extra-large shrimp, cleaned and sliced in half down through the back
8 ounces boneless chicken breast, cut into thin strips
1/4 cup vegetable oil, or as needed
1 tablespoon fresh ginger, minced
1/2 cup green onions, sliced into 1-inch lengths
1 tablespoon garlic, minced
4 ounces pork tenderloin, cut into thin strips

1/2 pound bean sprouts
1 red bell pepper, julienned
1 onion, sliced lengthwise
Salt and white pepper, to taste
2 eggs, lightly whisked
1 pound thin rice noodles, soaked in water for 1 hour and drained
1/2 cup chicken broth
2 tablespoons Madras curry powder
3 tablespoons fresh cilantro, minced

1. Combine sherry, soy sauce, sesame oil, cornstarch, and white pepper in a large bowl. Add shrimp and chicken, and marinate for 20 minutes at room temperature.
2. Coat a wok well with vegetable oil and stir-fry ginger, green onions, and garlic for 30 seconds. Add shrimp, chicken, and pork; toss quickly for 2 minutes. Remove with a slotted spoon and set aside.
3. Add more oil to wok if needed and stir-fry bean sprouts, red bell pepper, and sliced onions. Season with salt and white pepper, and cook for 2 minutes; remove and set aside.
4. Wipe out wok and add a bit more vegetable oil. Add eggs and rotate the pan to spread the eggs into a pancake. While egg is still partially fluid, add rice noodles to wok. Stir and fold noodles and break up eggs into noodles. Continue to stir to keep noodles from sticking to pan until noodles begin to wilt. Add chicken broth and curry powder, and season with salt and white pepper.
5. When noodles are steaming hot and tender, add shrimp, chicken, and vegetable mixtures and toss until everything is very hot and dispersed evenly. Garnish with cilantro.

Thai Braised Fresh Ginger Pork Curry

Serves 6

Tamarind paste is made from the seed pod of the Tamarind tree. The extracted pulp has a sweet-and-sour taste, and is popular in African, Asian, and South American cuisines.

1/4 cup fresh ginger, peeled and finely slivered
1 1/2 pounds boneless pork shoulder or boneless country-style ribs
2 tablespoons Thai red or yellow curry paste
1/4 cup light brown sugar
2 1/2 cups chicken broth
2 teaspoons turmeric
1 teaspoon Chinese dark soy sauce
1/2 teaspoon salt
1/4 cup shallots, thinly sliced
2 tablespoons garlic, minced
1 tablespoon tamarind paste soaked in 1/4 cup water (or use 2 tablespoons fresh lime juice)
Cooked jasmine rice or sticky rice

1. Place ginger in a small bowl and cover with warm water. Set aside for later use. Cut pork into 1-inch cubes and toss with curry paste and brown sugar in a 5-quart Dutch oven.

2. Place the pan over medium heat and cook for 15 minutes, stirring occasionally, until the pork browns lightly and renders some of its fat.

3. Combine broth, turmeric, soy sauce, and salt; add to pork. Bring to a simmer and then cook until meat is tender, uncovered, about 45 minutes, stirring occasionally.

4. Add the shallots and garlic. Add the ginger and soaking liquid to pork. Simmer 5 minutes, or until tender. Drain tamarind and stir in 2 tablespoons juice, or use lime juice. Season to taste for sweet, sour and salty flavors. Let stand for 20 minutes. Serve warm with rice.

RON'S TIP

Le Creuset French Oven

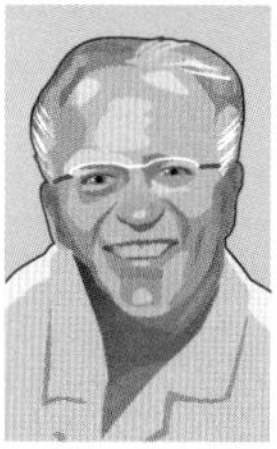

A good heavy pot — like this enamel-coated cast-iron pot — has all the benefits of a cast-iron pan with none of the maintenance and mess. The cast iron allows for even heating and excellent browning of foods. The enamel coating is nonreactive, so it allows for the use of acidic ingredients such as wine, lemon, or tomatoes without a change in color or flavor. It is also stick-resistant. The heavy lid fits tightly, which reduces the loss of nutrients and liquid, and traps all those delicious flavors in your food. The pot goes from stovetop to oven to tabletop — no need to switch pans. Le Creuset ovens are available in round, great for soups and stews, and ovals, perfect for roasts. They come in sizes ranging from 3½ quarts all the way up to 15 quarts.

Do-Ahead Appetizer Party

DIANE PHILLIPS

Bacon-Wrapped Dates • Champagne Cosmopolitan Cocktails
Crabby Bites with the Crabbiest of Spreads • Prosciutto Pinwheels
Baked Brie with Apricots and Dried Cranberries

Chef Diane shares some really fun recipes for easy entertaining in her do-ahead style. When the work is done in advance, you can relax and truly enjoy your guests. In addition to the recipes, Diane shares tips for preparing items one day — or up to two months — ahead. This appetizer party menu would be great any time of year — just add family and friends for the perfect gathering.

Bacon-Wrapped Dates

Serves 10 to 12

12 strips bacon, cut in half crosswise
24 dates, pitted
1/4 pound Parmigiano-Reggiano cheese, cut into small pieces

1. Cook the bacon in a large skillet over medium heat until it has rendered some fat and begins to turn translucent; don't let it brown at all. Remove from the pan and drain thoroughly on paper towels.
2. Make a slit in each date and stuff with a small piece of cheese. Wrap the date in a piece of bacon and secure with a toothpick, if needed. Place the wrapped dates in a baking dish.
3. Diva Do-Ahead: At this point, you can cover and refrigerate for up to 36 hours or transfer to zipper-top plastic bags and freeze for up to one month.
4. Preheat the oven to 375°F.
5. Bake the dates until the bacon is crisp, 10 to 12 minutes. Remove from the oven, drain the dates on paper towels, and set on a platter for serving. Thin shreds of leftover cheese make a super garnish.

Champagne Cosmopolitan Cocktails

Serves 8

1½ cups Cointreau liqueur
1½ cups cranberry juice cocktail
½ cup fresh lime juice
16 fresh raspberries
1 (750-milliliter) bottle champagne, chilled

1. In a large pitcher, mix together the Cointreau and juices. Refrigerate until chilled, or up to four days.
2. When ready to serve, pour 2 tablespoons of the juice mixture into a champagne flute, add two raspberries to the glass, and fill with champagne. Serve immediately.

NOTE

• Remember that icing champagne will get it colder in less time, so stick the bottles into a cooler filled with ice rather than loading the fridge when you need space to store your do-ahead items.

Crabby Bites with the Crabbiest of Spreads

Serves 12 to 16

CRABBY SPREAD *(Makes about 3 cups)*

1 (3-ounce) package cream cheese, softened
½ cup mayonnaise
2 scallions (white and tender green parts), finely chopped
2 teaspoons prepared horseradish
2 teaspoons Worcestershire sauce
2 teaspoons Old Bay seasoning
1 to 2 teaspoons dry white wine or dry vermouth, as needed
1 pound lump crabmeat, picked over for shells and cartilage
¼ cup fresh Italian parsley, chopped

CRABBY BITES

1 (17.5-ounce) package Pepperidge Farm puff pastry, defrosted
3 cups crabby spread
1 large egg, beaten with 2 tablespoons water

1. Make the crabby spread. In a medium bowl, beat together the cream cheese, mayonnaise, scallions, horseradish, Worcestershire, Old Bay, and wine until smooth. Gradually fold in the crabmeat, being careful not to break up the lumps too much. If the mixture is stiff, thin it with additional wine or some milk, and stir in the parsley.
2. Diva Do-Ahead: At this point, cover and refrigerate for at least 2 hours and up to 24 hours.
3. Make the crabby bites. Roll out each of the puff pastry sheets into a 16-inch square. Cut each square into 2-inch squares. Place a square into a muffin cup and spoon 1 teaspoon of the crab mixture into the center of the dough. Draw up the corners of the dough toward the center and twist together to seal. Brush with a bit of the egg wash. (If you are freezing the pastries, don't brush with the egg wash.) Repeat until you have used up all the pastry.
4. Diva Do-Ahead: At this point, you can cover and refrigerate for up to 8 hours or freeze in the tins, then transfer to zipper-top plastic bags and keep frozen for up to 5 weeks.
5. Bake the crabby bites. Preheat oven to 400°F. Bake until golden brown, about 12 to 14 minutes. If the pastries are frozen, place on a baking sheet lined with parchment paper or silicon liner, brush with the egg wash, and bake for 15 to 17 minutes.

Prosciutto Pinwheels

Serves 12 to 16

1 cup freshly grated Parmesan cheese
1 (17.5-ounce) package Pepperidge Farm frozen puff pastry sheets, defrosted
1/3 pound prosciutto, very thinly sliced

1. Sprinkle half of the cheese over your work surface and roll out a sheet of puff pastry into a 12x16-inch rectangle. Repeat with the remaining cheese and puff pastry sheet.
2. Lay half the prosciutto over each pastry sheet, covering it. Roll up each pastry sheet from the long side and seal the edges.
3. Diva Do-Ahead: At this point, you can cover and refrigerate for up to two days or freeze for up to two months.
4. Heat oven to 400°F. Cut the rolls, even if frozen, into 1/2-inch-thick slices and place on a baking sheet lined with a silicone liner, parchment paper, or aluminum foil.
5. Bake the pinwheels until golden brown, 10 to 12 minutes, or 15 to 17 minutes if frozen. Serve hot.

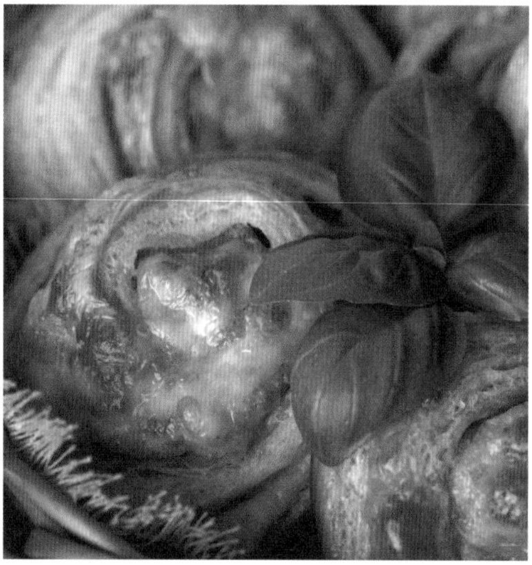

RON'S TIP

Silpat

Once used only by professional pastry chefs, Silpat baking sheets are now available to the home baker. You too can achieve professional results. This food-grade silicone surface is nonstick and never needs greasing. It allows anything — even the stickiest of cookies or cheeses, or the gooiest of candies — to glide right off without a hitch. It also helps keep the bottoms of delicate foods from overcooking or scorching. Sized to fit half-sheet, full-sheet, or true jelly-roll pans, Silpats are available for any need. Because a Silpat can be used in temperatures ranging from -40°F to 482°F, you can also freeze individual pieces of food on it and then easily transfer them. Silpat sheets are light and easy to store. They are also easy to clean — soap and water does the trick.

Baked Brie with Apricots and Dried Cranberries

Serves 10 to 12

1 (6- to 8-inch) wheel brie, rind left on
1 sheet frozen puff pastry, defrosted and rolled out into a 15-inch square
2 tablespoons cognac
1 cup apricot preserves
1 cup unsweetened dried cranberries
1 large egg beaten with 2 tablespoons milk, heavy cream, or water

OPTIONAL TOPPINGS

Substitute any of these for the apricot preserves and cranberries:
1 cup basil pesto, homemade or store-bought
1 cup sun-dried tomato pesto, homemade or store-bought
1 cup wild mushroom spread
1 cup raspberry jam, thinned with Chambord liqueur or another brandy, and topped with slivered almonds
1 cup orange marmalade, thinned with Grand Marnier
8 to 10 dried figs, soaked in sherry and coarsely chopped (drain off the sherry after the figs have plumped)
8 to 10 dried apricots, soaked in brandy and coarsely chopped (drain off the brandy after the apricots have plumped)

1. Place the brie in the center of the puff pastry.
2. In a small bowl, combine the cognac, preserves, and cranberries (or other optional toppings). Spread over the brie.
3. Bring the corners of the puff pastry toward the center of the brie and twist together into a decorative knot.
4. Diva Do-Ahead: At this point, cover or slip the pastry into a 2-gallon zipper-top plastic bag and refrigerate for at least one hour (up to 24 hours) so the puff pastry will relax, or freeze for up to 6 weeks. Defrost overnight in the refrigerator before continuing.
5. Preheat oven to 350°F.
6. Coat the inside of a 9- to 10-inch pie plate or quiche dish with cooking spray and place the brie in the center. Brush brie with the egg wash before baking. (You can also bake this on a baking sheet lined with a silicone baking liner, but the pie plate will help to keep the cheese in the pan, and you can surround it with baguette slices or crackers.)
7. Bake until the crust is golden, 35 to 45 minutes. Remove from the oven and let rest for 15 minutes before serving.

Savory Pies & Tarts

KATHERINE EMMENEGGER

Turkey and Vegetable Pot Pie with Chenin Blanc Herb Pastry
Balsamic-Roasted Heirloom Tomato and Parmesan Tart with Garlic and Lemon Aioli
Crab and Asparagus Bake with White Cheddar Pastry • Easy Crab Quiche

---

Who says pies and tarts have to be sweet? In this menu Chef Katherine features a classic turkey pot pie that your grandmother would be proud of you for making. The roasted tomato and Parmesan tart has a slightly French flair; it can be served year-round for dinner or an elegant brunch. The easy but sophisticated garlic and lemon aioli that tops this tart could also be used as a dip with fresh vegetables. The crab and asparagus bake with cheddar pastry on top is a sure winner, and the quiche is a great basic recipe that can change with your mood — so experiment!

Turkey and Vegetable Pot Pie with Chenin Blanc Herb Pastry

Serves 8

PASTRY *(Makes 2 [9-inch] rounds)*
2 1/4 cups all-purpose flour
1 teaspoon salt
1 tablespoon fresh thyme leaves, minced
1 tablespoon fresh oregano leaves, minced
11 tablespoons chilled unsalted butter, cut into 1/4-inch pieces
7 tablespoons vegetable shortening, chilled
4 to 5 tablespoons well-chilled chenin blanc wine

FILLING
4 tablespoons unsalted butter
1 large yellow onion, peeled and diced small
3 medium carrots, peeled and diced medium
2 ribs celery, washed and diced medium
1 cup celery root, diced medium
1 medium russet potato, peeled and diced medium
Salt and pepper, to taste
1/2 cup all-purpose flour
2 cups low-sodium chicken broth
1 1/2 cups whole milk
1/2 teaspoon dried thyme, or to taste
3 tablespoons dry sherry
1 1/2 pounds boneless, skinless turkey, cooked and diced medium
3/4 cup frozen peas, thawed
3 tablespoons fresh parsley leaves, minced

1. Preheat oven to 350°F.
2. Make the pastry. In the bowl of a food processor fitted with a steel blade, combine the flour, salt, and herbs using the pulse method. Add the butter and vegetable shortening a few pieces at a time using the pulse method until the mixture resembles coarse meal. Sprinkle 3 tablespoons of the wine over the mixture and pulse to combine. Feel the consistency and add more wine if necessary to just bind the dough. Do not overwork. Transfer the dough from the bowl onto a piece of plastic wrap. Divide in half and flatten into 2 disks. Wrap in plastic and refrigerate for 30 minutes. Transfer to a clean, dry work surface. Roll out the dough between 2 sheets of plastic wrap with a small amount of flour to 1/8-inch thick. Refrigerate until ready to assemble.
3. Make the filling. In a saucepan over medium-high heat, melt the butter and sauté the onions, carrots, celery, celery root, and potatoes until tender, about 5 minutes; season with salt and pepper. Add the flour to the pan, stir, and cook for about 1 minute. Whisk in the chicken broth, milk, and thyme; bring to a simmer. Stir constantly until the sauce thickens, about 5 minutes. Adjust the seasoning and stir in the sherry. Add the turkey, peas, and parsley.
4. Assemble and bake. Whether making individual pies or one large pie, cut the dough to 1 inch beyond the circumference of the pie dish and press into the pan. Pour the turkey mixture into the prepared dish(es) and top with a layer of rolled pastry. Trim the dough so it extends 1/2 inch beyond the pan edge. Fold the dough from the top and bottom layers together and tuck the overhanging dough so the folded edge is flush with the lip. Flute the edges all around. Cut at least three vent holes in the top dough. Bake until the pastry is golden brown and filling is bubbly, 30 minutes for large pies and 20 to 25 minutes for smaller pies. Serve hot.

Balsamic-Roasted Heirloom Tomato and Parmesan Tart with Garlic and Lemon Aioli*

Serves 4 as an entree or 6 to 8 as an appetizer

AIOLI *(Makes 3/4 cup)*
4 large garlic cloves, minced
1 large egg
1 tablespoon fresh lemon juice
1 tablespoon fresh Italian parsley leaves, minced
1/2 teaspoon salt
Freshly ground pepper, to taste
1/2 cup extra-virgin olive oil

TART
3 tablespoons extra-virgin olive oil
1 cup julienne yellow onion, julienned
2 each red and yellow bell peppers, washed, cored, seeded, and julienned
1 tablespoon garlic, minced
1 tablespoon fresh rosemary leaves, minced
1 tablespoon fresh basil leaves, chiffonade
1 tablespoon fresh thyme leaves, minced
Salt and freshly ground pepper, to taste
2 to 3 large heirloom tomatoes, washed, cored, and sliced 1/4-inch thick crosswise
1/4 cup balsamic vinegar
14 ounces frozen puff pastry, thawed in the refrigerator
12 to 16 pitted Kalamata olives, quartered
1/4 cup shredded Parmesan cheese

1. Make the aioli. In a blender, combine the garlic, egg, lemon juice, parsley, salt, and pepper; purée.
2. With the blender running, add the oil in a thin stream; the mixture will form a thick emulsion.
3. Store refrigerated in an airtight container until ready to serve; the aioli can be kept for a day.
4. Make the pastry topping. Preheat oven to 375°F.
5. In a large sauté pan, heat the oil over medium-high heat, and sauté the onions, bell peppers, and garlic; caramelize the mixture for approximately 20 minutes. Add the rosemary, basil, thyme, salt, and pepper; sauté 2 minutes more. Transfer from the heat and cool the mixture to room temperature.
6. On a parchment-lined baking sheet, arrange the tomato slices and brush with the balsamic vinegar. Oven roast for 15 to 20 minutes, until slightly dehydrated. Transfer from the oven and cool to room temperature.
7. On a clean, dry, lightly floured work surface, roll the chilled pastry out to about 1/4-inch thick, in a rectangle approximately 9x12 inches.
8. Place the pastry on a parchment-lined baking sheet and score the pastry with a sharp knife; scoring will keep the pastry from puffing too high.
9. Spread the cooled pepper mixture on the pastry, leaving a 1-inch border. Arrange the tomato slices, olives, and Parmesan cheese over the top.
10. Bake in the center of the oven until the pastry is golden brown, about 25 minutes. Let rest for 15 minutes before cutting.
11. Serve with the garlic and lemon aioli.

Crab and Asparagus Bake with White Cheddar Pastry

Serves 6

CRAB AND ASPARAGUS FILLING

5 large eggs, beaten
2 cups whole milk
Salt and pepper, to taste
1½ cups shredded white cheddar cheese or your favorite cheese
¼ cup finely diced yellow onion, lightly sautéed
1 pound fresh asparagus spears, trimmed and cut into 2-inch lengths, steamed to crisp tender
1 pound crabmeat, cleaned (or imitation crab)

WHITE CHEDDAR PASTRY TOPPING

½ cup water
½ cup whole milk
8 tablespoons unsalted butter
1 large pinch coarse salt
1 cup all-purpose flour
4 large eggs
1 cup shredded white cheddar cheese
Freshly ground pepper, to taste
Freshly grated nutmeg, to taste

1. Preheat oven to 350°F.
2. Prepare an 8x12-inch baking dish with a light coating of butter.
3. Make the filling. In a large bowl, whisk together the eggs and milk until thoroughly blended; season with salt and pepper.
4. Combine the cheese, onion, asparagus, and crabmeat in the prepared dish.
5. Pour the egg mixture evenly over the crabmeat mixture.
6. Make the pastry topping. In a medium saucepan over medium-high heat, combine the water, milk, butter, and salt; bring to a boil.
7. Add the flour and combine until a smooth dough forms; stir over low heat until it dries out and begins to pull away from the pan, about 2 minutes.
8. Place the dough in the bowl of an electric mixer fitted with a paddle. Beat the mixture for 15 seconds on medium speed. Add the eggs one at a time, beating thoroughly between each one.
9. Add the cheese and a pinch each of pepper and nutmeg; mix for just a few seconds more.
10. Transfer the pastry dough to a pastry bag fitted with a ½-inch star tip. Pipe the pastry over the crab and asparagus mixture in a lattice design.
11. Bake on the center rack of the oven for 22 minutes, or until the topping is puffed and golden brown and the filling is firm, and serve.

Easy Crab Quiche

Serves 6 to 8

PASTRY

1½ cups all-purpose flour
Pinch salt
½ cup unsalted butter, chilled and cut into small pieces
5 to 6 tablespoons ice water

CRAB FILLING

4 large eggs
2 cups half & half
Salt and pepper, to taste
⅛ teaspoon freshly grated nutmeg
½ cup coarsely shredded Monterey Jack cheese
½ cup Boursin cheese, crumbled
½ pound lump crabmeat, picked over for shell pieces
¼ cup chives, finely sliced

1. Make the pastry. Preheat oven to 400°F convection bake or 425°F for a standard oven.
2. In a food processor fitted with a steel blade, combine the flour and salt.
3. Using the pulse method, add the butter one or two pieces at a time until all butter is incorporated into the flour and the mixture resembles coarse meal.
4. Continuing with the pulse method, add enough water until it just begins to bind the pastry.
5. Turn the dough out onto a floured work surface, gather it into a ball, and press it into a disk. Seal in plastic wrap and refrigerate for 30 minutes.
6. Remove from the refrigerator and unwrap on a lightly floured work surface.
7. Roll the pastry to 13 inches in diameter.
8. Place in a 10½-inch pie pan. Lightly press the pastry dough into the pan. Trim the excess overhang from the edge, leaving enough to fold under and crimp decoratively. Line with foil and enough pastry weights to fill a third of the shell.
9. Bake in the preheated oven for 20 minutes. Remove the foil with the pastry weights.
10. Return the pastry to the oven to bake for an additional 5 minutes. Remove and cool.
11. Make the crab filling. Preheat oven to 350°F convection bake or 425°F for a standard oven.
12. In a large bowl, whisk the eggs and half & half until thoroughly blended; season with salt, pepper, and nutmeg.
13. Place half of the cheeses in the prebaked pastry and top with the crabmeat. Sprinkle the chives and remaining cheese evenly over the top.
14. Pour the egg mixture over the filling and press the cheese to coat.
15. Bake on the center rack of the oven for approximately 30 minutes, or until the filling is golden and baked through in the center.
16. Remove the quiche from the oven and let stand for 10 minutes before serving.

Decadent Dinner Party

PHILLIS CAREY

Baked Salmon Stuffed with Mascarpone Spinach
Risotto with Caramelized Butternut Squash, Bacon, and Sage Topped with Brown-Butter-Seared Scallops
Porcini-Crusted Filet Mignon with Tarragon Maitre d' Butter
Rack of Lamb with Dried Cherry-Green Peppercorn Sauce
Pumpkin Spice Trifle with Ladyfingers, Pecan Praline Pieces, and Mascarpone Cream

In this luxuriously elegant menu, Chef Phillis shares some amazing recipes for serving fine-dining restaurant meals at home. How about porcini-crusted filet mignon with tarragon butter? Risotto with butternut squash, bacon, and sage topped with seared sea scallops can be served as an entrée or an elegant starter. The baked salmon stuffed with mascarpone spinach would make anyone happy, and the rack of lamb with dried cherry-green peppercorn sauce makes a great focal point for the table. For dessert, a beautiful trifle with layers of ladyfinger cookies, pumpkin, mascarpone cheese, and pecan praline pieces can be assembled in a crystal footed bowl.

Baked Salmon Stuffed with Mascarpone Spinach

Serves 8

2 (5-ounce) bags fresh baby spinach
4 ounces cream cheese, room temperature
4 ounces mascarpone cheese, room temperature
Pinch freshly ground nutmeg
Salt and pepper
8 (6-ounce) salmon fillets
Olive oil
3 cups coarse fresh bread crumbs
1/2 cup unsalted butter, melted
1/2 cup freshly grated Parmesan cheese

1. Remove spinach from bags and place in a large glass baking dish and cover with plastic wrap. Poke one hole in the plastic and microwave on high power for 4 to 5 minutes, or until wilted. Drain, squeeze dry, and finely chop. Place in a bowl and add the cream cheese, mascarpone, and nutmeg. Season to taste with salt and pepper.

2. Cut one 3/4-inch-deep by 2½-inch-long slit down the center of the flesh side of each salmon fillet, forming a pocket for spinach mixture. Fill each slit with spinach, dividing equally among salmon fillets. This can be made up to 4 hours ahead. Cover and refrigerate.

3. Preheat oven to 450°F. Line a baking sheet with parchment. Brush salmon with olive oil and season with salt and pepper. Place the salmon on the prepared baking sheet. Mix the bread crumbs, melted butter, and Parmesan cheese in a medium bowl. Top each salmon fillet with bread crumbs, pressing to adhere. Bake salmon until opaque in center, 12 to 15 minutes.

Risotto with Caramelized Butternut Squash, Bacon, and Sage Topped with Brown-Butter-Seared Scallops

Serves 4 to 6

RISOTTO

2 pounds butternut squash, peeled and cut into 3/4-inch cubes
1 tablespoon brown sugar
2 tablespoons olive oil
Salt and pepper
5 cups chicken broth
Pinch saffron threads
3 slices thick bacon, diced
5 tablespoons unsalted butter, divided use
1/3 cup shallots, chopped
1 1/2 cups arborio rice
1/2 cup dry white wine
1 tablespoon chopped fresh sage
3/4 cup freshly grated Parmesan cheese

SCALLOPS

1/4 cup unsalted butter
8 to 12 large scallops, muscle removed, washed and dried
Salt and pepper, to taste

1. Make the risotto. Preheat oven to 400°F. Toss squash cubes with brown sugar and olive oil, and season with salt and pepper. Spread squash out on a parchment-lined baking sheet and roast in oven for 25 to 30 minutes, tossing once, until very tender. Set aside.
2. Place broth and saffron in a saucepan and bring to a simmer. In a 5-quart Dutch oven, cook the bacon until crisp. Remove to paper towels to drain. Drain off all but 2 tablespoons bacon fat and add 2 tablespoons butter. Add shallots and cook over medium heat for 10 minutes, or until shallots are tender. Stir in rice and toss with butter; cook, tossing often, for 2 minutes.
3. Stir in wine and cook about 2 minutes, stirring constantly or until wine has cooked in. Add a third of the broth and cook, stirring constantly, until broth is almost absorbed. Adjust heat under the pot so that the mixture just simmers. Continue cooking, adding more broth as the rice absorbs it, until the rice is just about tender, about 30 minutes total time. Season with salt and pepper.
4. Cook the scallops. Heat butter in a medium to large nonstick skillet over medium heat until butter is browned but not burned. Increase heat to medium high just before adding scallops to the pan. Season scallops with salt and pepper and sear 90 seconds per side, or until just cooked through and nicely caramelized.
5. When the risotto is done, stir in the sage and roasted squash, and heat through. Remove from the heat and stir in the remaining 3 tablespoons butter, cooked bacon, and cheese. Combine well.
6. Serve. Place seared scallops on top of risotto.

Porcini-Crusted Filet Mignon with Tarragon Maitre d' Butter

Serves 6

$^3/_4$ cup unsalted butter, softened
3 tablespoons fresh chives, chopped
1$^1/_2$ tablespoons fresh tarragon, chopped
2 cloves garlic, minced
1 teaspoon flaky or ground sea salt
1 ($^1/_2$-ounce) package dried porcini mushrooms
6 (1$^1/_4$-inch-thick) filet mignon steaks
Salt and pepper, to taste

1. Make the maitre d'butter. In a bowl combine the butter, chives, tarragon, garlic, and salt, mashing to combine well.

2. Prepare the porcini. Grind the dried mushrooms in a spice grinder to a fine powder. Transfer to a plate.

3. Cook the steaks. Preheat oven to 400°F. Season the steaks with salt and pepper, and press porcini powder into the meat, coating both sides well. Melt 2 tablespoons of the herb butter in a heavy skillet over medium heat. Add the steaks and cook 4 minutes per side. Transfer to the oven and roast for 8 to 10 minutes for medium-rare to medium.

4. Serve. Top steaks with a rounded tablespoon of the remaining herb butter.

Rack of Lamb with Dried Cherry-Green Peppercorn Sauce

Serves 4

1 tablespoon unsalted butter
1/3 cup minced shallots
1 tablespoon tomato paste
1 1/2 cups beef broth
1 1/2 cups chicken broth
1/2 cup dried bing or tart cherries
1/4 cup ruby port
1/4 cup brandy
3 tablespoons fresh rosemary, chopped, divided use
3 tablespoons fresh marjoram, chopped, divided use
1/2 teaspoon green peppercorns in brine, drained and chopped
2 (1 1/2 pounds each) 8-rib racks of lamb
3 tablespoon fresh parsley, chopped
Salt and pepper, to taste
2 tablespoons olive oil

1. Make the peppercorn sauce. Melt butter in medium saucepan over medium heat. Add shallots; sauté 2 minutes. Mix in tomato paste. Add broths, bring to a boil, and cook until reduced to 1¼ cups, about 25 minutes. Strain sauce into a small saucepan. Add cherries, port, brandy, ½ teaspoon rosemary and ½ teaspoon marjoram. Bring to a boil and cook until reduced to 1 cup, about 15 minutes. Mix in peppercorns and set aside.

2. Cook the lamb. Preheat oven to 425°F. Sprinkle racks of lamb with remaining rosemary, marjoram, and parsley, pressing to adhere. Sprinkle with salt and pepper. Heat oil in large skillet over high heat. Add a rack of lamb and brown on all sides, about 6 minutes. Place lamb, meat side up, in a small roasting pan and repeat with second rack. Roast until meat thermometer inserted into center registers 130°F for medium rare, about 18 minutes. Let stand 10 minutes. Cut the lamb between bones.

3. Serve. When ready to serve, bring the sauce back to a simmer and serve the lamb topped with sauce.

Pumpkin Spice Trifle with Ladyfingers, Pecan Praline Pieces, and Mascarpone Cream

Serves 10 to 12 • Make 1 day ahead

PRALINE

1 cup golden brown sugar
1/2 cup sugar
1/3 cup half & half
1 1/2 tablespoons unsalted butter
1 teaspoon vanilla extract
1/4 teaspoon salt
1 2/3 cups pecan halves

MASCARPONE CREAM

2 cups chilled heavy whipping cream
1 (8-ounce) container chilled mascarpone cheese
1/4 cup granulated sugar
1 teaspoon vanilla extract

FILLING

1 (15-ounce) can pure pumpkin purée
1/2 cup golden brown sugar
1/4 cup heavy whipping cream
1 teaspoon ground cinnamon
1/4 teaspoon freshly grated nutmeg
1/4 teaspoon ground ginger
1/4 teaspoon salt
1 1/2 (3-ounce) packages ladyfinger cookies
4 1/2 tablespoons dark rum, divided use

Special Equipment Needed:
Candy thermometer

1. Make the praline. Line a baking sheet with parchment paper or a Silpat. Bring both sugars and half & half to boil in heavy medium saucepan over medium-high heat, whisking to dissolve sugar. Reduce heat to medium low and simmer 5 minutes, whisking constantly. Add butter, vanilla, and salt. Attach candy thermometer to pan. Simmer without stirring until temperature registers 260°F, about 8 minutes. Remove from heat; immediately mix in pecans. Transfer to prepared sheet, spreading in single layer. Cool completely. Chop into 1/4-inch pieces. Reserve 1 cup for serving.

2. Make the mascarpone cream. Using an electric mixer, beat all ingredients in large bowl until firm peaks form. Set aside 1/2 cup cream for the filling.

3. Make the filling. Whisk pumpkin, brown sugar, cream, cinnamon, nutmeg, ginger, and salt in a large bowl to blend. Whisk in reserved 1/2 cup mascarpone cream.

4. Assemble. Spread 1/3 cup mascarpone cream over bottom of 8x5-inch trifle dish (12- to 14-cup capacity). Place layer of ladyfingers over cream in bottom of dish (about half of a 3-ounce package). Sprinkle 1 1/2 tablespoons rum over the ladyfingers. Spread 1/2 cup pumpkin filling over ladyfingers, spreading to edges. Sprinkle 1/3 cup praline on top and then spread with 1 cup mascarpone cream. Cover with another layer of ladyfingers. Sprinkle with 1 1/2 tablespoons rum, then spread with 1 cup pumpkin filling. Sprinkle 1/2 cup praline on top. Repeat 1 more time with 1 cup mascarpone cream, ladyfingers, 1 1/2 tablespoons rum, 1 cup pumpkin filling, and 1/2 cup praline. Spread with remaining mascarpone cream. Cover and chill overnight, or up to 2 days.

5. Serve. Uncover trifle. Sprinkle 1 cup praline decoratively over top (reserve any remaining praline for another use).

winter

winter menus

NOTE: Recipes highlighted with an asterisk (*) are vegetarian or can easily be adapted to be vegetarian.

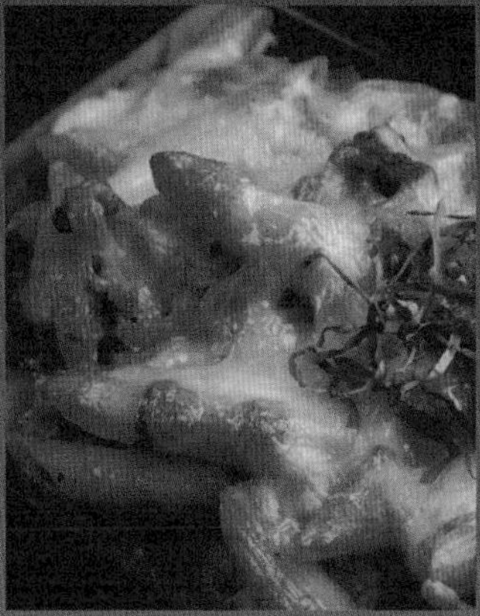

Comfy Winter Soups

MARY ANN VITALE

Irish Chicken Soup • Sweet Potato Soup with Buttered Pecans • Southwestern-Style Beef Stew
Tuscan Lentil and Barley Soup • Sicilian Artichoke and Pea Soup

Nothing beats a great bowl of soup on a winter day. It's comfort food at its best. This collection of recipes has something for everyone. The menu starts with chicken soup (an Irish version), then slips into a velvety sweet potato soup with buttered pecans. Hearty beef stew with a southwestern twist is followed by Mary Ann's famous Tuscan-style lentil and barley soup with a tomato broth base. The artichoke and pea soup brings home a strongly Sicilian style, one that parallels California cuisine. Mary Ann's diversity as a chef is celebrated in the not-so-humble bowl of soup.

Irish Chicken Soup

Serves 6 to 8

4 slices lean, smoked bacon, chopped
1 pound skinless, boneless chicken, cut into 1-inch pieces
2 tablespoons butter, unsalted
3 russet potatoes, peeled and cut into 1-inch cubes
3 onions, diced
Salt and freshly ground pepper, to taste
2½ cups chicken stock
3 cups milk
⅔ cup heavy cream
2 tablespoons Italian parsley, roughly chopped

1. In a heavy-bottomed pan on a medium-high heat, sauté the bacon until most of the fat has been rendered. Add the chicken and continue to cook until it is almost done, about 10 minutes. Add the butter, potatoes, and onions, and cook for 7 to 10 more minutes, stirring constantly. Season with salt and pepper.
2. Add the chicken stock and milk; bring soup to a boil. Reduce heat and simmer for 45 minutes. Blend in the cream and simmer for 5 minutes. Stir in parsley and serve.

Sweet Potato Soup with Buttered Pecans*

Serves 6 to 8 • Make garnish 3 hours ahead

4 tablespoons unsalted butter
3/4 cup onion, finely diced
2 large leeks, white and pale green parts only, washed well, drained, and chopped
2 garlic cloves, finely minced
2 large carrots, diced (about 1 1/2 cups)
1 1/2 teaspoons fresh ginger, grated
1/8 teaspoon nutmeg, freshly grated
1 bay leaf
Salt and pepper, to taste
3 pounds (about 3 large) red-skinned sweet potatoes (yams), peeled, cut into 1-inch pieces
1/2 pound russet potatoes, peeled and diced
6 cups chicken or vegetable broth
3/4 cup dry white wine
2 to 4 tablespoons brown sugar, depending on desired sweetness
1 1/2 cups orange juice

BUTTERED PECANS

2 tablespoons unsalted butter
3/4 cup chopped pecans
Salt, to taste

CRÈME FRAÎCHE GARNISH

1 cup whipping cream
1/2 cup sour cream
1 teaspoon fresh ginger, peeled and grated
1 1/2 teaspoons orange peel, grated

1. In a large heavy-bottomed pot, melt the butter. Add the onion, leek, garlic, carrots, ginger, nutmeg, and bay leaf. Season with salt and pepper. Stir constantly until the vegetables are softened. Add all of the potatoes, broth, wine, brown sugar, and orange juice. Simmer, covered, for 15 to 20 minutes, or until the potatoes are very tender. Purée the mixture with a hand blender until it is smooth, adding additional broth if necessary to obtain desired consistency. Recheck for seasoning.

2. Make the pecans. Melt butter in a skillet over medium-high heat. Add pecans and season with salt. Cook, stirring occasionally, for about 8 to 10 minutes, until golden brown. Transfer to a paper towel to drain.

3. Make the crème fraîche garnish. Combine all the ingredients. Let stand until thickened, about 3 hours. Cover and refrigerate.

4. Divide the soup among bowls and top each with crème fraîche and buttered pecans.

RON'S TIP

Trudeau Pot Clips

The Pot Clip attaches directly to the edge of a pot or a pan and holds utensils while you are cooking to avoid stovetop or kitchen-counter residue by directing the food drops back into the pot. The Trudeau Pot Clip is a great space saver because it eliminates the need for a spoon rest. It's made with a high-quality stainless-steel finish and high-heat-resistant silicone (up to 600°F/260°C) that remains cool to the touch. It's also dishwasher safe and available in a variety of colors.

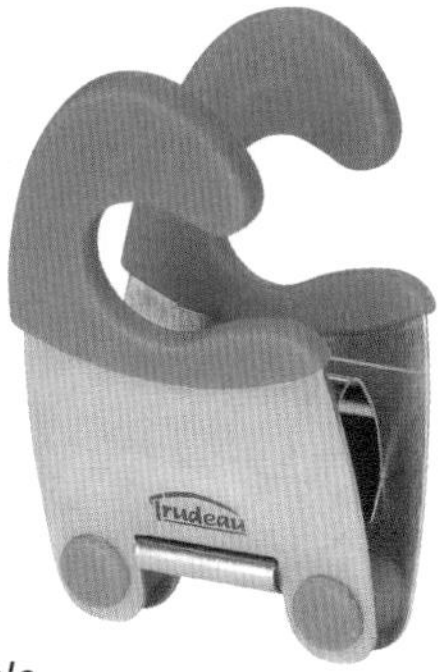

Southwestern-Style Beef Stew

Serves 4 to 6

FRESH SALSA

4 medium tomatoes, chopped
1/2 cup green onions, coarsely chopped
1 to 2 Anaheim peppers, chopped
1/4 cup cilantro, roughly chopped
Salt and freshly ground pepper, to taste

BEEF STEW

3 tablespoons olive oil
3 pounds beef stew meat, cut into 1/2-inch cubes
3 tablespoons flour
3 onions, chopped
4 garlic cloves, minced
1 red bell pepper, seeded and chopped
2 jalapeño peppers, seeded and chopped
2 to 3 Anaheim peppers, seeded and chopped
3 carrots, peeled and cubed
1 pound Yukon gold potatoes, peeled and cubed
1 (28-ounce) can whole tomatoes, plus liquid
1/2 pound green beans, cut into 2-inch pieces
4 cups beef broth
2 ears fresh corn, cut into 1-inch pieces
2 tablespoons fresh salsa
1 tablespoon chili powder
1 teaspoon ground cumin
1/4 teaspoon ground cayenne pepper
Salt and freshly ground pepper, to taste
2 cups shredded cheddar cheese, for garnish

1. Make the salsa. In a glass or ceramic bowl, mix the tomatoes, green onion, Anaheim peppers, and cilantro. Season to taste with salt and pepper.
2. Make the stew. Heat the olive oil in a heavy-bottomed ovenproof pot over medium heat. Toss the beef cubes with the flour and add them to the pot. Cook, stirring, until the beef is browned.
3. Add the onions, garlic, bell pepper, Anaheim peppers, carrots, and potatoes. Continue to sauté until the vegetables start to become tender. Add the tomatoes, green beans, and beef broth. Simmer for about 30 minutes, or until beef is tender.
4. Add corn, salsa, chili powder, cumin, and cayenne. Simmer uncovered for 10 to 12 minutes. Season with salt and pepper to taste.
5. Serve stew topped with cheddar cheese and fresh salsa.

RON'S TIP

William Bounds Pepper & Salt Mills

Salt and pepper are the foundation seasonings of every chef — and a good mill is an essential tool for any kitchen. William Bounds offers a large variety of excellent mills that are not only attractive, but also have an innovative ceramic mechanism that evenly crushes pepper or salt. The three-step adjustable ring allows you to choose fine, medium, or coarse settings, which will not slip as you grind away.

Tuscan Lentil and Barley Soup

Serves 8 to 10

1¼ cups dried lentils
½ pound pancetta, finely chopped
2 tablespoons unsalted butter
2 large onions, chopped
2 carrots, diced small
2 celery stalks, diced small
6 cups chicken broth
1 (14.5-ounce) whole peeled plum tomatoes, mashed by hand
1 bay leaf
¼ cup barley
Salt and pepper, to taste
2 tablespoons Italian parsley, roughly chopped
2 tablespoons extra-virgin olive oil

1. Rinse and sort lentils; set aside.
2. In a heavy-bottomed soup pot, sauté pancetta until most of the fat has been rendered. Add the butter and heat until melted. Add the onion, carrots, and celery, and sauté until the onion is soft. Add the reserved lentils to the pan. Stir in the broth, tomatoes, bay leaf, and barley. Season with salt and pepper to taste.
3. Bring this mixture to a boil; reduce heat to low. Simmer, covered, stirring occasionally, until lentils are tender and barley is soft, about 50 to 60 minutes. Remove from heat. Discard the bay leaf; check the seasoning. Stir in the parsley and olive oil.

Sicilian Artichoke and Pea Soup*

Serves 4 to 6

4 artichoke hearts, fresh or frozen
1 lemon, juiced (use with fresh artichokes only)
1/4 cup olive oil
1/2 white onion, minced
3 cloves garlic, minced
1/2 pound asparagus, cut on a 1-inch bias
Salt and freshly ground black pepper, to taste
5 cups rich chicken broth
2 tablespoons Italian parsley, roughly chopped
1 pound fresh peas, shelled, or frozen peas
1/2 pound fava beans
1/2 pound capellini spaghetti, broken into small pieces
1 1/4 cup freshly grated Parmesan cheese

1. Prepare the artichokes. If using fresh artichokes, remove the stems and all the outer green layers, leaving only the tender inner leaves. Turn them on their sides, and, with a sharp knife, cut about 1½ inches off the top. As you trim the artichokes, drop them into cold water with the lemon juice added.

2. Make the soup. In a heavy-bottomed soup pot, heat the olive oil on medium-high heat; add the onion and sauté for 2 minutes. Stir in the garlic and continue cooking for 1 minute. Toss in the artichokes and asparagus, season with salt and pepper, and sauté for another 5 minutes, or until golden. Add the chicken broth and parsley, bring to a boil, and simmer for 25 minutes, or until the artichokes are tender. Add the peas, fava beans, and spaghetti, and continue to cook for 5 to 7 minutes, or until the pasta is tender. Serve with Parmesan cheese.

Demystifying Convection Cooking

KATHERINE EMMENEGGER

Rosemary Dijon Roasted Vegetables • Mini Wild Mushroom and Blue Cheese Puffs
Three-Cheese Potatoes au Gratin
Garlic-Crusted Prime Rib Roast with Creamy Horseradish Sauce
Pear and Cranberry Pecan Crisp

Convection cooking is prized for its superb results and reduced cooking times. Meats have a beautiful caramelized surface and they retain moisture, taste better, and shrink less. Baked goods have a nicer surface finish and smoother texture, and they rise better — although they may not cook faster. Convection cooks food with heated air that is circulated in the oven in different "modes" or patterns, allowing foods to cook more evenly. Selecting the correct mode is the key to convection cooking. Reduce the oven temperature by 25 degrees and use low-sided pans or flat baking sheets to expose as much surface area as possible to the circulating air, and you will get great results. "Pure convection" is best for baking, roasting, and cooking several different items together. "Convection bake" is used for heavy, dense foods or large items like a turkey. All convection recipes can also be made in a conventional oven. The items will take about 25 percent longer to finish. Alternatively, the temperature can be increased by 25 degrees. Try these recipes and you'll be cooking convection with conviction!

Rosemary Dijon Roasted Vegetables*

Serves 6

ROSEMARY DIJON GLAZE

2 tablespoons vegetable oil
1/4 cup whole-grain Dijon mustard
3 garlic cloves, minced
1 tablespoon fresh rosemary leaves, minced
Salt and pepper, to taste

VEGETABLES

1/2 pound cippolini onions, cleaned and trimmed, (Trader Joe's has them in a bag ready to use)
1/2 pound baby carrots, steamed to crisp tender
1/2 pound brussels sprouts, washed, trimmed, and cross-scored in the stem

1. Make the glaze. In a bowl, combine all ingredients.
2. Preheat oven to 400°F pure convection setting.
3. Prepare the vegetables. In a large bowl, combine all ingredients and coat evenly with the rosemary Dijon glaze. Arrange the vegetables in a single layer on two parchment-lined baking sheets.
4. Roast for 40 minutes, or until the vegetables are crisp on the outside and tender on the inside, turning occasionally. Transfer to a dish and serve.

Mini Wild Mushroom and Blue Cheese Puffs*

Makes about 2 dozen

- $^1/_2$ cup water
- $^1/_2$ cup whole milk
- 8 tablespoons unsalted butter
- 1 large pinch coarse salt
- 1 cup all-purpose flour
- 4 large eggs
- 1 cup crumbled blue cheese
- $1^1/_2$ cups reconstituted dried porcini mushrooms, rinsed, drained, and diced small
- Freshly ground pepper, to taste
- Freshly grated nutmeg, to taste

1. Preheat oven to 400°F pure convection setting.
2. Line two baking sheets with parchment paper.
3. In a medium saucepan over medium-high heat, combine water, milk, butter, and salt; bring to a boil.
4. Add the flour and combine until a smooth dough forms; stir over low heat until it dries out and begins to pull away from the pan, about 2 minutes.
5. Place the dough in the bowl of an electric mixer fitted with the paddle attachment. Beat the mixture for 15 seconds on medium speed. Add the eggs one at a time, beating thoroughly between additions.
6. Add the cheese, mushrooms, and a pinch each of pepper and nutmeg; mix for just a few seconds more.
7. Transfer the dough to a pastry bag fitted with a $^1/_2$-inch round tip and pipe tablespoon-size mounds onto the lined sheet trays about 2 inches apart.
8. Bake on the center rack of the oven for 22 minutes, or until puffed and golden brown. Transfer to a platter and serve hot.

Note: The puffs can be refrigerated for up to 3 days or frozen for up to 3 months. Reheat in a 350°F oven until heated through.

Three-Cheese Potatoes au Gratin*

Serves 8

2 tablespoons unsalted butter
1 small yellow onion, peeled and minced
2 garlic cloves, minced
3 cups heavy cream
4 sprigs fresh thyme leaves, minced
Salt and pepper, to taste
Butter, for the baking dish
4 pounds russet potatoes, peeled and cut into 1/8-inch thick slices
1/2 cup (about 2 ounces) white cheddar cheese, shredded
1/2 cup (about 2 ounces) Asiago cheese, shredded
1/2 cup (about 2 ounces) Gruyère cheese, shredded

1. Preheat oven to 350°F convection bake setting.

2. In a saucepan over medium-high heat, melt the butter and sauté the onions until softened, about 5 minutes. Add the garlic and sauté 30 seconds more. Add the cream, thyme, salt, and pepper; bring to a simmer. Cook for 2 to 3 minutes; remove from the heat and set aside to cool.

3. In a 3-quart buttered baking dish, layer the sliced potatoes, sprinkling some of the cheeses between the layers and reserving some for the top. Pour the cream mixture over the potatoes and sprinkle the remaining cheese over the top. Cover the dish with foil and place in the oven. Bake for 30 minutes. Remove the foil and bake for an additional 20 minutes, or until browned and bubbly.

4. Remove from the oven and let stand for 5 minutes before serving.

Garlic-Crusted Prime Rib Roast with Creamy Horseradish Sauce

Serves 6

HORSERADISH SAUCE *(Makes about 2 cups)*

1 (6-ounce) jar prepared white cream-style horseradish
1/2 cup mayonnaise
1 teaspoon sugar
1/2 teaspoon salt
1/2 cup heavy whipping cream, whipped to soft peaks

ROAST

1 (8 1/2-pound) prime rib roast, bone-in, top fat trimmed, let stand at room temperature for 2 hours maximum before roasting
2 tablespoons vegetable oil
Coarse salt and coarsely ground black pepper, to taste
6 large garlic cloves, minced

1. Preheat oven to 400°F pure convection setting.
2. Make the horseradish sauce. In a bowl, combine all ingredients and fold together. Place in a serving bowl. Set aside.
3. Prepare the meat. In a roasting pan with a rack, place the roast, fat side up. Coat the roast with the vegetable oil and season with the salt, pepper, and garlic. Position the oven rack in the bottom third of the oven. Insert a probe thermometer or ovenproof thermometer into the thickest part of the meat.
4. Cook the meat. Roast the meat for 20 minutes. Reduce the oven temperature to 350°F pure convection setting, and roast until the internal temperature is 130°F for rare. (As an added measure, check an instant-read thermometer inserted into thickest part of meat after about 1 1/2 hours.)
5. Transfer the roast to a platter and cover loosely with foil; let rest for 15 to 20 minutes; the temperature will rise about 5 to 10 degrees as the roast stands.
6. Serve. Slice the roast and serve with the creamy horseradish sauce.

Pear and Cranberry Pecan Crisp

Serves 8

TOPPING

1½ cups all-purpose flour
½ cup toasted pecan pieces
½ cup firmly packed light brown sugar
¼ teaspoon ground cinnamon
¼ teaspoon freshly ground nutmeg
1 stick softened unsalted butter

FRUIT FILLING

1½ cups tawny port
1 cup dried cranberries
8 ripe Bartlett pears, about 2½ pounds, peeled, cored, and sliced
¼ cup granulated sugar
Unsalted butter, softened (for the ramekins)

1. Make the topping. In a large bowl, combine all the ingredients, working the topping into a crumbly mixture with your hands. Set aside.
2. Preheat oven to 350°F pure convection setting.
3. Make the fruit filling. In a small saucepan over medium high heat, bring the port to a simmer. Remove the pan from the heat and add the dried cranberries. Let stand to plump the dried cranberries and cool, about 20 minutes. Drain the cranberries.
4. In a large bowl, combine the pears, drained cranberries, and sugar. Divide the fruit into 8 (8-ounce) buttered ramekins and place them on a baking sheet. Evenly sprinkle the topping over the filling. Bake for 40 minutes, or until topping is crispy.
5. Serve with your favorite vanilla ice cream.

Tamales 5 Ways

KATHERINE EMMENEGGER

Masa, Corn Husks, and Tamale Assembly • Salsa Verde Chicken Tamales
Cajun Crab Tamales • Traditional Spicy Shredded Pork Tamales
Oaxaca Cheese and Sweet Potato Tamales • Grilled Pineapple and Macadamia Nut Tamales

---

Tamales are a Mexican delicacy usually made at Christmas time but enjoyed year-round. It is customary for several families or multiple generations to come together for a full-day event, making hundreds of tamales to share over the holidays. Traditional fillings are generally savory, such as spicy pork, beef, or chicken salsa verde. This menu features less common tamales, too: Cajun crab as well as vegetarian-friendly Oaxaca cheese and sweet potato versions. A dough of ground corn, referred to as "masa," surrounds the filling. The bundle is packaged in a corn husk that has been soaked in hot water. The entire package is then rolled, tied, and steamed to maintain a delicate texture. Chef Katherine includes a special treat — using a sweet filling of pineapple and macadamia nuts as a dessert-style option. Tamales are definitely worth the effort it requires to make them, so give them a try and create a holiday tradition.

Masa, Corn Husks, and Tamale Assembly

Makes about 3 dozen tamales • Needs 1 hour pre-soaking time

Use these instructions for all the tamale recipes

4 cups packed masa mix
1 tablespoon baking powder, best if fresh
2 teaspoons salt
4 cups beef, chicken, or vegetable broth, or fruit juice, liqueur or other sweet liquid for dessert masa
$1\frac{1}{3}$ cups vegetable shortening or lard
2 bags dried corn husks, soaked in hot water for 1 hour, silk removed, rinsed, and drained

1. Make the masa. In a deep bowl, combine the masa, baking powder, and salt. Pour the broth or other liquid into the masa a little at a time, working it in with your fingers.
2. In the bowl of an electric mixer fitted with the paddle attachment, whip the vegetable shortening or lard until fluffy; add the masa and combine until just mixed.
3. Assemble the tamales. Use the largest husks. Lay the husk flat on a plate or work surface with the smooth side up and the narrow end facing you. Scoop 2 tablespoons of the masa onto the husk. If you are making a filled tamale, lay a piece of plastic wrap over the masa and press with your palm. Remove the plastic wrap and reserve for the remaining tamales. Add about 1 or 2 tablespoons of the filling down the center of the masa. Bring the long sides of the husk together to encase the filling in masa, fold the bottom of the husk up, and roll the husk, but not too tightly.
4. Stand the tamales up in a large steamer or colander with the open end up. Do not pack too tightly. Load the steamer into a large pot containing 2 inches of water. The water should not touch the tamales. Lay a damp cloth over the tamales and cover with the lid. Bring to a simmer to steam the tamales for about 1 hour, checking periodically to make sure the water level is consistent.
5. The tamales are done when the masa pulls cleanly away from the husk. The tamale should be tender, yet firm and not mushy. Serve with accompaniments, such as salsas, sour cream, or more of the filling.

Pressure-cooking directions: To steam in a pressure cooker, load tamales on a trivet with 1 cup of water at 8 psi for 15 to 20 minutes. Reduce the pressure with the natural release method (remove from heat source and allow the temperature to drop naturally, approximately 10 minutes). Check for doneness.

Salsa Verde Chicken Tamales

Makes about 3 dozen tamales

SALSA VERDE

5 pounds tomatillos, husked and cored
4 serrano or jalapeño peppers, cored, and seeded, or more to taste
2 tablespoons vegetable oil
2 large yellow onions, diced small
4 garlic cloves, minced
1 cup cilantro leaves, minced
1 tablespoon chili powder, or to taste
Salt and pepper, to taste

CHICKEN

6 cups cooked, shredded chicken

1. Make the salsa verde. In a food processor, purée the tomatillos and serrano peppers.
2. Heat the oil in a medium saucepan over high heat and sauté the onion and garlic for 5 minutes. Stir in the puréed mixture and simmer for 20 minutes. Remove from the heat and set aside to cool. Add the cilantro and chili powder. Season with salt and pepper.
3. Prepare the chicken. In a large bowl, combine the shredded chicken with 2 cups of the salsa verde. Refrigerate until ready to use.
4. Make the masa. Follow the directions on page 179, but replace the 2 cups of the stock with 2 cups of the salsa verde.
5. Cook the tamales. Assemble and steam as directed on page 179.
6. Serve. Plate the tamales and serve with the remaining salsa verde.

Cajun Crab Tamales

Makes about 3 dozen tamales

1/4 cup grapeseed oil
1 1/2 cups yellow onion, diced
1 1/2 cups celery, diced
1 1/2 cups red bell pepper, diced
3/4 cup mayonnaise
1/4 cup Louisiana hot sauce, or to taste
1 lemon, juiced
4 green onions, root ends removed, thinly sliced
2 tablespoons fresh Italian parsley leaves, minced
Salt and freshly ground black pepper, to taste
Cayenne pepper, to taste
1 pound crabmeat, picked over for shells and cartilage

1. In a large sauté pan, heat the oil over medium-high heat and sauté the onions, celery, and pepper until softened, about 5 minutes. Set aside to cool.
2. In a bowl, combine the sautéed vegetables with the remaining ingredients; mix well.
3. Make the masa. Follow the directions on page 179.
4. Cook the tamales. Assemble and steam as directed on page 179.
5. Serve. Plate the tamales and serve with your favorite hot sauce or mustard.

Traditional Spicy Shredded Pork Tamales

Makes about 3 dozen tamales

PORK

4 pounds pork shoulder, bone-in (Boston butt), rinsed and dried
Kosher salt, pepper, and chili powder, to taste
1 tablespoon vegetable oil
2 large yellow onions, julienned
3 garlic cloves, crushed
3 cups vegetable broth

SAUCE

2 tablespoons vegetable oil
1 large yellow onion, diced small
2 garlic cloves, minced
1 (28-ounce) can tomato purée
2 tablespoons ground cumin, or to taste
3 tablespoons ancho chili powder, or to taste
1 tablespoons dry oregano, crumbled, or to taste
Salt and cayenne pepper, to taste

1. Make the pork. Season the pork with the salt, pepper, and chili powder.
2. Heat the oil in a large pot over medium heat and brown the pork on all sides. Transfer the meat to a platter. Add the onions and garlic to the pot and sauté until translucent. Return the meat to the pot and add the vegetable broth. Cover and braise over low heat until the meat is fork-tender, about 2 to 3 hours. This can also be done in a pressure cooker in less time (see page 191).
3. Transfer the meat to a platter to cool. Shred the meat and set aside.
4. Strain the stock and reserve the onions and garlic; discard the liquid.
5. Make the sauce. In the same pot used for the pork, heat the oil over medium heat and sauté the onions and garlic for 3 to 4 minutes. Add the tomato purée, cumin, ancho chili powder, oregano, and reserved onions and garlic from the broth. Simmer for 20 minutes. Adjust the seasoning with salt and cayenne pepper.
6. Cool and combine the sauce with the pork.
7. Cook the tamales. Assemble and steam as directed on page 179.

Oaxaca Cheese and Sweet Potato Tamales*

Makes about 3 dozen tamales

3 tablespoons vegetable oil
1 large yellow onion, peeled and diced small
2 poblano or other mild green peppers, cored, seeded, and diced small
4 ears sweet white corn, husked and kernels cut away from the cob (about 4 cups)
Salt and pepper, to taste
3/4 cup unsalted butter
3 cups milk, or more as needed to adjust the thickness of the masa
3 cups packed masa
1/2 pound instant or quick-cooking grits
2 teaspoons baking powder
1/4 cup brown sugar
Salt, to taste
3/4 pound Oaxaca cheese or mozzarella cheese, shredded
2 medium sweet potatoes, baked or microwaved until soft, peeled, mashed, and cooled
Prepared salsa (Stonewall Kitchen Spicy Corn Salsa is good)

1. In a large sauté pan, heat the oil over medium-high heat and sauté the onion for 2 to 3 minutes. Add the peppers and corn; sauté until golden brown. Season with salt and pepper; set aside to cool.
2. In a saucepan over medium heat, combine the butter and milk; bring to a simmer.
3. In a large bowl combine the masa, grits, baking powder, sugar, salt, cheese, sweet potato, and the sautéed mixture.
4. Fold the hot milk into the masa mixture with a spatula until combined well.
5. Make the masa. Follow the directions on page 179, but rather than spread the masa, roll it into a log shape.
6. Cook the tamales. Assemble and steam as directed on page 179.
7. Serve. Plate the tamales and serve with your favorite salsa.

Grilled Pineapple and Macadamia Nut Tamales

Makes about 3 dozen tamales

MASA

1 Masa Dough recipe (see page 179)
3 cups pineapple juice
1/2 cup Coco Lopez or Coco Real coconut cream (found in the liquor section of grocery stores and commonly used in piña coladas)
2/3 cup packed light brown sugar
1 tablespoon pure vanilla extract

FILLING

1 pineapple, peeled, cored, and sliced into rings
Grapeseed oil, for grilling
1 1/2 cups macadamia nuts, toasted and chopped
1 cup sweetened shredded coconut, toasted

WHIPPED CREAM

1 cup heavy whipping cream
1 teaspoon pure vanilla extract
1 tablespoon powdered sugar

1. Preheat a grill pan to high and oil it.
2. Prepare the pineapple. Grill the pineapple on both sides until well marked but still juicy. Transfer to a tray and cool. Dice the pineapple small.
3. Make the masa. Follow the directions on page 179, but replace the broth with the pineapple juice and Coco Lopez cream. Stir the sugar and vanilla into the masa. Then fold in the diced pineapple, macadamia nuts, and coconut.
4. Cook the tamales. Assemble and steam as directed on page 179, but rather than spreading the masa, roll it into a log shape.
5. Make the whipped cream. Chill the bowl and wire whip of an electric mixer. In the chilled bowl, combine all ingredients and whip until firm peaks form.
6. Serve. Plate the tamales and top with the whipped cream.

Authentic Italian Dinner from La Taverna

MARY ANN VITALE

Stuffed Mushrooms • Bruschetta Pomodoro • Garlic Smashed Potatoes
Steak Toscano • Shrimp Scampi with Garlic Pasta • Almond Cake • Strawberry Vin-Santo Sauce

Mary Ann Vitale was one of the first chef instructors at Great News! Cooking School more than 16 years ago. Today, in addition to teaching at Great News!, she is chef and owner of La Taverna, an authentic Italian restaurant in a cozy neighborhood of La Jolla. In this collection of recipes, Mary Ann creates a classic Tuscan dinner — including stuffed mushrooms, bruschetta, steak Toscano, and shrimp scampi. True to Mary Ann's style, these recipes feature bold flavors, quality ingredients, and traditional appeal.

Stuffed Mushrooms*

Serves 4 to 6

1 pound mushrooms, white button or portobellinis
4 tablespoons unsalted butter, melted
8 ounces feta cheese, mashed
1/2 cup cream cheese
1/2 cup freshly grated Parmesan cheese
1/4 cup Italian parsley, chopped
1/2 cup garlic croutons, crushed

1. Preheat oven to 350°F.
2. Remove stems from the mushrooms. Brush melted butter over the mushroom caps, completely covering them, inside and out.
3. Combine all of the other ingredients in a bowl until blended.
4. Stuff each mushroom with the mixture and brush butter over the tops. Place mushrooms on a baking sheet.
5. Bake at for 10 to 15 minutes, or until golden brown and bubbly.

Bruschetta Pomodoro*

Serves 4 to 6

6 slices firm white bread (day-old is best)
Extra-virgin olive oil, for brushing on bread
1 pound (about 8) ripe plum tomatoes, chopped
5 to 6 garlic cloves, finely chopped
1/4 cup fresh basil, chopped or torn, plus more for garnish
1/4 cup extra-virgin olive oil
Salt and freshly ground pepper, to taste

1. Brush the day-old bread with olive oil on both sides. Toast the bread in the oven, under the broiler, or preferably on a grill until the slices are golden brown. This will dry the bread out to just the right texture. (Never toast your bread in the toaster!)
2. Combine the tomatoes, garlic, and basil with the olive oil and season with salt and freshly ground pepper to taste.

3. Scoop some of the tomato mixture on each slice of warm toast.
4. Serve. Sprinkle with extra basil and serve warm.

Garlic Smashed Potatoes*

Serves 4 to 6

1 pound small red potatoes, quartered
12 whole roasted garlic cloves, smashed
1/2 cup heavy cream
2 tablespoons unsalted butter
3/4 teaspoon salt
1/4 teaspoon freshly ground black pepper
1 tablespoon chives, chopped (optional)

1. In a saucepan, cover unpeeled potatoes with cold water and bring to a boil. Cook potatoes until just fork tender. (Do not overcook the potatoes or they will be watery.)
2. Drain the potatoes well, return them to the pan over low heat, and stir until they are dry and no water remains in the bottom of the pan.
3. Add garlic cloves, cream, butter, salt, and pepper. Using a large spoon, stir the potatoes, smashing them against the side of the pan, until all ingredients are combined but potatoes are still lumpy.
4. Preheat oven to 400°F.
5. Pour potatoes into a buttered 8x8-inch baking dish. Bake potatoes for 7 to 10 minutes, or until golden brown on the top.
6. Garnish with chives, if desired.

Steak Toscano

Serves 4 to 6 • Requires 1 to 2 hours or up to 2 days to marinate

2 (2-pound) porterhouse steaks
6 tablespoons olive oil
2 tablespoons kosher salt
2 teaspoons freshly ground pepper
2 tablespoons garlic, minced
2 tablespoons rosemary, minced
Lemon wedges, for garnish

1. Mix together the oil, rosemary, salt, pepper, and garlic in a small bowl. Pat the steaks dry with a paper towel. Put the steaks in a shallow bowl or a dish and rub the mixture all over the meat.

2. Marinate at room temperature for 1 to 2 hours — or better still, cover in the refrigerator for up to 2 days. Turn the meat from time to time to coat both sides evenly.

3. Remove the steaks from the refrigerator at least an hour before cooking.

4. Drain off any excess oil from the steaks.

5. Heat a grill pan over moderately high heat. Place steaks on the grill pan and cook until well seared on one side, 6 to 8 minutes. Turn the steaks over and sear on the second side for 6 to 8 minutes. Lower the flame to medium and cook turning once, 10 to 15 minutes for rare. To check for doneness, make a 1/4-inch cut into the thickest part of the meat and take a peek. Remove the meat from the heat, cover with foil, and allow it to rest for 10 minutes before serving. Garnish with lemon wedges.

Shrimp Scampi with Garlic Pasta

Serves 4 to 6

12 ounces dry thin spaghetti
2 tablespoons unsalted butter
2 tablespoons olive oil
1 pound shrimp (16-20 count per pound)
8 cloves garlic, thinly sliced
1/4 cup Italian parsley, chopped, plus more for garnish
Salt and freshly ground pepper, to taste
1/2 cup dry white wine
2 cups heavy whipping cream

1. Cook spaghetti in boiling salted water for 4 to 5 minutes, or until slightly firm. Drain and set aside.
2. In a large hot skillet, melt the butter and olive oil. Then add the shrimp, garlic, and parsley, and season with salt and pepper. Sauté for just a few minutes, or until the shrimp are golden brown. Remove the shrimp from the pan and set aside.
3. Deglaze the skillet. Add the wine and stir until all browned bits are loosened from the pan and the wine starts to cook away.
4. Slowly whisk in the cream, and adjust the salt and pepper to taste. Stir until the sauce bubbles and begins to thicken. Return the shrimp to the sauce and cook for an additional 2 minutes.
5. Add the pasta to the sauce and stir until the pasta is hot and the sauce is creamy. Sprinkle with parsley and serve immediately!

RON'S TIP

All-Clad Skillets

No chef is any good without a good skillet. The layered metal bonding construction of All-Clad's design makes for exemplary cooking performance. It consists of a core of aluminum sandwiched between an 18/10 stainless-steel interior and exterior. The aluminum is key in the conduction of heat, insuring even heating from edge to edge. The stainless-steel surface is nonreactive (no "off" flavors or change in colors when cooking acidic foods). The light-colored surface makes it easy to see the level of browning of the fond (the brown bits that form on the bottom of the pan) that is the basis for a superb sauce or gravy. The magnetic stainless-steel exterior can be used on a gas or electric burner, or on an induction stovetop. The riveted handle is strong and will stay cool while you are cooking on the stovetop. This versatile pan can also be put in the oven or under the broiler.

Almond Cake

Makes 1 (9-inch) cake

1/2 cup cake flour
1/2 cup finely grind yellow cornmeal, plus more for sprinkling pan
1 teaspoon baking powder
1/4 pound (1 stick) plus 3 tablespoons unsalted butter, room temperature
1 1/4 cups powdered sugar, plus more or dusting cake
1/2 cup natural almond paste
4 egg yolks
2 whole eggs
1/2 teaspoon pure almond extract
1/4 teaspoon pure vanilla extract
Pinch salt
1 lemon, zest grated
1 orange, zest grated

1. Preheat oven to 350°F.
2. Sift together the flour, cornmeal, and baking powder into a large bowl. Set aside.
3. Using a stand mixer, combine the butter, sugar, and almond paste. Beat the ingredients until the mixture is very fluffy, light, and pale in color — 6 to 8 minutes. While beating on medium speed, add the egg yolks, one at a time, and then the whole eggs, one at a time, mixing well after each addition and scraping down the sides of the bowl with a rubber spatula. Beat in the almond and vanilla extracts and salt. Reduce the speed to low and add the flour mixture, one-third at a time, beating well after each addition until thoroughly incorporated. Fold in the lemon and orange zests.
4. Butter an 8 1/2x4 1/2x2 1/2-inch loaf pan or 9-inch springform pan and sprinkle with extra cornmeal. Pour the batter into the pan. It is not necessary to level the surface. Bake the cake for about 45 minutes, or until golden brown and a tester inserted in the center comes out dry. Remove from the oven and let the cake cool in the pan for 15 minutes. Then while the cake is still warm, turn it out onto a wire rack and let cool completely.
5. Serve. Sprinkle a light dusting of powdered sugar over the top before serving.

Strawberry Vin-Santo Sauce

Makes 2 cups

1 pound fresh strawberries, hulled, quartered (about 4 cups)
1/4 cup granulated sugar
2 tablespoons Vin-Santo Muscat wine or cream sherry
1/4 teaspoon pure vanilla extract
1/4 teaspoon lemon peel, grated

1. Purée strawberries in a food processor. Transfer to a large, heavy saucepan. Stir in the sugar, Vin Santo, vanilla and lemon peel.
2. Simmer over medium-low heat, stirring often until sauce is reduced to 2 cups, about 15 minutes. Let cool (sauce can be prepared up to two days ahead). Cover and refrigerate.
3. Delicious over ice cream or panna cotta!

Pressure Cooking Made Easy

KATHERINE EMMENEGGER

Texas Chili • Spicy Black Beans • Barbecue Pulled Pork Sandwiches with Coleslaw
Grandma's Chicken Soup • Peanut Butter-Fudge Cheesecake

Everything old is new again. Risotto in 7 minutes? Artichokes in 15? Beef stew in 20? Using a pressure cooker allows you to reduce your cooking time by 40 to 70 percent. Due to the sealed environment, the pressure cooker gets hotter and heats food more quickly, allowing foods to retain more of their natural vitamins, minerals, and FLAVOR. New equipment advances include updated safety valves that allow greater accuracy in timing, multiple pressure settings, and elimination of explosions. So don't be shy — try a pressure cooker!

Texas Chili

Serves 4

CHILI

2 medium yellow onions, peeled and diced
3 tablespoons vegetable oil
6 cloves garlic, minced
3 pounds beef chuck, cut into 1-inch cubes
Salt and pepper, to taste
3 tablespoons fresh oregano leaves, minced
2 tablespoons smoky paprika
2 tablespoons ground cumin, or to taste
2 tablespoons chili powder, or to taste
1 canned chipotle chile, minced
2 cups beef broth, or more as needed
1 cinnamon stick
2 tablespoons dark brown sugar, or to taste
2 (28-ounce) cans crushed tomatoes
2 tablespoons masa harina
1½ ounces Mexican chocolate, chopped

GARNISHES

Grated queso fresco, cilantro leaves, lime wedges

1. In a 6-liter or larger pressure cooker over medium heat, sauté the onions in the oil until softened, about 5 minutes. Add the garlic and sauté 1 minute more.
2. Pat the beef dry and season with salt and pepper.
3. Transfer the beef to the pot and brown well, stirring frequently. Stir in oregano, paprika, cumin, chili powder, chipotle, broth, cinnamon, and sugar. Bring to a boil. Add the tomatoes but do not stir.
4. Lock the pressure cooker lid in place and adjust the heat to high. Bring the pressure cooker to 15 p.s.i., stabilize the pressure, and time for 16 minutes. Use the natural release method to release the pressure (remove the pan from the heat source and allow the temperature to drop naturally). After about 10 minutes, carefully remove the lid.
5. Adjust the seasonings and add the masa harina and chocolate; simmer for another 10 minutes, uncovered, to thicken.
6. Serve garnished with the queso fresco, cilantro, and lime.

Spicy Black Beans*

Serves 6

BLACK BEANS

2 tablespoons grapeseed oil
1 large yellow onion, peeled and diced
2 garlic cloves, minced
2 canned chipotle peppers in adobo sauce, finely diced
1/3 cup fresh cilantro leaves, minced
1 tablespoon fresh oregano leaves, minced
2 cups dried black beans, cleaned, picked over, and rinsed
5 cups vegetable stock
Salt and black pepper, to taste
2 tablespoons lime juice
2 tablespoons light brown sugar
Sour cream, for garnish
Cilantro leaves, for garnish

1. In a 6-quart or larger pressure cooker, heat the oil over medium heat and sauté the onion until it softens, about 5 minutes. Add the garlic and chipotle peppers; cook 1 minute more. Stir in the cilantro, oregano, beans, stock, salt, and pepper.
2. Bring to a simmer, stir, and lock the lid in place; bring to 15 p.s.i. Adjust the heat to stabilize the pressure and cook for 25 minutes.
3. Transfer the pressure cooker from the heat and use the natural release method (remove the pan from the heat source and allow the temperature to drop naturally). Carefully unlock the lid and test beans for doneness. If necessary, cover and return the pot to pressure; cook for an additional 2 to 3 minutes, again using the natural release method to reduce pressure. Continue until the beans are done to your liking.
4. Stir in the lime juice and sugar. Adjust the seasoning and serve with sour cream and cilantro.

NOTES ABOUT COOKING BEANS

- No need to presoak
- Fill the pressure cooker no more than halfway
- A small amount of oil will retard foaming during cooking
- Adding a small amount of salt to the beans at the beginning of the cooking process will help the beans retain their shape and keep their skins intact.

RON'S TIP

WMF Pressure Cookers

Pressure cookers have come a long way in the past few decades. By cooking under pressure, you can reduce your cooking time up to 70 percent and also reduce energy costs. Because it is an enclosed system, you can also cook with less liquid, so foods cook in their own juices, retain their vitamins and minerals, and have a more intense flavor. WMF pressure cookers have advanced safety features to prevent pressure buildup. They are made in Germany of 18/10 stainless steel, and they come in sizes ranging from 3 to 8.5 liters. They're especially great for preparing vegetables, soups, stews, chili, and tougher cuts of meats.

Barbecue Pulled Pork Sandwiches with Coleslaw

Serves 8 • Refrigerate overnight

DRY RUB

2 tablespoons black pepper
3 tablespoons brown sugar
3 tablespoons paprika
1 tablespoon onion salt
1 tablespoon garlic salt
Cayenne pepper, to taste

PORK

3 tablespoons grapeseed oil
4 pounds boneless pork shoulder, cut into 4- to 5-inch pieces

COLESLAW DRESSING

1/2 cup vegetable oil
1/4 cup cider vinegar
1/4 cup fresh lemon juice
2 teaspoons dry mustard
Hot sauce, to taste (your favorite)
Cayenne pepper, to taste
1 teaspoon celery seeds
Salt and freshly ground black pepper, to taste

COLESLAW

1/2 pound green cabbage, shredded
1/2 pound red cabbage, shredded
2 large carrots, peeled and coarsely shredded
2 green onions, washed and thinly sliced

BRAISING LIQUID

1 cup cider vinegar
1 cup vegetable stock
2 tablespoons Worcestershire sauce
2 cups Dr Pepper

HONEY BARBECUE GLAZE

1 cup honey
1 1/2 cups ketchup
1 teaspoon liquid smoke, optional
2 tablespoons Dijon mustard
1/4 cup cider vinegar
Salt, cayenne, and black pepper, to taste

ASSEMBLY

Kaiser rolls

1. Make the dry rub. In a bowl combine all the ingredients and set aside until ready to use.
2. Place the meat on a baking sheet. Sprinkle the rub over the surface of the meat; cover with plastic wrap and refrigerate overnight.
3. Make the coleslaw and dressing. In a small bowl, combine all dressing ingredients and mix well. In a large bowl, combine the slaw ingredients, add the dressing, mix well, and chill until ready to serve.
4. Cook the pork In an 8-quart or larger pressure cooker over medium-high heat, heat the oil and brown the pork on all sides. Add the braising liquid ingredients; bring to simmer. Lock the pressure cooker lid in place.
5. Bring the pressure to 15 p.s.i., stabilize by adjusting the heat. Set a timer for 45 minutes. Use the natural release method to reduce the pressure (remove the pan from the heat source and allow the temperature to drop naturally). Check for doneness and, if needed, continue pressure cooking in 10- to 15-minute increments. Transfer the pork to a bowl to cool. Remove the visible fat and shred the pork.
6. Make the barbecue glaze. In a small saucepan over medium low heat, combine all ingredients and simmer until desired thickness is achieved.
7. Assemble the sandwiches and serve. Combine the pork with some of the glaze, reserving the rest of the glaze for the sandwiches. Place some of the pork on the rolls, and top with slaw and more of the glaze.

Grandma's Chicken Soup

Serves 10

BROTH

1 large yellow onion, root and stem end removed, sliced in half crosswise
2 ribs celery, cut into 2-inch-long slices
2 carrots, peeled and sliced into 2-inch-long slices
1 bunch parsley
6 cups water
1 (4-pound) chicken, rinsed and drained

SOUP

2 tablespoons vegetable oil
1 cup celery, diced
1 cup yellow onion, diced
3/4 cup carrots, diced
4 quarts chicken broth
2 cups dry pasta (egg noodles or your favorite cut)
1 cup cooked chicken meat, diced
1 cup Roma tomatoes, seeded and diced
Salt and pepper, to taste
2 teaspoons Italian parsley, minced

1. Make the broth. The broth can take up to a third less time to prepare in a pressure cooker, and it will retain the rich and full-bodied flavor desired for wonderful soups.
2. Over an open flame or under the broiler, brown the cut part of the onion until dark in color. This adds flavor and color to the broth.
3. In an 8-quart or larger pressure cooker, combine all the broth ingredients, placing the chicken breast side up.
4. Lock the lid in place and bring to 15 p.s.i. Stabilize the pressure by adjusting the heat. Set a timer for 20 minutes. Use the natural release method to reduce the pressure (remove the pan from the heat source and allow the temperature to drop naturally). After about 10 minutes, carefully remove the lid.
5. Move the chicken to a platter to cool. Remove the meat from the bones and return the bones to the pressure cooker. Add enough water to bring the pot to two-thirds full. Reserve the meat for the soup or other uses.
6. Return the cooker to 15 p.s.i. and set the timer for 20 minutes more, using the natural release method. Strain the broth; discard the bones and vegetables.
7. Make the soup. In an 8-liter or larger pressure cooker, heat the oil and sauté the celery, onions, and carrots. Add the chicken broth and bring to a simmer. Add the pasta, stir, and lock the lid in place. Bring to 8 p.s.i. and stabilize the pressure by adjusting the heat. Set a timer for 5 minutes.
8. Use the quick release method to reduce the pressure. (Place the cooker in a sink and run cold water over the lid and side of the pan, but not the valve. This stops the cooking process.) Carefully remove the lid. Add the chicken and tomatoes, and simmer 2 minutes more.
9. Serve. Adjust the seasoning with salt, and pepper, and garnish with the minced parsley. Serve.

Peanut Butter-Fudge Cheesecake

Makes 1 (7-inch) cheesecake • Refrigerate for 6 hours or overnight

CRUST

1 1/2 cups graham cracker crumbs
1/4 cup unsalted butter, melted

FILLING

2 (8-ounce) packages cream cheese, room temperature
1 cup sour cream
3/4 cup granulated sugar
3 large eggs
6 ounces semisweet chocolate, melted
1 cup creamy peanut butter

1. Make the crust. In a bowl, combine the graham cracker crumbs and butter until blended. Press the crumbs over the bottom and up side of a 7-inch springform pan; refrigerate for 30 minutes to set.
2. Make the filling. Using an electric mixer fitted with the paddle attachment, beat the cream cheese until fluffy. Add the sour cream, sugar, and eggs.
3. Divide the batter in half. Add the chocolate to one half and the peanut butter to the other half.
4. Pour the fillings into crust simultaneously and swirl gently with a spoon.
5. Completely enclose the springform pan in plastic wrap and then in aluminum foil.
6. In a 6-quart or larger pressure cooker, bring 1 cup of water to a boil.
7. Set the steamer basket in the bottom of the pressure cooker and carefully lower the covered cake into it.
8. Lock the lid in place and bring to 8 p.s.i. Adjust the heat to stabilize and time for 45 minutes. Remove from the heat and use the natural release method (remove the pan from the heat source and allow the temperature to drop naturally).
9. Transfer the cheesecake from the pressure cooker and remove the foil and plastic wrap. Cool the cheesecake to room temperature. Refrigerate for at least 6 hours or overnight before cutting and serving.

RON'S TIP

Kaiser Bakeware Springform Pans

A great homemade cheesecake is hard to beat. Kaiser makes a whole line of outstanding professional-quality bakeware for use by the home baker. The steel base allows for even and gentle heating, and the latest nonstick technology produces a superior scratchproof surface that allows you to cut right on the pan. The unique rim construction means no fiddling to set the ring into the base. The rim also makes the pan leak-resistant — it works perfectly for cooking in a water bath. The hefty clasp has a lifetime warranty and is easy to use. Available in traditional round sizes ranging from 7 to 12 inches in diameter, the pans also come in square and rectangular shapes. But don't use these pans just for cheesecakes. Use them for baking cakes, breads, tortes, or anything that is difficult to remove from a regular pan.

Elegant Holiday Party

DIANE PHILLIPS

Savory Bread Pudding • Sweet and Spicy Nuts • Mango-Cranberry Salad with Blue Cheese
Red, White, and Green Pesto Torte • Roast Beef Tenderloin with Garlic-Herb Marinade
Port Wine Reduction Sauce • Hot Apple Cake with Cream Cheese Frosting and Toasted Caramel Pecan Sauce

Everyone occasionally needs help putting together a holiday dinner party, so Chef Diane created this menu with her Diva Do-Ahead tips to ease the workload while guests are over. Start with her sweet and spicy nuts and a festive tricolored torte. Enjoy the star of the meal — the roast beef tenderloin — with a side of savory bread pudding. For a sweet ending to the perfect meal, save room for the hot apple cake with cream cheese frosting and toasted caramel pecan sauce.

Savory Bread Pudding*

Serves 8 to 10 • Refrigerate at least 4 hours before baking

3 tablespoons unsalted butter
1 tablespoon olive oil
2 large onions, thinly sliced
1 tablespoon granulated sugar
2 teaspoons dried thyme
1 1/2 teaspoons salt
1/2 teaspoon freshly ground black pepper
3 cloves garlic, mashed
5 large eggs
2 cups heavy cream
5 shakes Tabasco sauce
1 teaspoon Worcestershire sauce
6 cups white bread cubes with crusts removed
1 cup (about 1/4 pound) Gruyère or imported Swiss cheese, chopped
1/4 cup fresh parsley, chopped
1/2 cup freshly grated Parmesan cheese

1. Coat a 13x9-inch baking dish with nonstick cooking spray. In a large skillet, heat the butter and oil over medium heat until the butter melts and the foam subsides. Stir in the onions, coating with the butter, and cook until they begin to turn translucent. Sprinkle with the sugar, thyme, salt, pepper, and garlic and cook, stirring, until the onions become golden. Remove from the skillet.

2. Diva Do-Ahead: At this point, cool the mixture, cover and refrigerate for up to 2 days, or freeze for up to 2 weeks.

3. In a large bowl, whisk together the eggs, cream, Tabasco, and Worcestershire. Stir in the bread, Gruyère, onion mixture, and parsley. Pour into the prepared dish and sprinkle the top evenly with the Parmesan cheese.

4. Diva Do-Ahead: At this point, cover the mixture and refrigerate for at least 4 hours, or up to 24 hours. Bring to room temperature before continuing.

5. Preheat oven to 350°F. Bake until golden brown and bubbling, 45 to 55 minutes. Let rest for 5 minutes before serving.

6. Diva Do-Ahead: At this point, cool the cooked bread pudding, cover, and freeze for up to 1 month. Defrost overnight in the refrigerator, and then reheat in a 325°F oven, covered with foil, for 30 minutes.

Sweet and Spicy Nuts*

Makes about 2 cups

2 tablespoons unsalted butter
3 tablespoons granulated sugar, divided use
1 teaspoon seasoned salt
1/2 teaspoon garlic salt
1/8 teaspoon cayenne pepper
2 cups pecan or walnut halves or whole almonds

1. Melt the butter in a 12-inch nonstick skillet over medium heat. Stir in 2 tablespoons sugar, seasoned salt, garlic salt, and cayenne and cook, stirring, until the spices give off some aroma, about 1 to 2 minutes. Add the nuts and toss until well coated, about 4 minutes.
2. Remove from the heat and place the nuts in a glass bowl. Sprinkle the remaining 1 tablespoon sugar over the nuts and toss until coated.
3. Diva Do-Ahead: At this point, cool and transfer to zipper-top plastic bags, and freeze indefinitely.

NOTES
• If you would like to make nuts for salads, chop them before cooking in the butter and seasonings.
• It is important to use dried spices with the nuts because they become fragrant in the butter and will adhere to the nuts. Fresh herbs and spices are terrific in other recipes, but not here.

Mango-Cranberry Salad with Blue Cheese*

Serves 10 to 12

DRESSING
1 1/2 cups vegetable oil
2/3 cup rice vinegar
2 tablespoons granulated sugar
1 1/2 teaspoons salt
1 teaspoon freshly ground black pepper

SALAD
4 (10-ounce) packages mixed greens
1 large ripe mango, peeled and finely chopped
1/2 cup red onion, finely chopped
1 cup unsweetened dried cranberries
2 cups Sweet and Spicy Nuts (see recipe above)
1 cup crumbled blue cheese (Gorgonzola, Maytag, or Point Reyes)

1. Make the dressing. In a medium bowl, whisk together all the dressing ingredients until thickened.
2. Diva Do-Ahead: At this point, you can cover and refrigerate the dressing for up to 2 weeks.
3. Assemble and serve. Place the greens and remaining ingredients in a large salad bowl and toss with vinaigrette to taste. Serve immediately.

Red, White, and Green Pesto Torte*

Serves 12 to 16 • Needs 1 hour to chill

BASIL PESTO

2 cups fresh basil leaves
1 cup freshly grated Parmesan cheese
1/4 cup pine nuts
3 cloves garlic, peeled
1/2 cup olive oil

SUN-DRIED TOMATO PESTO

1 1/2 cups oil-packed sun-dried tomatoes
6 medium-size cloves garlic, peeled
1 cup packed fresh basil leaves
1 cup freshly grated Parmesan cheese
1/2 cup olive oil
2 tablespoons balsamic vinegar

CREAM CHEESE

2 (8-ounce) packages cream cheese, softened
1 pound (4 sticks) unsalted butter, softened
1 tablespoon Worcestershire sauce
1 tablespoon garlic salt

GARNISHES

Fresh basil leaves
Oil-packed sun-dried tomatoes, drained and cut into strips
Fresh baguette slices or crackers

1. Make the basil pesto. In a blender or food processor, process the basil, cheese, pine nuts, and garlic together until broken up. With the machine running, gradually add the oil and process until smooth. Scrape down the bowl and process for another 30 seconds.

2. Diva Do-Ahead: At this point, you can pour the basil pesto into a jar, float ½ inch of olive oil on the top, and refrigerate for up to 5 days. Pour off the oil and stir before using. Pesto freezes beautifully and will keep for up to 2 months. An easy way to freeze small portions is to line muffin cups with plastic wrap and fill each with 1/2 cup of pesto. Cover the tins with plastic and freeze until the pesto is firm. (It will not be rock hard.) Once frozen, remove it from the muffin cups and transfer to zipper-top plastic bags. When you are ready to use some pesto, remove a "puck" or two from the freezer and thaw for about 30 minutes at room temperature. If you decide to freeze the pesto, you can forgo the step of pouring the half-inch of oil over the top.

3. Make the sun-dried tomato pesto. In a food processor, combine the tomatoes, garlic, basil, and Parmesan, and process for about 1 minute. With the machine running, gradually add the oil and vinegar, and process until thoroughly incorporated. Scrape down the bowl and process for another 30 seconds.

4. Diva Do-Ahead: At this point, you can pour the tomato pesto into a jar and refrigerate for up to 7 days, or freeze for up to 2 months.

5. Prepare the cream cheese. In a large bowl with an electric mixer, or in a food processor, combine the cream cheese and butter. Add the Worcestershire and garlic salt, and blend until smooth.

6. Assemble the torte. Line a 4- to 6-cup mold (or a loaf pan, soufflé dish, or lotus bowl) with plastic wrap, letting 4 inches hang over the edge. Wet your hands with warm water and pat a 1/2-inch layer of the cream cheese mixture into the bottom.

7. Spread a 3/4-inch layer of one of the pestos over the cream cheese. Spread with another 1/2-inch layer of the cream cheese mixture. Cover with a 3/4-inch layer of the other pesto.

8. Continue to layer the cream cheese and pestos, ending with the cream cheese. Fold the plastic wrap over the top of the mold.

9. Diva Do-Ahead: At this point, refrigerate for at least 1 hour or up to 2 days to firm up the torte. Or freeze in a zipper-top plastic bag for 2 months, then defrost overnight in the refrigerator before garnishing and serving the torte.

10. Serve. Unmold the torte onto a serving plate, and garnish with basil leaves and sun-dried tomato strips. Serve with baguette slices or crackers.

VARIATION

Buy 2 packages of goat cheese and storebought containers of basil pesto and sun-dried tomato pesto. Mash the goat cheese and press one-third of it into the bottom of a plastic wrap-lined mold. Top with a 3/4-inch layer of one pesto and spread another third of the goat cheese evenly over that. Top with a 3/4-inch layer of the other pesto and evenly cover with the remaining goat cheese. Refrigerate, unmold, and decorate. You can also make this using just one type of pesto if you prefer.

NOTES

- The size of your mold will determine the number of layers you have. This will give you three layers of cream cheese and a layer each of the pestos if you use a soufflé dish or loaf pan. If there are leftovers, they freeze beautifully, or slather them on crusty bread and run under the broiler.
- This elegant appetizer can be shaped into almost anything. During the holidays, use a star-shaped baking dish for the mold, and for larger parties you can make several small tortes to place around the entertaining space. For an elegant decoration, cut sun-dried tomatoes into petals to form a flower head, and add a basil stem and leaves to complete it. If you like, you can also add pine nuts as the center of the flower. Or just use basil leaves for decoration.

Roast Beef Tenderloin with Garlic-Herb Marinade

Serves 8 • Needs 8 to 36 hours to marinate

This piece of meat, while costly, is a show-stopper and there is hardly any waste. Since it has no fat, it will need a bit of marinating to give it some flavor. It can be roasted the day before the party and served at room temperature with your choice of sauce, or served warm — it's really up to you. Many wholesale clubs like Costco sell whole beef tenderloins for $50 to $70, and, since one will serve a lot of people as a main course, it's really not as big a splurge as you might think.

To trim the roast, remove the silver skin (a tendon sheath that surrounds the center portion of the meat). This is easily done with a sharp knife; cut close to the skin and peel the silver skin off the meat. Also remove any fat extending down the roast and connecting a thin strip of meat to the center portion. You can cut off this thin strip of meat and freeze it for kebabs and stir-fries because it cooks much faster than the rest of the tenderloin. If you decide to roast this piece, remove it from the pan and cover it with aluminum foil after it reaches 130°F on an instant-read meat thermometer.

The trimmed meat should weigh about 4 to 5 pounds. The tapered end portion of the roast will cook more quickly than the center. To help prevent this, fold the tapered piece under itself, and it will cook to medium, not medium-rare. You can serve this portion to those who don't like their meat pink.

Roast your beef in a heavy-duty roasting pan, which will leave some caramelized pan juices for you to turn into a nice *au jus* or gravy. Tying the roast with silicone loops or cotton string every 1½ inches will ensure that it cooks evenly and the meat stays compact for easy carving. You can ask your butcher to do this for you.

MARINADE

(Makes about 1½ cups, enough for 4 pounds of meat)

½ cup olive oil
2 tablespoons red-wine vinegar
½ cup soy sauce
4 cloves garlic, minced
2 teaspoons dried thyme
1 bay leaf
1 teaspoon freshly ground black pepper

TENDERLOIN

1 (4- to 5-pound) trimmed beef tenderloin, tapered end tucked under and roast tied with silicone loops or cotton string every 1½ inches
Port Wine Reduction Sauce (see page 199)

1. Make the marinade. In a small glass bowl, whisk together all the ingredients.
2. Diva Do-Ahead: At this point, you can cover and refrigerate the marinade for up to 5 days.
3. Put the prepared meat in a 2-gallon zipper-top plastic bag; pour in the marinade and seal.
4. Diva Do-Ahead: At this point, refrigerate for at least 24 hours and up to 36 hours. Bring to room temperature before continuing.
5. Preheat oven to 400°F. Drain the meat and pat it dry. Place in a heavy-duty roasting pan and roast until an instant-read meat thermometer inserted in the thickest part registers 135°F, 45 to 55 minutes. When taken out at this temperature, your roast will be medium-rare to medium when it finishes resting.
6. Remove the meat from the oven, cover with aluminum foil, and let rest at least 15 minutes.
7. Diva Do-Ahead: At this point, cool the roast completely, cover, and refrigerate overnight. Bring to room temperature before continuing. Slice and serve with the Port Wine Reduction Sauce or a sauce of your choice.

Port Wine Reduction Sauce

Makes about 3 cups

$^{1}/_{2}$ cup (1 stick) unsalted butter, softened, divided use
$^{2}/_{3}$ cup chopped shallots
8 sprigs fresh thyme, or $1^{1}/_{2}$ tablespoons dried
$^{1}/_{2}$ cup cabernet sauvignon wine
1 cup ruby port wine
4 cups beef stock, or beef broth
$^{1}/_{4}$ cup all-purpose flour

1. In a $2^{1}/_{2}$-quart saucepan, melt half of the butter over medium heat. Add the shallots and thyme and cook, stirring, until the shallots soften, 3 to 4 minutes. Pour in the cabernet, port, and broth, and bring to a boil. Reduce the heat to medium and simmer until the sauce begins to thicken, about 30 minutes. Strain through a fine-mesh strainer.
2. Diva Do-Ahead: At this point, you can let cool, cover, and refrigerate for up to 5 days or freeze for up to 2 months. Defrost and reheat gently before continuing.
3. In a small bowl, blend together the flour and remaining butter to form a smooth paste.
4. Bring the sauce to a boil, and then add the flour mixture a tablespoon at a time, bringing the sauce to a boil after each addition. Add only enough of the flour mixture to get the sauce to the thickness you prefer. Remove from the heat and serve.
5. Diva Do-Ahead: At this point, you can let cool, cover, and refrigerate for up to 5 days. Reheat gently.

NOTE

• Sometimes this sauce can have a pronounced wine flavor after boiling it down. This has to do with the wine, not the recipe. To counteract this, deglaze the roasting pan with the sauce — the drippings from your roast will round out the flavors.

RON'S TIP

Mauviel Roasting Pans

The right roasting pan makes all the difference in how well your meats are cooked. A heavy, good-quality pan is essential to any roasting recipe. Constructed of three plies — a layer of aluminum sandwiched between a stainless-steel interior and exterior — the Mauviel roaster can be used on any stovetop, including induction, allowing you to sear and brown your meat. From there you can transfer the pan right into the oven for final cooking. The pan is oven-safe up to a whopping 680°F. After removing your food, put the pan back on the stovetop to make a sauce or gravy. The riveted stainless-steel handles make lifting easy. In addition to roasting, you can use this pan to make lasagna for a crowd, and you can take advantage of its generous capacity whenever you need a water bath for a cheesecake, custard, or crème brûlée.

Hot Apple Cake with Cream Cheese Frosting and Toasted Caramel Pecan Sauce

Serves 14 to 16

BATTER

4 sticks unsalted butter
2 cups granulated sugar
4 eggs
3 cups all-purpose flour
1/2 teaspoons ground nutmeg
2 teaspoons ground cinnamon
2 teaspoons baking soda
5 medium Granny Smith apples, peeled, cored, and finely chopped
1 cup pecans, chopped
1 tablespoon vanilla paste or pure vanilla extract

CREAM CHEESE FROSTING *(Makes about 6 cups)*

1/2 cup unsalted butter, softened
1 (8-ounce) package cream cheese
5 cups confectioners sugar
2 teaspoons vanilla paste or pure vanilla extract
Milk or water (to thin frosting)

PECAN CARAMEL SAUCE *(Makes about 2 cups)*

4 tablespoons unsalted butter
1/2 cup pecan halves, toasted
1 cup firmly packed light brown sugar
1 cup whipping cream

1. Make the batter. Preheat oven to 350°F, and grease a 13x9-inch cake pan, or line a 15x10-inch jelly-roll pan with a silicone baking liner.

2. Beat the butter and sugar in a large bowl until light and fluffy. Beat in the eggs until well blended. Add flour, spices, and baking soda, and beat until just incorporated. Mix in the apples, nuts, and vanilla.

3. Spoon batter into prepared pan. Bake for 35 to 40 minutes for the 13x9-inch pan, 25 to 30 minutes for the jelly-roll pan. Remove to a rack to cool. Wrap the cake in foil and refrigerate or freeze.

4. Diva Do-Ahead: Cake can be refrigerated for 3 days, or frozen for up to 2 months. Reheat the cake, covered with foil, in a 350°F oven for 10 minutes before serving.

5. Make the frosting. In the bowl of an electric mixer, combine the butter and cream cheese until creamy. Add the sugar one cup at a time, beating until the mixture is spreading consistency. Add the vanilla and blend until thoroughly combined. Add milk or water to obtain a good spreading consistency, if necessary.

6. Diva Do-Ahead: Frosting can be refrigerated for 1 week or frozen for up to 3 months.

7. Make the caramel sauce. Melt the butter in a medium saucepan over medium high heat. Add the pecans and toast them in the butter for about 3 minutes. Add in the brown sugar, and stir until it melts. Add the whipping cream, and cook, stirring constantly, until the sauce boils and the sugar dissolves.

8. Diva Do-Ahead: Sauce can be refrigerated for up to 1 week. Reheat in the microwave at 50 percent power or over low heat on the stovetop.

9. Serve. Frost the cake. Place a warm piece onto a dessert plate. Serve with a scoop of vanilla ice cream and spoon hot caramel pecan sauce over all.

Ridiculously Delicious Risotto

PHILLIS CAREY

Italian Sausage and Wild Mushroom Risotto
Risotto Milanese with Saffron (for Risotto Balls, Cakes, or Tortes with Roasted Red Pepper Sauce)
Jalapeño Jack Corn Risotto with Grilled Chile-Lime Chicken
Sun-Dried Tomato Risotto with Seared Scallops and Truffle Oil
Lemony Risotto with Shrimp and Grilled Asparagus

Risotto conjures up images of someones' Italian grandmother in the kitchen slowly stirring a large pot of rice and singing while she does it. "Cooking is love," and it requires love and some patience to make good risotto. Risotto is short-grain arborio rice, high in natural starch. The starch gives the rice a creamy consistency, yet the individual grains remain firm. It is a classic Italian comfort food that has become one of Americas' gourmet favorites.

Italian Sausage and Wild Mushroom Risotto

Serves 6 to 8

2 tablespoons olive oil
1 pound sweet Italian sausage, casings removed
8 ounces portobello mushrooms
8 ounces fresh shiitake mushrooms
1 teaspoon fresh thyme, chopped
1 teaspoon fresh oregano, chopped
1 1/2 cups Madeira, divided use
1/2 cup unsalted butter, divided use
1 1/2 cups onion, chopped
4 cloves garlic, minced
2 cups arborio rice
7 cups hot chicken broth
1 cup freshly grated Asiago cheese
2 tablespoons Italian parsley, chopped

1. Heat oil in a large nonstick skillet over medium-high heat. Add crumbled sausage and sauté until beginning to brown, about 3 minutes. Trim stems and scrape out black gills from the portobello mushrooms. Cut into 1/2-inch pieces. Remove stems from shiitake mushrooms and dice. Add mushrooms to sausage along with thyme and oregano. Sauté until mushrooms are tender, about 10 minutes. Add 1/2 cup Madeira and boil until almost absorbed. Set aside.

2. Melt 1/4 cup butter in heavy large pot over medium-high heat. Add onion and garlic, and cook until tender, about 5 minutes. Add rice and cook and stir 2 minutes, until rice grains are glistening. Add remaining 1 cup Madeira and simmer until absorbed, about 2 minutes.

3. Add 1 cup hot broth and simmer, stirring, until almost absorbed. Continue to cook, stir and add broth by the cupful, until the rice is just tender, about 25 minutes. Stir in sausage mixture. Stir in remaining 1/4 cup butter and season to taste with salt and pepper. Sprinkle with cheese and parsley; serve immediately.

Risotto Milanese with Saffron (for Risotto Balls, Cakes, or Tortes with Roasted Red Pepper Sauce)*

Serves 6 to 8

RISOTTO MILANESE

1/4 teaspoon saffron threads
6 cups hot chicken or vegetable broth, divided use
3 tablespoons olive oil
1 cup onion, finely chopped
2 cups arborio rice
1 cup dry white wine
Salt and pepper, to taste
3 tablespoons unsalted butter
3/4 cup freshly grated Parmesan cheese
1 1/2 cups frozen baby peas, thawed (if serving as Risotto Milanese)

RED BELL PEPPER SAUCE

4 red bell peppers, roasted and peeled
1 clove garlic
1 teaspoon granulated sugar
1 cup mayonnaise

RISOTTO BALLS (ARANCINI), CAKES, AND TORTES

Vegetable oil, for frying Arancini
2 to 4 large eggs, divided use
Fine dry bread crumbs
12 ounces Italian fontina cheese, cut into 1/2- to 3/4-inch cubes
Olive oil, for frying Risotto Cakes
Butter, for preparing pans for Risotto Tortes

1. Prepare the saffron. In a bowl, place 1 cup of broth and add the saffron. Set aside to steep.
2. Make the risotto. Heat olive oil in a Dutch oven over medium-high heat. Add onions and cook, stirring often, until tender, about 8 minutes. Add the rice and stir for 1 minute.
3. Add the wine and cook, stirring constantly, until wine has been absorbed. Add 2 cups of the remaining hot broth and cook, stirring often, while broth simmers until almost all is absorbed. Add the saffron broth and cook, stirring often, until that broth is absorbed. Continue adding broth 1 cup at a time and cooking and stirring until the rice is tender, about 40 to 50 minutes. Season to taste with salt and pepper; stir in butter and Parmesan cheese.
4. If serving as Risotto Milanese, stir in peas and warm through. If planning to make the risotto balls, cakes, or tortes, transfer the cooked risotto to a bowl and let cool at least 1 hour or up to overnight in refrigerator.
5. Make the Red Bell Pepper Sauce. In a food processor, purée the roasted red peppers, garlic and sugar. Stir mixture into mayonnaise. Refrigerate up to 3 days.
6. Make the Risotto Balls (Arancini), Risotto Cakes, and Risotto Tortes.

- **Risotto Balls.** Heat the vegetable oil in a deep fryer, or heat 3 inches of oil in a pot on top of the stove to 375°F. Stir 2 eggs into cooled or cold risotto. Using 2 to 3 tablespoons of the rice mixture, form a ball. Stuff a piece of fontina cheese into the center of the ball, forming the rice all the way around the cheese; ball may be refrigerated at this point for 8 hours. Whisk 2 eggs in a bowl and place 2 cups bread crumbs in another bowl. Dip rice balls into egg to coat and then carefully roll in bread crumbs. Fry rice balls a few at a time until golden brown. Remove and drain on a rack. Serve hot, warm, or at room temperature as is or with roasted red pepper sauce for dipping.
- **Risotto Cakes.** Stir 2 eggs into cooled or cold risotto. Whisk 2 eggs in a flat bowl and place 2 cups bread crumbs in another flat bowl. Form risotto into cakes or patties. Coat rice cakes with egg and then gently turn in bread crumbs. Place 1/4 inch olive oil in a nonstick skillet and heat over medium-high heat. Add rice cakes to hot oil in batches and cook until brown and crispy on both sides. Remove and blot with paper towels. Serve warm drizzled with roasted red pepper sauce.
- **Risotto Tortes.** Preheat oven to 350°F. Using 1 tablespoon butter for each pan, butter 2 (8-inch) cake pans well and coat with bread crumbs. Stir 2 eggs and cheese cubes into cooled rice. Spread rice in prepared pans, pressing down to smooth top. Cover pans with foil and bake 20 minutes. Uncover and bake 20 minutes longer, or until rice is firm. Invert onto serving plates. Cut into wedges to serve hot.

Jalapeño Jack Corn Risotto with Grilled Chile-Lime Chicken

Serves 6 • Needs to marinate 1 to 3 hours

CHICKEN

6 boneless chicken breast halves
2 serrano chile peppers, minced
2 cloves garlic, minced
1 tablespoon fresh ginger, minced
3 tablespoons fresh lime juice
6 tablespoons vegetable oil
Salt and pepper, to taste

RISOTTO

2 tablespoons unsalted butter
3 garlic cloves, minced
1/4 teaspoon ground cumin
1 1/2 cups arborio rice
5 cups hot chicken broth
1 (16-ounce) bag (3 cups) frozen sweet corn, thawed
1/3 cup whipping cream
1 1/2 cups jalapeño Jack cheese, grated
Salt and pepper, to taste
2 tablespoons fresh cilantro, chopped

1. Prepare the chicken. Trim and pound chicken breasts to an even ½ inch thickness.

2. Make the marinade. In a shallow dish, whisk together the serrano, garlic, ginger, lime juice, and oil. Add salt and pepper to taste. Add chicken, turning to coat. Cover and refrigerate at least 1 hour and up to 3 hours.

3. Make the risotto. Melt butter in heavy saucepan over medium heat. Add garlic and cumin; sauté 1 minute. Mix in rice and toss 2 minutes.

4. Add 1 cup hot broth and stir until absorbed. Add more broth, 1 cup at a time, until rice is almost done, simmering and stirring constantly. Stir in corn and more broth, if needed, and cook until rice is tender and mixture is slightly thick and creamy, stirring frequently — it will take 30 to 40 minutes.

5. Stir in the cream and cheese until the mixture is heated through. Season to taste with salt and pepper.

6. Cook the chicken. Remove from marinade and grill 3 to 4 minutes per side to cook through.

7. Serve. Cut chicken into strips and serve on top of risotto. Garnish with cilantro.

Sun-Dried Tomato Risotto with Seared Scallops and Truffle Oil

Serves 4 to 6

RISOTTO

1 ounce sun-dried tomatoes (not in oil), cut into strips
1 cup water
5 cups chicken broth
1 cup onion, finely chopped
1 clove garlic, minced
4 tablespoons olive oil
1½ cups arborio rice
½ cup dry white wine
⅓ cup freshly grated Parmesan cheese
3 tablespoons unsalted butter

SCALLOPS

12 to 18 large sea scallops
Salt and pepper
1 tablespoon olive oil
White truffle oil
2 tablespoons fresh parsley, minced

1. Make the risotto. Simmer tomatoes in water in a medium saucepan for 1 minute. Let stand 15 minutes. Drain, reserving liquid, and chop. Combine reserved tomato liquid and broth in a saucepan and bring to a simmer.

2. In a large saucepan or Dutch oven, cook the onion and garlic in olive oil until tender. Add the rice and stir until each grain is coated with oil. Stir in tomatoes and wine. Continue stirring and adding broth, 1 cup or so at a time, until rice is tender (about 30 minutes). Stir in cheese and butter.

3. Make the scallops. Remove the foot or tough muscle from each scallop (if still attached) and season with salt and pepper. Heat olive oil in a large nonstick skillet over medium heat. Add scallops and cook until well browned on the outside and just opaque on the inside, about 1 to 2 minutes per side depending on thickness. (Scallops can also be grilled — thread onto double bamboo skewers, season with salt and pepper, brush with oil, and grill 1 to 2 minutes per side.)

4. Serve. Top rice with scallops, drizzle scallops with just a touch of truffle oil, and sprinkle with parsley. Serve immediately.

Lemony Risotto with Shrimp and Grilled Asparagus

Serves 4 to 6 • Marinate up to 4 hours

SHRIMP AND ASPARAGUS

12 to 18 extra-large raw shrimp, shelled and deveined
3 tablespoons olive oil, divided use
2 tablespoons fresh lemon juice
1 clove garlic, minced
2 tablespoons Italian parsley, chopped
12 to 18 stalks asparagus
Salt and pepper, to taste

RISOTTO

2 tablespoons olive oil
1 cup onion, chopped
1 1/2 cups arborio rice
5 cups hot chicken broth
6 tablespoons fresh lemon juice
4 teaspoons grated lemon zest
1/2 teaspoon freshly ground black pepper
3 tablespoons unsalted butter
1/2 cup freshly grated Parmesan cheese
2 tablespoons Italian parsley, chopped
Salt and pepper, to taste

RON'S TIP

Chef'n Citrus Presses

A good citrus press is an essential kitchen tool. One of the best hand pressers available is the Chef'n FreshForce Citrus juicer. The ingenious extra gear mechanism is the key. It allows you to achieve maximum juicing power with minimal hand strain, producing 20 percent more juice than with other manual juicers. The easy-to-squeeze handle is very comfortable to use, and the stainless-steel pressing plate won't chip, rust, or react with acidic juices. The press can be used for lemons, limes, or small oranges.

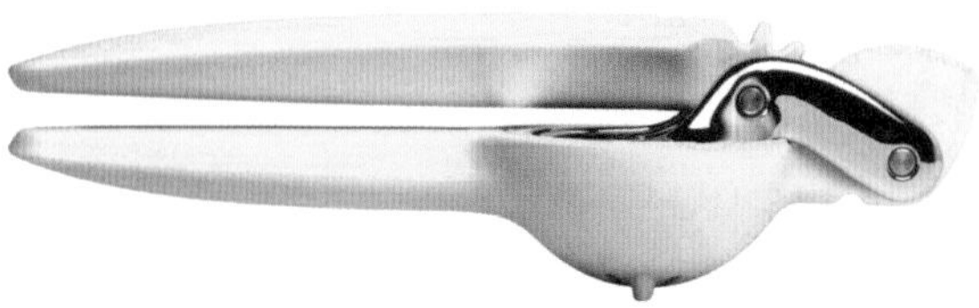

1. Prepare the shrimp. Place the shrimp in a shallow dish. Combine 2 tablespoons oil, lemon juice, garlic, and parsley. Pour over shrimp, tossing to coat. Cover and refrigerate for up to 4 hours. Thread shrimp on bamboo skewers that have been soaked in water for 20 minutes. Just before cooking rice, grill shrimp for about 3 minutes per side. Toss asparagus with remaining oil and season with salt and pepper. Grill asparagus for 7 to 10 minutes alongside shrimp, until just crisp-tender.

2. Make the risotto. Heat oil in a Dutch oven over medium-high heat. Add the onion and sauté until tender, about 4 minutes. Add rice; stir 1 minute.

3. Add 1 cup hot broth and lower heat to keep mixture just simmering. Stir often and add broth 1 cup at a time. Keep stirring often and add lemon juice, zest, and pepper along with a quarter cup of broth. Keep stirring and cooking until rice is just tender, adding more broth if necessary.

4. Remove rice from heat and stir in butter and cheese. Season with salt and pepper.

5. Serve. Divide rice among bowls or plates and top each with three grilled shrimp and three asparagus stalks. Sprinkle with parsley; serve immediately.

One-Dish Wonders

PHILLIS CAREY

Chili Tortilla Casserole • Mexican Chicken Lasagna
Turkey Divan with Broccoli and Parmesan Sauce
Three-Cheese Italian Sausage and Penne Bake

Lots of us remember growing up with Mom or Dad's casserole for dinner. We all liked the simplicity of a one-dish meal that contained all of the elements of a balanced meal — and it made life easy for working parents everywhere. Chef Phillis shares a diverse assortment of casserole recipes, including chili tortilla, turkey divan with broccoli and Parmesan sauce, Mexican chicken lasagna, and an Italian version with sausage and penne pasta. These are definitely not your mother's casseroles!

Chili Tortilla Casserole

Serves 6 to 8

1½ pounds lean ground beef
1 onion, chopped
1 (15-ounce) can tomato sauce
1 (15-ounce) can kidney beans, drained
1 tablespoon chili powder
½ teaspoon garlic powder
1 (2.2-ounce) can sliced olives
1 (4-ounce) can diced green chiles
8 corn tortillas, cut into quarters
2 cups grated cheddar cheese
½ cup beef broth or water
¼ cup green onions, chopped
1 cup sour cream

1. Combine the ground beef and onions in a 2½-quart casserole. Cook, covered with wax paper, in the microwave oven on high for 5 to 6 minutes, or until beef loses its pink color, stirring and breaking the meat up twice. Drain well.
2. Stir in the tomato sauce, kidney beans, chili powder, garlic powder, olives, and chiles. Microwave, covered, on high 3 minutes just to warm.
3. Arrange half of the tortillas in the bottom of a greased 9x13-inch oval dish. Pour half the beef-and-bean mixture over the tortillas. Cover with half the cheese. Repeat with a layer of tortillas and then remaining beef-bean mixture. Pour the beef broth or water over all.
4. Microwave, covered with parchment paper, on high for 12 minutes. Sprinkle with the remaining cheese and cook, uncovered, for 1 to 2 minutes, or until hot through and cheese is melted. Sprinkle with green onions and let stand 5 minutes before serving topped with a dollop of sour cream.

NOTE
• This may also be cooked covered in a 350°F oven for 25 minutes. Uncover and sprinkle with cheese and bake another 10 minutes, or until heated through and bubbly.

Mexican Chicken Lasagna

Serves 9 to 12

FILLING

2 cups small-curd cottage cheese
2 eggs
1/3 cup cilantro, chopped
1 (4-ounce) can diced green chiles

SAUCE

2 tablespoons vegetable oil
1 medium onion, chopped
2 cloves garlic, minced
1 medium red bell pepper, diced
2 (16-ounce) jars saucy mild salsa
2 tablespoons chili powder
1 teaspoon ground cumin

LASAGNA

1 (8-ounce) package no-cook lasagna noodles
4 cups cooked chicken, cut into bite-size pieces
1 1/2 cups shredded sharp cheddar cheese
1 1/2 cups shredded Jack cheese

1. Make the filling. In a bowl, combine the cottage cheese, eggs, cilantro, and diced chiles. Mix well. Set aside.
2. Make the sauce. Heat oil in a 4-quart saucepan or Dutch oven. Add the onion, garlic, and red bell pepper. Cook, stirring often, until onion is soft but not brown. Add salsa, chili powder, and cumin; bring to a boil. Reduce heat to medium and boil gently, uncovered, stirring often, until mixture is reduced to 4 cups, about 10 minutes.
3. Prepare the lasagna. Cook lasagna noodles 4 or 5 at a time in a large pot of boiling salted water for 4 to 5 minutes, or until softened and just tender. (Do not use these noodles dry, as the directions say!) Drain noodles and rinse with cold water to stop cooking. Place on plastic wrap; do not allow noodles to touch. Set aside.
4. Assemble. Arrange one-third of the noodles over the bottom of a 9x13-inch baking dish; spread with half the filling, then cover with half the chicken. Spoon one-third of the sauce over the chicken and sprinkle with 1/2 cup each of the cheeses. Repeat layers, using one-third of the remaining noodles, the remaining filling and chicken, 1/2 cup each of the cheeses, and one-third of the sauce. Top with remaining noodles and sauce.
5. Cook the lasagna. Bake covered with foil at 375°F for 40 minutes. Uncover, sprinkle with remaining cheeses, and bake another 10 minutes. Let stand at least 5 minutes before cutting and serving.

Turkey Divan with Broccoli and Parmesan Sauce

Serves 6

1 (16-ounce) bag fresh broccoli florets
12 turkey scallops (thin slices of turkey breast)
Salt and pepper, to taste
2 tablespoons olive oil
1 1/2 cups chicken broth
1/4 cup unsalted butter, plus more for coating dish
1/2 cup freshly grated Parmesan cheese, divided use
1/2 cup toasted slivered almonds
1/4 cup flour
1 cup whole milk
1/8 teaspoon ground nutmeg
3 tablespoons dry sherry
1/2 cup heavy whipping cream

1. Steam or microwave broccoli just until tender but still bright green in color. Pound turkey slices between 2 sheets of plastic wrap until very thin. Season well with salt and pepper.
2. Heat oil in a large skillet and cook turkey for 2 to 3 minutes per side, or until just cooked through. Remove turkey to a plate. Add chicken broth to skillet and boil down to 1 cup, scraping up any browned bits from the bottom.
3. Preheat oven to 350°F. Butter a 2-quart casserole dish and arrange broccoli in a single layer in bottom of pan. Sprinkle with 1/4 cup Parmesan and arrange turkey slices evenly over the broccoli; sprinkle with almonds.
4. For sauce, melt butter in a medium saucepan over medium heat. Add flour and stir 1 minute. Add the reduced chicken broth and milk, whisking until smooth and thickened. Season to taste with salt, pepper, and nutmeg. Stir in 1/4 cup Parmesan and the sherry. Set aside to cool somewhat.
5. Whip the cream until soft peaks form and then fold into the cheese sauce. Pour evenly over the turkey and bake until bubbly and golden brown, about 35 minutes.

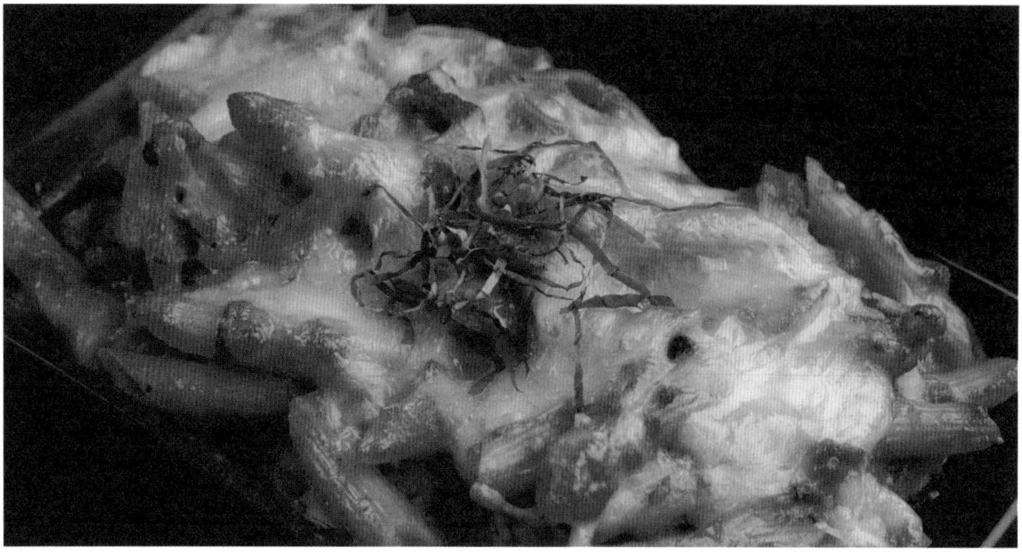

Three-Cheese Italian Sausage and Penne Bake

Serves 8 to 12

4 tablespoons extra-virgin olive oil, divided use
1 pound sweet Italian sausage, casings removed and coarsely crumbled
1 pound hot Italian sausage, casings removed and coarsely crumbled
4 cups onions, thinly sliced
1 3/4 teaspoon salt, divided use
3/4 teaspoon freshly ground black pepper
1 tablespoon garlic, minced
1/2 cup vodka
2 (16-ounce) cans whole tomatoes, crushed with juice
1/2 teaspoon dried oregano
1/2 teaspoon dried thyme
1/2 cup heavy whipping cream
1 pound penne pasta
15 ounces ricotta cheese
1 cup freshly grated Parmesan cheese
1/4 cup fresh basil leaves, julienned
1 1/2 cups grated mozzarella

1. Preheat oven to 350°F. Heat 2 tablespoons oil in a large skillet or Dutch oven over high heat. Add the sausages and cook, stirring, until browned, 4 to 5 minutes. Add the onions, 3/4 teaspoon salt, and pepper. Cook, stirring occasionally, until the onions are just soft, about 5 minutes. Add the garlic and cook, stirring, for 1 minute.
2. Add the vodka, tomatoes, oregano, and thyme; reduce the heat to medium-low and simmer, uncovered, stirring occasionally, for 40 minutes. Stir in the heavy cream and simmer for 5 minutes. Remove from the heat.
3. Cook the pasta in a large pot of boiling water with the remaining 1 teaspoon salt until *al dente*, 7 to 10 minutes. Remove from the heat and drain well.
4. Combine the ricotta, Parmesan, and basil with the remaining oil in a large bowl. Add pasta and coat evenly. Add the sausage mixture and mix well.
5. Transfer the mixture to a 9x13-inch baking dish. Sprinkle with mozzarella. Bake until bubbly and golden, about 45 minutes.

Traditional Holiday Desserts

KATHERINE EMMENEGGER

English Toffee • Spicy Cashew and Macadamia Nut Brittle
Holiday Peppermint Chocolate Cheesecake Bars • Chocolate Raspberry Linzer Torte
Bûche De Noël (Christmas Log Cake)

The holidays are a special time of year when everyone indulges in their favorite desserts. It is also the perfect time to spend in your kitchen making edible gifts for your family and friends. The English toffee and the spicy cashew brittle featured here make excellent gifts, as do the peppermint chocolate cheesecake bars. The Bûche De Noël, a Christmas classic, is a rolled, stuffed sheet cake that looks like a tree log. (It tastes great!) The chocolate raspberry Linzer torte has the style and elegance of old Europe. These treats will delight your family and friends from Thanksgiving to New Years.

English Toffee

Makes about 24 pieces

1 cup slivered almonds, toasted
2 cups granulated sugar
1/4 cup water
1 cup unsalted butter
2 teaspoons pure vanilla extract
1/2 teaspoon baking soda
12 ounces semisweet chocolate, coarsely chopped

1. Line a 9x12-inch sheet tray with foil and lightly oil the surface. Arrange the almonds over the surface of the prepared tray.
2. In a heavy medium saucepan, combine the sugar, water, and butter; bring to a boil, stirring constantly. Monitoring with a candy thermometer, bring the mixture to the hard-crack stage, 290°F to 300°F. Then immediately remove the pan from the heat. Add the vanilla extract and baking soda.
3. Pour the mixture evenly over the almonds.
4. While the toffee is hot, sprinkle the chocolate evenly over the surface. Press the chocolate with an offset spatula to aid in melting; after about 5 minutes, the chocolate will be soft enough to spread in an even layer over the surface of the toffee.
5. Cool completely. Break the toffee into irregular pieces.
6. Store the toffee in an airtight container at room temperature for up to 1 month.

Spicy Cashew and Macadamia Nut Brittle

Makes about 2 pounds

½ cup water
3 cups granulated sugar
1 cup light corn syrup
½ cup roasted and salted cashews, broken or whole (unsalted can also be used)
½ cup roasted and salted macadamia nuts, broken or halves (unsalted can also be used)
4 tablespoons unsalted butter
1 tablespoon pure vanilla extract
2 teaspoons baking soda
½ teaspoon cayenne pepper, or to taste

1. Lightly butter or oil two sheet trays or line with Silpats.
2. In a 2-quart saucepan over medium heat, combine the water, sugar, and corn syrup; whisk until the sugar dissolves. Insert a candy thermometer into the pan. Simmer the sugar until the temperature of the mixture reaches 230°F; add the nuts and stir to coat. The temperature will drop slightly.
3. Continue to simmer until the temperature reaches 300°F, the hard-crack stage. Transfer from the heat and add the butter, vanilla, baking soda, and cayenne pepper.
4. Stir to combine. The mixture will become foamy looking.
5. Immediately distribute half of the mixture to each tray and spread evenly with a metal spatula.
6. Let cool 1 hour.
7. Break into pieces and place into gift boxes or an airtight container. The brittle can be stored for several weeks.

Holiday Peppermint Chocolate Cheesecake Bars

Makes 24 bars • Chill before serving

CRUST

2 sleeves chocolate graham crackers, finely ground in a food processor, about 2 cups
1 1/4 sticks unsalted butter, melted

TOPPING

2 cups sour cream
1/4 cup granulated sugar
1 tablespoon lemon juice

FILLING

1 1/2 pounds cream cheese, softened
1/2 cup granulated sugar
3 large eggs, beaten
2 teaspoons pure vanilla extract
1/2 cup mini chocolate chips, plus more for garnish
1/2 cup candy cane, crushed into pea-size pieces, plus more for garnish

1. Preheat oven to 350°F.
2. Make the crust. Prepare a 13x9x2-inch metal baking pan with nonstick spray.
3. In a bowl, combine the graham cracker crumbs and melted butter. Transfer the crumb mixture to the pan and press evenly onto the bottom of the pan.
4. Bake for 10 minutes to set. Transfer from the oven to a rack to cool.
5. Make the topping. In a bowl combine all ingredients. Set aside.
6. Make the filling. In the bowl of an electric mixer fitted with the paddle attachment, cream the cream cheese and sugar. Add the eggs and vanilla; mix until well blended. Fold in the chocolate chips and crushed candy cane.
7. Spread the filling evenly over the cooled crust.
8. Bake until just set in center and the edges are puffed, about 35 minutes. Transfer to a rack and cool to room temperature.
9. Spread the topping evenly over the top of the cheesecake and return it to the oven for 10 minutes to become smooth.
10. Remove from the oven, let cool to room temperature, and then refrigerate, uncovered, until well-chilled.
11. Serve. Garnish with additional chocolate chips and crushed peppermints. Cut the cheesecake into 24 bars and serve.

Chocolate Raspberry Linzer Torte

Serves 8

FILLING

1 (12-ounce) jar seedless raspberry jam

PASTRY

1 3/4 sticks unsalted butter, softened
1/2 cup granulated sugar
3 large egg yolks
2 cups all-purpose flour
1 teaspoon cinnamon
1/2 teaspoon salt
1/4 cup unsweetened cocoa powder
1 1/2 cups hazelnuts, toasted, skinned, and finely ground

GARNISHES

Powdered sugar
Whipped cream

1. Preheat oven to 375°F.
2. Make the filling. In a small saucepan over medium-low heat, warm and thin out the jam.

3. Make the pastry. In the bowl of an electric mixer fitted with the paddle attachment, cream the butter and sugar until light and fluffy. Add the egg yolks and beat until smooth.
4. In a bowl, combine the flour, cinnamon, salt, and cocoa powder. Add the dry ingredients to the creamed butter and mix until just combined. Add the hazelnuts and combine.
5. Use three-quarters of the dough for the bottom of the torte and reserve the rest for the lattice top. In an 11-inch, removable-bottom tart pan, evenly press the dough in the bottom and up the side.
6. Roll the remaining dough between two sheets of wax paper into a round slightly thicker than 1/8 inch. Place the dough on a sheet tray and freeze for 15 minutes.
7. Evenly spread the cooled jam over the bottom of the tart shell.
8. Transfer the pastry from the freezer and remove the top sheet of wax paper. With a pastry wheel or sharp knife, slice 1/2-inch-wide strips across the pastry. With a long metal spatula, transfer the strips in a lattice pattern over the jam. Trim the ends at the edge of the pan.
9. With the remaining dough, prepare a 1/4-inch thick strip to press around the rim and cover the ends of the lattice strips.
10. Bake on the center rack for 25 to 30 minutes, or until lightly browned. Transfer the torte from the oven to a cooling rack; cool.
11. Serve. Remove the rim of the pan, dust with the powdered sugar, and serve with whipped cream.

Bûche De Noël (Christmas Log Cake)

Makes 1 (12-inch) log

CHOCOLATE BUTTER CREAM FROSTING (FOR THE FILLING AND ICING)

1/2 cup unsalted butter, softened
3 1/4 cups powdered sugar
1/2 cup unsweetened cocoa powder
1/8 teaspoon salt
1 teaspoon pure vanilla extract
1/4 cup buttermilk

CAKE

5 eggs, separated
1/4 cup granulated sugar
1 teaspoon vanilla extract
1/4 cup all-purpose flour
1/4 teaspoon salt
1/4 cup cocoa powder

GARNISHES

Powdered sugar or cocoa powder
Meringue mushrooms or other decorations

1. Make the frosting. In the bowl of an electric mixer fitted with the paddle attachment, cream the butter until light and fluffy.
2. In a bowl, sift together the sugar, cocoa, and salt; add to the butter. Mix well and then add the vanilla and buttermilk. Mix until very smooth. Set aside.
3. Preheat oven to 350°F. Spray a 12x9-inch sheet tray with nonstick cooking spray and line with parchment paper or wax paper. Spray again with the nonstick cooking spray.
4. Make the cake. In the bowl of an electric mixer fitted with the whisk, whip the egg whites to stiff peaks. Transfer the whites to a clean, dry bowl.
5. In the same mixer bowl with the whisk, whip the yolks and the sugar until thick and smooth. Add the vanilla extract and combine.
6. In a bowl, sift the flour, salt, and cocoa. Add the dry ingredients to the egg yolk mixture; mix well.

7. Fold half of the egg whites into the yolk-and-flour mixture to lighten the mix. Then fold the remaining whites into the batter.
8. Pour the batter into the prepared sheet tray and spread evenly.
9. Bake for 15 to 20 minutes. Remove from the oven and cool on a rack for 5 minutes. Then invert the cake onto a new, oiled sheet of parchment paper to cool 10 minutes more. Remove the top sheet of used paper.
10. Spread about half of the frosting evenly over the cooled cake. Using the bottom sheet of parchment paper like a sushi mat, carefully roll the cake along the long edge into a tight cylinder. Discard the paper, and carefully place the cake on a serving tray.
11. Finish the cake. To create a log effect, cut the ends of the cake at an angle and place the trimmed parts against the log to look like cut-off branches. Attach them with butter cream.
12. Frost the outside of the log. Use a fork to make irregular lines on the cake to give the effect of bark.
13. Refrigerate the cake for 20 minutes to set the frosting. Then cover loosely with plastic wrap and keep refrigerated overnight.
14. Before serving, dust the cake with cocoa powder and/or powdered sugar. Decorate with meringue mushrooms, royal icing candy decorations, or fondant decorations.

Great Food! Index

Great News! Recipe Index

PASTA AND RICE

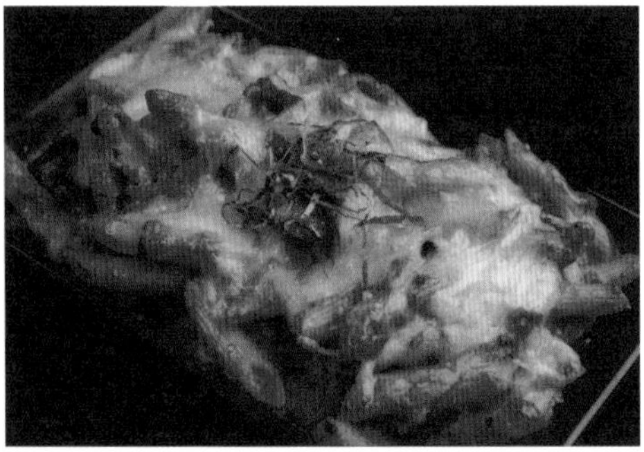

SALADS

SAUCES

SIDE DISHES

SOUPS

VEGETARIAN (AND RECIPES THAT CAN EASILY BE ADAPTED TO BE VEGETARIAN)

Photo Credits

Michael D. Pawlenty/Chefs Press: 1, 4, 5, 6, 7, 8, 11, 12, 13, 22–23, 27, 36, 42, 46, 71, 82–83, 104, 112, 121, 124–125, 128, 153, 164–165, 185, 210, 215, 220, 222, 224
Photo Styling: Jessica Rhomberg
All-Clad: 19, 187
Bigstock: 26, 33, 35, 47, 48, 53, 54, 55, 57, 61, 64, 65, 66, 67, 68, 70, 72, 73, 74, 75, 76, 77, 87, 88, 89, 93, 94, 96, 99, 100, 106, 113, 118, 120, 129, 130, 131, 134, 135, 136, 138, 140, 141, 142, 143, 149, 154, 160, 162, 174, 175, 176, 177 , 179, 182, 183, 188, 192, 195, 204, 205, 209, 211, 213, 218, 219
Breville: 144
CDN: 93
Chef'n: 206
Chicago Metallic: 32, 37
Cuisipro: 139
Dreamstime: 18, 34, 38, 39, 41, 51, 52, 58, 59, 60, 62, 63, 69, 79, 81, 91, 97, 102, 103, 105, 114, 115, 116, 117, 122, 123, 148, 152, 156, 168, 171, 172, 178, 181, 184, 212, 214, 217, 223
Emile Henry: 110
Epicurean: 43
iStockphoto: 17, 31, 49, 108, 132, 133, 145, 147, 150, 157, 158, 161, 179, 186, 187, 197, 202, 203, 208, 216, 221
Kaiser: 193
Kyocera: 54
Le Creuset: 149
Mauviel: 199
Microplane: 50
Rösle: 95
Scanpan: 29
Silpat: 152
Taylor: 40
Trudeau: 100, 169
Vic Firth: 109
William Bounds: 170
WMF: 190
Wüsthof: 44